HOSPITALITY AND AUTHORING

T0308850

HOSPITALITY AND AUTHORING

An Essay for the English Profession

Authoring Part II

RICHARD HASWELL
JANIS HASWELL

UTAH STATE UNIVERSITY PRESS
Logan

© 2015 by the University Press of Colorado

Published by Utah State University Press
An imprint of University Press of Colorado
5589 Arapahoe Avenue, Suite 206C
Boulder, Colorado 80303

 The University Press of Colorado is a proud member of
The Association of American University Presses.

The University Press of Colorado is a cooperative publishing enterprise supported, in part, by Adams State University, Colorado State University, Fort Lewis College, Metropolitan State University of Denver, Regis University, University of Colorado, University of Northern Colorado, Utah State University, and Western State Colorado University.

∞ The paper used in this publication meets the minimum requirements of the American National Standard for Information Sciences—Permanence of Paper for Printed Library Materials. ANSI Z39.48–1992

ISBN: 978-0-87421-987-6 (paper)
ISBN: 978-0-87421-988-3 (ebook)

Library of Congress Cataloging-in-Publication Data
Haswell, Richard H.
  Hospitality and authoring : an essay for the English profession / Richard Haswell, Janis Haswell.
    pages cm
  "Authoring Part II."
  Includes bibliographical references and index.
  ISBN 978-0-87421-987-6 (pbk.) — ISBN 978-0-87421-988-3 (ebook)
  1. English language—Rhetoric—Study and teaching (Higher) 2. English language—Study and teaching (Higher) 3. Classroom environment. 4. Teacher-student relationships. I. Haswell, Janis Tedesco. II. Haswell, Janis Tedesco. Authoring. III. Title.
  PE1404.H374 2015
  808'.042071—dc23
                          2014028857

24 23 22 21 20 19 18 17 16 15   10 9 8 7 6 5 4 3 2 1

Cover photogragh: Nicolai Fechin's "Beautiful Corner" icon cabinet in the Taos Art Museum at Fechin House, Taos, NM. Photo by the authors.

Any gathering of two or more ought to be fraught with the love of life.

—Thomas Aquinas

CONTENTS

ACKNOWLEDGMENTS

We thank David Higham Associates for our use in chapter 7 of Paul Scott materials published by University of Chicago Press, Cambria Press, Heinemann, and Granada; and *Science* for permission to reproduce the graph of baby-length growth in chapter 10. *College Composition and Communication* kindly allowed us to use some parts of our 2009 essay, "Hospitality in College Composition Courses." Glenn Blalock, who coauthored that article with us, has long supported and informed our interest in hospitality. We also thank Rebecca Lyons for her help in interviewing students and transcribing their comments, analyzed in chapter 6, and Michael Spooner for drawing our attention to the Chinook legend explored in chapter 1. Thanks to the Taos Art Museum for granting us permission to use our photograph of Nicolai Fechin's cabinet on the cover. This is the "beautiful corner" cabinet in the Fechin House in Taos, displaying family and holy icons and, according to Fechin's design, featuring welcoming doors carved with images of pineapples, traditional symbol of hospitality.

HOSPITALITY AND AUTHORING

INTRODUCTION

Where ask is have, where seek is find,
Where knock is open wide.
                    —Christopher Smart

Hospitality happens, even in English courses. But take care. Hospitality here is not necessarily the same as hospitality there.

In March 2013, Rich signed up for a massive open online course (MOOC), mildly hyped by Duke University as English Composition I: Achieving Expertise. The first assignment was to write a 300-word essay called "I Am a Writer." Two days later, before Rich had started that oddly redundant task, he received an even odder e-mail from Denise Comer, the coordinator of the course. It begins,

> Dear Richard H. Haswell,
> I am so very much enjoying reading through the "I am a Writer" posts, and I am learning so much about you as writers and about writing around the world. Thank you for sharing your experiences with writing and for helping to establish a productive class atmosphere by being so supportive and encouraging with your classmates.

This was odd because of the thanks extended to Rich for "sharing" and "helping" and "being so supportive and encouraging"—when he had done none of those things. Odd because of the unexplained switches in referring to the reader: from the singular "Richard H. Haswell," to all the enrollees in the course, then back to the singular. So when Rich first read "you as writers," he had the startling thought that his brand-new teacher was diagnosing him with multiple personalities. Most odd because the teacher claims to be "so very much enjoying reading through" the essays submitted for a course that, at this point, had an enrollment of 67,530.

These rhetorical curiosities can be dissected with tools supplied by current discourse analysis, which has a long history, though a much more modest scholarly enrollment. This book offers a new tool: the practice, history, and theory of hospitality.

DOI: 10.7330/9780874219883.c000

What kind of light does hospitality throw on Comer's letter? Obviously, the letter sends familiar signals of welcome. With express warmth and friendliness, it helps two strangers connect, ushering a new guest (Rich) into a sheltering house (the course). It even offers a gift exchange, of sorts, common in traditional hospitality, with the guest "sharing" experiences and the host reciprocating with her expression of enjoyment in receiving them. An understanding of the history of hospitality, however, quickly sees through these rhetorical gestures, which are just trappings of hospitality.

In acts of genuine, traditional hospitality, host and guest—strangers to each other—meet in the flesh, one on one, weaponless hands clasping. Here the meeting is digitized and Comer and Rich have never met and do not know how far apart, in real miles, they are. Comer does not even know they are meeting. The personal hello is a pose. How can you personally greet 67,530 people in a week, much less read through their essays? Also in traditional hospitality, the empathy of the host for the houseless guest is heartfelt. Here Comer knows nothing and therefore feels nothing about Rich or her other enrollees. Rhetorically, she has no recourse but to switch immediately to a mass "you."

Perhaps most telling, in the deep and private exchange that constitutes traditional hospitality, the host never asks the guest for personal information, not even the guest's name. Here, with her first words ("Dear Richard H. Haswell"), Comer reveals that the real host is not her but a computerized program that has remembered Rich's name, including the middle initial, from the instant he signed up. Later, but not much later, the computer will encourage Rich to join the "Signature" track, at a reduced "introductory" price of $39, and to fill out a personal "profile." It is no surprise that Google.com, which survives on personal information for advertising purposes, helped underwrite this Duke MOOC.

Duke's English Composition I: Achieving Expertise betrays other parallels with the ways of traditional hospitality, most of them diabolical inversions. The MOOC allies not with the eighteenth-century code of "knock is open wide" but with the twentieth-century code of what we will call colonial, entertainment, or entrepreneurial hospitality. This is given away by the advertisement tone of Comer's letter, the distinctive mix of fake and effusive ("so very much enjoying reading through"). Historical hospitality has degenerated into "the hospitality trade," where knock is just a prospect to make money. The point is that discursive traditions of hospitality are still alive, occasionally in their age-old form but usually so altered that most people do not recognize the connections. Like prestidigitation, meaning is conveyed by conventional expectations and then by the absence of them. Sleight of hand turns into slight of hand.

AUTHORING

This book, however, does not explore hospitality just to further discourse analysis. We take up hospitality in its full-bodied sense: as a physical, cultural, ethical act with personal, social, and educational consequences. We open the door to hospitality because, among other functions, it serves as the foundation for the act and activity of authoring and for the teaching of authoring. This is hospitality's major importance for the English profession.

As the central human act that underlies all major components of English studies—composition, literature, linguistics, and creative writing—authoring would seem in no need of explanation. But in fact authoring has plenty of the mysterious about it. In ways similar to hospitality, authoring is an act of legerdemain. Humans pull words, paragraphs, whole essays, hard-nosed speeches, soft-spoken poems, condensed reports, three-volume novels, plagiarized patches, verbalized dreams, all out of a mental hat. Or out of some material cultural semiosphere; the difference doesn't matter. Magical or not, mental or not, social or not, authoring is an act that has to have happened. Suddenly the words are before us, real doves, fluttering around the screen or perched on the page. Automatically, we try to grasp them. Their presence has been begot, godlike, by authoring. How was that trick done?

In a previous book, we invited the English profession to consider authoring as paid authors and student authors actually experience it (Haswell and Haswell 2010). The consideration asked for some rethinking. We argued that two necessary energies of authoring, potentiality and singularity, have been neglected by the field. In the present book we hazard a third energy of authoring, hospitality. Hospitality is a social and ethical relationship not only between host and guest but also between writer and reader or teacher and student. Hospitality initiates acts of authoring, although how well it maintains and completes them is moot (see chapter 9). As an ageless social custom that eases two strangers into deep conversation, hospitality is the necessary companionable gesture to every genuine act of literacy.

So hospitality stands as a beginning point for a serious look at English classroom practice. Alongside the sanctioned trinity of vectors that make up text—context, writer, and audience—we propose a second trinity: potentiality, singularity, and hospitality. Maybe without them the author's fingers can still gesture, but the dove of discourse will be papier-mâché, without a beating heart.

POTENTIALITY AND SINGULARITY

For readers unfamiliar with our previous book, and there are many, here is a sketch of our take on potentiality and singularity.

Potentiality feeds much of authoring, from motivation to creativity to language itself. Working authors want to keep their potential to keep on writing. They want to wake up tomorrow with their drive to generate original and worthy text still healthy. A writer's potential is not a trick that, once learned, is guaranteed to work in the future. It must be nurtured, sustained, and guarded. It can atrophy and it can disappear forever.

In a word, potentiality is mathemagenic, an activity that serves for future learning. It is a capacity of human language itself, one that allows the continued production and reception of new utterances. It is also a capacity of the human brain to process new information and of human social groups to handle new situations. In English courses, student potential includes, for instance, the desire to keep on reading serious literature after the course is over, or the capability to transfer and adjust writing skills to later writing tasks. Teachers hope and even expect this kind of future for their students, but little in their syllabus is designed to foster or maintain potentiality and some of it, such as assigning pieces of literature beyond the knack or disposition of students to like, works actively against that future. Instruction can be anathemagenic. Technically, potentiality is theoretical because it always depends on the future. You can stop keeping a journal, but your potential for journal keeping may or may not have stopped.

Singularity, by contrast, is a physical fact. Singularity may be the one given that is accepted by the most fields of thought. That each person is unique with a unique personal history, that each moment a person spends at any spot in the world is unique and has never happened before and will never happen again, these are axioms in history, philosophy, brain studies, psychotherapy, physical sciences, political sciences, life-course studies, linguistics, and discourse analysis, among other fields of thought. In matters of language, singularity is a fact that helps nurture potentiality. Authors and readers are kept going by the knowledge that nearly every sentence they write and read is new. Even rereading a piece of discourse is new, because everything has changed since the previous reading—world, reader, purpose for reading, knowledge of the text.

English teachers don't really disbelieve the fact of singularity, but the last forty years have seen them shelve it in favor of nonsingular notions such as linguistic structure, literary period, discourse community, cultural trend, and mass communication. English classes dwell, for instance, on group interpretation, collaborative authorship, and historical, cultural, and ideological suasion. Instructional focus is on the collective and the normative, not on the individual and unique. Over these years, the one most crucial and far-reaching fact of English studies has been neglected, that the huge majority of sentences people write every day—and therefore the huge majority of sentences people read every day—are singular, have never seen light before. And "people" here includes students.

In gist this book starts with the universal fact—call it normative, if you wish—that at any moment any writer has the potential to produce singular text. As the singular reader receives the singular text offered by the singular writer, potentiality will actualize, the dove will appear.

At this point we ask a simple question: What social situations encourage the making and taking of singular texts? A moment's thought reveals that the answer is not simple. Inside the walls of the academy, many instructional situations actively discourage singularity in texts. In reading student essays, literature teachers may be looking for opinions and terminology repeated from their lectures or from the assigned texts, and may be reading so fast that they register a novel opinion as inappropriate. Machine scoring of essay examinations rewards students who use high-frequency topic-relevant words and therefore punish the student who uses singularly chosen words, even if they are relevant to the topic.

Outside the walls of the academy, the degree to which rhetorical situations entertain singular texts varies widely. A "few words" spoken at a wedding reception or a "rousing speech" at a political gathering may be badly received unless packed with common-stock ideas and delivered in a familiar, even hackneyed, style. On the other hand, research articles submitted to professional journals are expected to be sui generis and even multiple submissions are forbidden. It may be that a survey of standard genres would find that in the vast majority of formal discourse contexts, within and outside the academy, singular discourse is expected, from the daily journalistic need for new news items to the instructional need of unplagiarized student papers in English courses. Otherwise the ongoing potentiality of the genres themselves would die.

Still, is there one social situation most hospitable for singularity and potentiality in language use? What other than hospitality itself?

THE USES OF HOSPITALITY

Although *hospitality* is a word that has appeared rarely in English studies during the last forty years, in other fields scores of books have been devoted to it.[1] Devoted to hospitality's traditional practice, that is, which is distinct from offering friends nibbles and drinks before dinner or from selling motorists a room with a king-size bed and wireless Internet access. In the most minimal expression of its time-honored way, hospitality takes place when two strangers, one host and one guest, sit down privately together and, in mutual respect, freely and peacefully exchange gifts for each other's comfort, benefit, or entertainment. Gifts might consist, it is important to note, of information, wit, jokes, poems, or other language offerings. And the act of sitting down together, it is also important to note, may be literal, fictional, or symbolic. Hospitality can start taking place where hand is shaken, greeting exchanged, book opened, syllabus handed out, tutor space broached—any place or time where knock is open wide.

It is important to repeat that we mean hospitality as it is exercised in the traditional way, at sites where a host privately offers shelter, food, entertainment, and information to a stranger, not hospitality in the current sense of lodging travelers for money, wining and dining friends, or missionizing in foreign lands. The attributes of traditional hospitality are not balancing the ledger, evening the social score, or harvesting souls. They are goodwill, generosity, welcome, opening to the other, trust, mutual respect, privacy, talk, ease, gift exchange, elbow room, risk, marginality, social retreat, and embrace of change. Traditional hospitality is the opposite of Goody Two-shoes.

Most people today have stopped inviting total strangers into their house not because they dislike the old ways but because they are afraid. An act of generosity and charity, yes, but traditional hospitality is also an act of courage, transgression, disruption, resistance, or rebellion. And it is always a site for learning. One essential motivation for genuine hospitality—this also will bear repeating—is gaining new experience and new knowledge.

OUR ARGUMENT

We assume that when student and teacher meet—strangers to each other—two singular people of potential meet in some sort of socialized venue. The exchange can take any number of forms—superficial, formal, etiquette centered, business focused. But it can also be hospitable, in the deep traditional sense. Only from this last is learning and literacy likely to ensue. English teaching can be improved, this book argues, if it occupies various hospitable sites wherein teacher and student enter into complex, interactional, mutually enriching relationships such as reader and writer, student and teacher, host and guest. A reasonable, even self-evident argument, it would seem. Yet despite the fact that many modern thinkers—philosophers, theologians, historians, psychologists, sociologists, educationalists—have explored hospitality as central to human learning, this book's argument runs counter-field and will not be easy. We have taken some care with it.

First, the long history of hospitality needs to be traced (chapter 1, "Modes of Hospitality in History"). In part this is because there are at least three traditions still viable: Homeric, or warrior, hospitality; Judeo-Christian, or biblical, hospitality; and Central and Eastern Asian, or nomadic, hospitality. There are others, but we will focus on these three. The traditions are easily confused because all have undergone severe change with the spread of middle-class values, capitalistic venture, material wealth, military conflict, human population, and transportation technology. Their historical change can be called a debasement since it has largely erased the moral hazards and rewards entailed in the praxis of traditional hospitality. There, when host and guest are unknown to each other, even a passing encounter runs a risk. Yet both are needy: the guest lacking shelter, food, or guidance, the host limited perhaps by ignorance, entrenchment, authority, narrow view, or unfulfilled restlessness.

Modern debasement of the praxis has led to a current age needing to be reminded that hospitality is more than an outmoded social formality, like curtseying or tipping the hat. Hospitality has lasting depth and seriousness—socially, ethically, philosophically, and spiritually (chapter 2, "The Totality of War, the Infinity of Hospitality"). No one knew this better than post–World War II philosopher Emmanuel Levinas (1969), who pointed out that the opposite of hospitality is not incivility but war. War runs on ruse, force, and spectacle, while hospitality requires honesty, free will, and privacy. War loves the ambush and the interrogation cell, absolute opposites to hospitality's open embrace and unforced sanctum. War blocks, demonizes, or destroys the Other, while hospitality spreads arms to the Other in a gesture of acceptance so basic, says Levinas, that it stands as the root of ethical understanding and behavior. Without hospitable openness to others, people are trapped in totality—assumed to be finite, therefore countable, therefore controllable, therefore exploitable, therefore recruitable. This is why war governments and war corporations hate private acts of hospitality and sometimes criminalize them (see what happens to you if you invite a lonely foreign student to dinner who later is found to be acquainted with someone whom the government thinks might be a terrorist). Totalitarian organizations everywhere know the fundamental truth that people without hospitality are not boors but pawns.

Given the historical trends and philosophical grounds of hospitality, it perhaps comes as no surprise that the present system of higher education, for which students are counted and billed, is profoundly antihospitable. It is a system, however, that teachers can challenge in good faith because traditional hospitality is profoundly pro-learning (chapter 3, "Hospitality in the Classroom"). Generally, three acts of hospitality work in postsecondary classrooms. "Intellectual hospitality" welcomes and makes room for new ideas coming from any direction, including from students, and undercuts the fatal expectation that knowledge transfer is a one-way street from teacher to student. "Transformative hospitality" assumes that both student and teacher will be altered by their meeting, countering the image of teachers as books full of knowledge, available to be opened and read but fixed in time, not a word or comma open to change. "*Ubuntu* hospitality," applicable to student and teacher, reflects the receptive and compassionate state of mind that deep down knows the stranger shares our humanness (*ubuntu* is the native folk ethic that allowed the South African Truth and Reconciliation Commission mandate to work). These hospitable acts signal a new set of classroom Rs: risk taking, restlessness, resistance, and retreat.

In sum, traditional hospitality, still with us in many forms, operates as an essential means of authoring, in the way people receive the world, the way writers receive readers, the way readers receive writers, and the way teachers receive students. It entails a wealth of models, enactments, and classrooms. Since it operates by trust rather than force, it can easily be forgotten or perverted. In chapter 4, "Inhospitable Reception: The Critic as Host," we examine a goal central to literature courses: training in literary criticism. Traditional hospitality encodes a reader who mirrors the open pages of the book with something like open arms. Professional literary critics, and sometimes the classrooms that produce them, often ignore that code. They are readers trained more in suspicion than in respect, welcoming new books with notable inhospitality. A fascinating example is the reception of Michael Ondaatje's (1982) *Running in the Family*, a history of his family roots in Sri Lanka. Initially some critics responded negatively. We identify their reception as scholarly colonization, illustrating an inversion well known in the history of contemporary hospitality. The guest-reader wrests control of the text from the author and assumes the role of host-critic. Initially foreigner and guest, the critic cannibalizes the writer, once native and host. No reciprocal exchange ensues. Imitating a dynamic long familiar to students of first world dominance over third world states, academic scholarship pursues an intellectual imperialism that the knife-edge of ethical hospitality easily dissects. Literary scholarship, once the genteel art of explaining texts, is now a matter of deconstructing, transforming, and "rewriting" them. Can traditional hospitality offer a counter-model of reading that respects the autonomy of both author and critic? Should that counter-model be taught in college English courses?

The dynamics of literary imperialism is perhaps most problematical when English teachers respond to the writings of their own students (chapter 5, "Hospitable Reception: Reading in Student Writing"). Is the "teacher-student relationship," long revered by the profession, compatible with the "writer-reader relationship," long analyzed by the profession? When the literature or composition teacher reads a student's essay, should the teacher function as host or guest? Answers to these questions require a new classification of hospitality, along synchronic rather than diachronic lines. We categorize hospitality as commercial, traditional, or radical. Teacher response to student writing may then be viewed as hospitable trade, hospitable sharing, or hospitable sacrifice. When we consider examples of student texts and possible responses to them, the range of options now available to teacher-readers has disturbing implications. Perhaps the most radical is a reversal of the orthodox pedagogical position that student writers must locate and then follow the demands of their readers. In contrast, hospitality suggests that student writers should write with the expectation that their audience, including their teacher, initially will trust, interpret, and respect what they have to say. Teacher readers, as well as student readers, might entertain as a model what we call "surrendered reading," an act that parallels Jacques Derrida's (2000) "unconditional hospitality." Since surrendered reading of student writing probably lies at the outer critical bourns of most English teachers, we analyze several actual cases of student writing. We conclude the chapter by recommending that literature and composition teachers try a radical—and traditionally hospitable—pedagogy: "risky response."

Radical enough, such instructional acts are perhaps not as disturbing as a classroom fact of which literature and composition teachers may be perfectly unaware. That is the authoring that their students are doing on their own (chapter 6, "Ten Students Reflect on Their Independent Authoring"). With the help of student researcher Rebecca Lyons, we conducted interviews with three graduate students and seven undergraduates, who spoke about their extracurricular authoring life. At the end of the interviews, we asked three questions. While composing, do the authors envision someone else reading their work? Does that image of a reader affect what they are writing? And do they ever think of themselves as hosting a reader? The answers are unsettling. In their academic writing, these authors write to please the teacher and no one else. In self-sponsored writing, their conscious audience is hardly less narrow. They write for a parent or a friend or, most commonly, for themselves. But they virtually never think of their writing self as a "host" and their readers as "guests." Why not? Has a school-sponsored vision of audience shaped their self-sponsored writing from the beginning? On their "own," do student authors still operate in the academic world wherein the author (as teachers tell them) should write *for* an audience, a world where the writer must give the audience what it wants? With "independent" student authors we may be seeing another way that formal education has spread the debasement of traditional hospitality. But we also see into the opinions of a faction of English students (how large is it?) who are authoring on their own—independent, fractious, enthused with writing, and highly critical of English teachers and the way we teach.

What about authors who are even more independent of schooling—authors now making a living by their words? Are the connections between authoring and hospitality a matter of concern or application among working writers? Paul Scott (1986), author of the Raj Quartet and other novels, provides some remarkable insights into these questions from the writer's point of view (chapter 7, "The Novel as Moral Dialogue"). Most fundamentally, he illustrates how hospitality throws light on a debate that extends back to the classical Greek rhetoricians, the moral relationship between writer and reader. In pondering the colonial encounter between British guest and native host in India, Scott comments on the need for the author's "moral imagination" to ensure hospitable equality between writer and reader. The evidence for his striving to achieve that equality emerges from his arduous draft revisions and his voluminous body of letters.

We have mentioned the dark side of hospitality, the way its mode and morality can so easily be advantaged, compromised, and undermined—corrupted, we would say—into social practices little supportive of traditional hospitality and sometimes greatly harmful to it, practices such as private entertainment, colonialism, or the "hospitality" trade. But even uncorrupted hospitality has its limits. The boundaries are tested in the next two chapters. Where hospitality ends and something else begins is often a personal matter, an offbeat verge about which the coauthors had better speak for themselves. In chapter 8 ("Outside Hospitality: The Desire to Not Write") Rich narrates a month in his life when the brute realities of his location did not welcome his desire to write. The place offered him a compelling topic to write on, yet in the end gave him a strong motive not to write about it. Perhaps illustrating Giorgio Agamben's insistence that potentiality cannot be true potentiality unless it retains the power "to not be" (1993, 34), Rich never did pursue the topic. The wretched poverty of the provincial town of Ayacucho, Peru, in 1970 may seem remote from the current U.S. English classroom, but the way the harsh conditions of the place overrode any reasonable efforts at hospitality is germane. In fact, the conditions could be called normal. Today traditional hospitality is a tenuous plant—perhaps it has always been—easily and usually trodden into the dirt when any will-o'-the-wisp material good or expedient goal beckons. The situation isn't that *much* lies outside hospitality and its link with authoring and instruction—it's that almost everything does.

In chapter 9 ("Beyond Hospitality: The Desire to Reread"), Jan considers another limit of hospitality and literacy. By its nature, the act of hospitality is fleeting. The singular and parlous engagement of stranger-host and stranger-guest soon wears off or wears away. The longer host and guest engage, the less they are strangers. Even in Near East and African cultures, where hospitality is such a given, the host can ask the guest to leave after a prescribed length of stay, often three days. And what is more ephemeral than a first draft or a first read? Yet, although both are never to be repeated, second drafts and second readings also happen. Chapter 9 asks what readers do after their initial yen to explore worlds, to encounter the Other, is satisfied. How does their desire to read turn into a desire to reread? Reading is, in the words of Peter Brooks (1984), a form of desire *for* meaning and *of* meaning, but Brooks does not consider how long that desire lasts. If that desire is a gift of the author-host to the reader-guest, the form of the gift is not just the text. Rather, the gift must involve the author's need to convey meaning that is dear to him or her—meaning discovered in the act of writing itself. It is true that authors such as Michael Ondaatje and J. R. R. Tolkien, while composing, discover the presence of the singular reader, the stranger-guest who will receive their singular gifts. But the potential of their texts is never fully actualized, and the meaning of their books cannot be found, with only one reading. The gift of desire changes as the relation between reader and writer changes from hospitality to friendship. Rereading outlasts hospitality because the desire of the reader for meaning outlasts it. Yet in the current classroom, "reading assignments" are almost licenses to steal cheap gifts for someone else, an act of theft that happens only once. Student readers are expected to draw the meaning from the text only once, not to reenact the infinite desire of the author, where the essence of reading lies.

The last two chapters, however, reaffirm hospitality and its permanent effects on literacy. It could be contended that with all these writer-reader and teacher-student relationships, traditional hospitality, outmoded as it is today, functions only as a model or metaphor. This argument does not stand scrutiny, however (chapter 10, "Tropes of Learning Change"). Without doubt, most comparisons used to explain writing or English teaching, such as dancing or traveling, are purely metaphoric, since normally writers and readers, teachers and students, do not dance or travel in books or classrooms, not actually. But although the hospitable gesture—for instance, on the first day of class the teacher reading aloud an essay she wrote as a student—may serve any number of symbolic ends, it also *is* an act of hospitality. Current hospitality functions much like the old sunken paths in many rural areas of Britain appreciated by ecologist Richard Mabey (1990). Formed by centuries of use, and now a familiar metaphor for cultural practices long gone, such as cattle droving, they are still being used. "Because they are alive there is a continuity between what they were and what they are" (95). And their continued use means their continued social and material change. "Habit," says Mabey, "becomes habitat" (96). Or becomes "habitus" in Pierre Bourdieu's (1984) sense of an evolving social structure that "organizes practices as well as the perception of practices" (170).

Wherever it takes place, the hospitable gesture is not an outmoded or isolated act but a living moment in *history* with historical roots and historical ramifications, a material *site* with material allowances and effects, and a cultural *narrative* with expected plot lines. To the degree that hospitable acts of authoring and hospitable acts of teaching share *kairos*, place, and story with acts of traditional hospitality, they are, literally, hospitality in action. English teachers, for instance, hold in common a number of narratives of learning taking place over time. This book argues that these constructions might be improved by integration with narratives of learning assumed by traditional hospitality. The profession, for instance, speaks about growth of student learning and growth of scholarly knowledge in terms of clearing the hurdles, crossing the border, climbing the ladder, marking height on the door frame, or learning the ropes. These tropes all describe the student or scholar learner as winning or succeeding. Students and scholars think they are fulfilling prerequisites, passing tests, developing skills, mastering scholarship, and getting published. But these narratives, constructed or not, imply that past learning alone counts, or that learning can be formulated and regimented, or that growth is by nature uniform, none of which is true. Hospitality tells stories with very different images of change. They speak of welcoming the stranger, for instance, sudden spiritual conversion, reversal of expertise, dumping of past knowledge. Which narratives are the more useful for the English profession? Which better fit the actual experience of active learners? Which better foster and maintain the singularity and potentiality of students and teachers?

All narratives are also situated, of course. Certain spaces on campus, other than the classroom itself, lend themselves especially well to enactments of hospitality. In English departments some are obvious, like the teacher's office or the tutor carrel in the writing center. But can the ordinary English classroom enact hospitality? Chapter 11 ("The Multiple Common Space Classroom") argues that reconceptualizing institutional space in terms of hospitality is aided by Italian philosopher Giorgio Agamben's (1993) notion of *agio* ("ease"), or the space members of a hospitable community provide one another to allow change according to singular personal inclinations. Community elbow room is created and legitimized by hospitality as it has been practiced in most cultures, and is easily adapted to academic spaces. No doubt much of the academic community would look with suspicion on the creation of such spaces, although they involve simple steps toward maintaining and developing the singular potential of everyone involved. But where hospitable multiple common spaces have been constructed, both the physical space and its effect on users have lasted.

ROOM TO LEARN

The chapters in this long essay are founded upon the premise that the book, the text, is a hospitable site where the potential and the singular fuse. The writer begins as host, the reader as guest, the book as the abode where potentiality actuates yet never is used up. "Incommensurable," says Edmond Jabès (1991) in his usual gnomic way, "is the book's hospitality" (100).

In her essay "Mr. Bennet and Mrs. Brown," thinking of the need of the writer to establish connections with the reader, Virginia Woolf (1988) says, "Both in life and in literature it is necessary to have some means of bridging the gulf between the hostess and her unknown guest on one hand, the writer and his unknown reader on the other." If we take it seriously, that gulf can be daunting. But a good host-writer, Woolf continues, solves how to get into touch with a guest-reader by "putting before him something which he recognizes, which therefore stimulates his imagination, and makes him willing to co-operate in the far more difficult business of intimacy" (34). The writer finds welcoming ways to pave the reader's entrance into the writer's world.

"It is of the highest importance that this common meeting-place should be reached easily," Woolf (1988, 34) rightfully observes. Most destructive to such a meeting place is the assumption of superiority, whether granted on the part of the reader or demanded on the part of the writer. For the writer-reader hospitality to work, there must be "a close and equal alliance between us" (38).

The hospitality entailed in the "common meeting-place" of author and reader brings us to the doorstep of the English classroom, where exercising hospitality, creating a "multiple common space," will obviously be more than presenting a smiley face and letting students introduce themselves, more than erecting an anteroom to the institution or a halfway house leading to legitimated society. In some ways the hospitable classroom will be unfamiliar and unsettling. It will be opposite and oppositional. It will be a place where teachers and students are less concerned with identification of themselves to each other than with dis-identification, with looking through social identities to the singular Other. Agamben put this transgressive blend of potentiality, singularity, and hospitality as concisely as possible: "What the state cannot tolerate in any way is that the singularities form a community without affirming an identity" (1993, 86). Or in the terms of Levinas (1969), the infinity formed when singular Self meets singular Other in hospitality, thereby forming an ongoing community, challenges the totality imposed when established orthodoxies regulate behavior, thereby affirming a permanent identity.

Travelers with only one horse no longer ride-and-tie the sunken lanes of England and no longer, night befallen, knock at the door of a squatter's house on the common expecting that the owner will freely offer them a place to sleep out of the weather. But some of the habitus of that old hospitality remains and can be used in English courses today. Today giant MOOCs with their pseudo-hospitality have not yet swallowed the traditional English classroom, which remains open to change in an opposite, resistant direction. This extended essay explores some ways that a true hospitable classroom community can be transformed (without resort to magic) through sites such as assigned reading, one-on-one conferencing, interpretation, syllabus, reading journal, topic choice, literacy narrative, writing center, program administration, teacher training, and many other passing habitations. There are no hotel guarantees framed on the inside of the doors to these chapters. They merely offer a few potentials, possibilities of change that might make college more of an institution where singular students and singular teachers create a room to learn with room to learn.

Note

1.   In composition studies, for instance, we can locate only four articles: Davis 2001; Heard 2010; Jacobs 2008; Haswell, Haswell, and Blalock 2009. There are a few more if we add the remarkable situated discourse studies of Rosemary Winslow (1996, 1999, 2004). No monograph-length study of hospitality exists in language, literacy, literature, or writing studies.

1

MODES OF HOSPITALITY IN HISTORY

Responsibilité aliene; hospitalité allege.
  —Edmond Jabès

A hospitable site with room to learn is neither alchemy nor futuristic vision. It is a reality of the past still alive. For millennia, in every country around the world, hospitality customs have taken root. Over and over in every culture's literature, the customs have supplied staple, central scenes. This chapter would have been superfluous for any but the last three generations of the Western world. In redrawing the professionally established dynamic between student and teacher according to an ethic of hospitality, we turn to a long and rich tradition that, today, happens to need retelling.

The definition of *hospitality* in the *Oxford English Dictionary* (1971) dons a beatific face: "the reception and entertainment of guests, visitors, or strangers with liberality and good will." But scholars such as Emile Benveniste (1973), who have traced the roots of the English word, draw an etymological history of intrinsic conflict, of both fear and attraction, repulsion and union. The Indo-European *ghostis* meant a stranger to be welcomed or feared, the Greek *xenos* a home host or alien guest, the Latin *hostis* a stranger or enemy and *hospes* a stranger or foreigner. To this day in French "host" and "guest" are conveyed by the same word, *hôte*.

The foundational English word *host* is also polysemous and fractious. Does it mean a host with open arms or a host with leveled arms? As we will see, the contradictions persist in social practices of hospitality. For the moment, however, we will focus on host as "one who receives or entertains another." The word *entertain* comes from *inter* and *tenere*, to hold together. Rather than offering the guest diversion or merriment, the host offers attention, empathy, welcome, and then understanding. With the reception of the guest into the host's home, two worlds meet and hold together: the world of the insider and the world of the outsider. Derrida (1993, 10) calls the guest the *arrivant*, a useful term

DOI: 10.7330/9780874219883.c001

since it combines a sense of both showing up (*elle arrivera demain*, she will arrive tomorrow) and occurring by chance (*il est arrivé que*, it happened that). The host is at home and in possession, while the guest—the chance appearer, the outsider, the traveler, the refugee, the immigrant, the homeless, the pilgrim—is dispossessed. Dispossessed but not empty-handed. For the guest opens up the host's world with the unfamiliar, the unknown, the unexpected, the new, the informative—often with stories.

But make no mistake. Hospitality's face may be one of liberality and goodwill, but the hospitable gesture aligns along the edge of a knife. Because the host is on home territory, he or she might fear to welcome an arrivant who, as the linguistic roots of *guest* remind us, could be an innocent stranger but might be a hostile intruder intending to take the host hostage or, in one of the earliest recorded possibilities, a god in disguise testing the host's hospitality. To limit the possibilities, the host might demand that the guest reveal his or her name, but that is a step running contrary to the customs of hospitality because it hints at some degree of mastery or violence (Kearney 1999).

The risk is not solely on the part of the host. The needy guest must cross the threshold and trust the host's good intentions (Rosello 2001, 75). Prolonged or forced stay might turn guest into servant or slave. Hospitality, this temporary shared residence of insider and outsider, is "à la fois menace et don" (Montandon 1999, 11), a simultaneous threat and gift applying to both welcomer and welcomed. The challenge, as Julia Kristeva (1991) reminds us, is to realize that the "foreigner" arrives "when the consciousness of my difference arises, and he disappears when we all acknowledge ourselves as foreigners" (1). As in Conrad's *The Secret Sharer*, knowing that the foreigner is already within, the host will not distrust the guest but instead risk meeting and communion.

THREE HISTORIC MODES

The central moral axis of traditional hospitality—equality in dignity, privilege, and value of stranger-host and stranger-guest—is complex and can turn like a double-edged knife. Therefore our rhetoric framing of it must be precise. We begin by clarifying modes and reviewing history.

One primary mode is Homeric, or warrior, hospitality. In the *Iliad* hospitality revolves around feasting. Equitable sharing of meat marks a celebration of victory, an act of thanksgiving to the gods, and an acknowledgment of the role and prestige of each warrior. Of course, other bounty is distributed—or, in the case of the female war trophies Chryseis and Briseis, disastrously redistributed. But underneath, two dynamics shape the politically loaded social interactions of hospitality in the *Iliad*: prestige and equality (Rundin 1996, 192, 194). Agamemnon wields control over the distribution of bounty because he commands the most men; he is the most privileged among the privileged and, as host, the sole gift giver (Reece 1993, 35). Yet equity in enjoying the spoils of war is crucial, for not only is bounty a measure of glory and fame, it also solidifies bonds of loyalty among independent bands of warriors and between warriors and kings. Feasting, as John Rundin (1996, 193) notes, is a "dominant element in the network of exchange" and strengthens pledges of service in the Greek camp, thereby assuring the continued commitment to their shared goal of victory over Troy.

Clearly, Homeric or warrior hospitality functions in a closed circle. It is conservative in the sense of solidifying and perpetuating the power of those already privileged. Gift giving happens only between relative equals. Anyone marginal to the warrior class—women, the poor, the nonmilitary, and the powerless—have no place at the feast: "The feast is an occasion for men in the realm of men" (Rundin 1996, 190). Perhaps it is not surprising that this militaristic mode best fits the current notion of hospitality as entertaining and rewarding one's friends, relatives, and allies rather than welcoming strangers.

In the biblical tradition of hospitality, we find a less exclusionary mode of host-guest relations. In the Old Testament story of Abraham and his angelic visitors at Mamre (Genesis 18), entertainment means providing strangers with food, water, and shelter to cleanse the body and refresh the spirit, then fellowship and community by widening the family or social circle to include them. The strangers, however, may be disguised, only appearing to be ragged and weary. Once revitalized under the terebinth trees of Mamre, the three guests reveal themselves in a truer guise—angels who can give Abraham a gift in turn: the promise of a son. The Jewish lesson persisted, and the New Testament is careful to warn, "Be not forgetful to entertain strangers: for thereby some have entertained angels unawares" (Hebrews 13:2).

In a larger Christian sense, moreover, feeding the hungry, clothing the naked, and visiting the sick is undertaken not in hopes of entertaining angels in disguise but in service to Christ himself (Matthew 25:34–46). The guest, the stranger, even the enemy, is now wreathed with an ethos of utmost dignity. Those who respect and protect that dignity will be welcomed into their eternal home by the original Host: "'Come unto me all you who labor . . . My Father has many mansions'" (John 14:2). "Where knock is open wide" is both an image and an action of *caritas*, the core Christian virtue. Thus believers are charged not with simply welcoming the arrivant but with loving him or her as "neighbor," as the parable of the Good Samaritan makes clear. In this tradition, the host who supplies shelter and kindness is the initial giver of gifts, but the guest or stranger reciprocates with gifts of her or his own. Whether in the form of shelter, feasting, useful knowledge, or granted wishes, gift exchange expresses the soul of biblical hospitality.

Unfortunately, over time, as religious institutional practices came to dominate behavior and motives, the mutual and often unforeseen trading of gifts gradually devolved into a one-sided beneficence. Caritas became charity. The church feeds the poor, the pastor folds the sheep, and neither expects anything in return except for devotion. The traditional biblical mode of hospitality provides a crucial point throughout this book: that hospitality, in teaching or literacy, is not commensurate with the kind of charitable display that in modern enactments maintains a hierarchic barrier between the moneyed and the needy.

Study of the Homeric and biblical traditions unearths the bones of Western culture, a framework around which centuries of social interactions took shape. But hospitality has functioned outside the West as well, and so we turn to our third mode, nomadic hospitality. This is the sort that held sway for millennia throughout much of Africa, Central Asia, and eastern Europe and that is still practiced, for instance, by the Bedouin of the Middle East. Here a nomadic host offers tent and food to persons who are wandering, for whatever reason, away from their own tent. Or perhaps they are just tentless. Both host and guest are on the move. But the guest is treated with extreme respect. Traditionally, it is forbidden for the host to ask any questions about the guest.

As in other early traditions of hospitality, there is an exchange of gifts. Along with food, drink, and shelter, the host offers information about his region useful to the wanderer. The guest offers a gift in return, in the form of communication: gossip, political news, information about the movement of other nomadic groups, land-boundaries, and even market conditions and business deals—potentially gifts that the host can use when he is traveling outside his own nomadic range. In short, there is an exchange of information, a kind of intellectual hospitality, helpful to both for their future wanderings. The essential difference with Homeric and biblical hospitalities is that with two nomads the status of host and guest is impermanent and reversible. When their migratory paths may again intersect, the earlier host can easily be the guest, the guest the host.

All three modes continue into the twentieth century, roughly aligning with what Jacques Derrida has called "political" and "ethical" hospitality.

Political hospitality involves a limited, guarded, and strategic exchange between host and guest, much like the Homeric warrior model. Ethical hospitality, at least in its pre-Roman form, encompasses an unconditional, decentered, and transformative experience for both guest and host, as in biblical and nomadic models. Political hospitality and ethical hospitality mark clearly conflicting practices, and it will be productive to explore the pitfalls of these modes before exploring their applicability to the English classroom.

HOSPITALITY CORRUPTED

When first considering hospitality as an expression of the spiritual life, it is easy to romanticize how it has historically functioned. We might envision the kind of monastic hospitality Kathleen Norris (1993) describes in *Dakota: A Spiritual Geography*. The Benedictine monks are model hosts because they are totally unprepossessing. Excluding no one, asking nothing, they welcome all people who have set out on life's journey and in transit arrive at the monastery walls. In this light, hospitality isn't something you do or achieve, but "something you enter . . . someone you become" (Pratt and Homan 2002, 38). For Catholic priest Henri J. M. Nouwen, who shares his life with mentally disabled persons, the ideal of hospitality renews his sense of vocation. "The minister as host heals, sustains, and guides." This is possible only when the host dares to renounce any desire for maintaining control, for having all the answers. Only then do "you have nothing to lose but all to give" (1972, 51). In short, the host takes on the vulnerability of the arrivant.

But it is a mistake to relegate hospitality to more simple, trusting, or naïve times.[1] There may have been no historical period when ethical hospitality was natural or easy or common, and examples abound of hospitable practices, understood and affirmed within a society or culture, being violated by the members of those same communities.

For example, evidence suggests that nomadic hospitality has not atrophied as much as has Homeric and biblical hospitality traditions in the West. But catastrophic events in the Middle East are helping it to catch up. Even before the Gulf Wars, Lois Beck, who studied the nomadic Qashqa'i of southwest Iran in 1977, describes urban incursions into the old cultural ways. For one instance, she narrates how the Bedouin family of Habib Aqa were unexpectedly visited by twelve near strangers. Although Aqa was in the middle of threshing and winnowing his wheat crop, work was stopped, a goat was slaughtered and roasted, and that night the hosts slept in the open air, giving up their tent to the guests

(1982, 433–434). Aqa's guests were urbanites, a retired army officer and his family who arrived in a Jeep station wagon and clearly were exploiting the situation. As Beck explains, there are many accounts of Westernized groups taking advantage of this deep-rooted cultural practice of the Bedouin. Even within traditional nomadic modes hospitality can insinuate Blake's clash between the Devouring and the Prolific (1973, plate 16).

It takes little imagination to recognize how warrior or Homeric hospitality degenerates into the degrading and violent experience of what scholars have called colonial hospitality. Under the political, military, economic, and missionary drive of European expansion, strangers arriving in foreign lands began relationships as guests but quickly commandeered the role of host. The arrivant became an invader, occupier, or colonizer (Derrida 1993, 34)—often all three. Here the foreign guest, even with excellent intentions, violates the hospitality code by attempting to rescue, to "save," the native host from native traditions and ways of life. Such rescue inevitably turns violent when the otherness of the native does not signify promise but only difference, a difference to be feared and labeled "savage" and "ignorant" (Sharon-Zisser 1999, 316–318). Colonial hospitality betrays ethical hospitality not because the role of host and guest are inverted but because there is no reciprocal exchange or equitable redefinition of roles as the new host devours and cannibalizes the natives, who were once hosts but now are perpetual and powerless guests in their own land (Rosello 2001, 28–30).

Vestiges of warrior hospitality can also be found in nationalist and racial presumptions about privilege that exclude newcomers from elite circles of power. In her masterful study of government practices and artistic representations of French immigration policies in the 1990s, Mireille Rosello likens Derrida's "ethical hospitality" to instances of personal or "private hospitality," when individual citizens offer sanctuary to immigrants and refugees. Such actions are characterized by mutual acts of generosity between hosts and guests and a selflessness that transcends economic gain or legal constraint (2001, 10–11). Rosello then applies Derrida's sense of political hospitality to what she sees as the "official hospitality" of the French government, which through normative and prescriptive discourse reduces guests to undocumented aliens, the *sans-papiers*, represented as endangering the language, economic health, and culture of French citizens (6–8). While the aliens could prove a valuable asset (were they already wealthy or educated enough, or willing to work at manual jobs for cheap wages), the state frames its relationship with them as a pragmatic exchange, weighing the fear and risk against potential benefits (12).

The perils of biblical hospitality can be found in the patriarchal elements of its roots and the privileges thereof; it was "man's work and man's reward" (Haggerty 2010, 56). The host was usually male and his home was a site of possession and therefore of power. Women in the home were only surrogate hosts, dispensing the true host's hospitality. Neither could they be guests. They were, in fact, captives possessed and powerless, commodities like goods or currency (Pilardi 2010, 73)— Chryseis and Briseis once again. No starker illustration is necessary than the Old Testament story of Lot and his two visitors who need saving from the lecherous mob of Sodom. To guarantee the safety of his guests, Lot offers to hand over his virgin daughters to the townspeople (Genesis 19:8). Undismayed by this display of male power, the visitors reveal themselves to be angels who save Lot, his wife, and daughters from God's sulphurous fire.

In practice, Bedouin hospitality is clearly patriarchal, and has been at least since the second century BCE, when it was the foundation for the culture of the Pentateuch fathers, the line of Abraham. But in structure, it does not have to be. Indeed, structurally nomadic hospitality may lend itself to gender egalitarianism more than other forms of hospitality because of the reversibility of host and guest. Joachim Manzi (1999) argues that as a model for social behavior, it is uniquely open for accepting the female Other on equal terms. This is not Tracy McNulty's (1999) argument, which sees the Old Testament female hostess (Sarah, Jael, Judith, Lot's unnamed wife) as a form of excess that "insists upon the discontinuity inherent in the relation between the human and the divine" (para. 76), an excess that helps preserve ethical hospitality from becoming a hospitality of pure law. In the history of Judaic hospitality, McNulty argues, the beginning of the end of ethical hospitality was signaled with the Decalogue (in which hospitality does not figure), the start of Israel's long transformation from nomadism to nationhood.

Contrary to regarding hospitality as a male privilege, some feminists have advanced the view that hospitality involves an essentially feminine role, that within the home women continue the old hospitable ways by giving of their work time so that others can attend to wage-earning and entertainment (Diprose 2009). The symbol of hospitality might in fact be the caring and receiving mother who dwells in the home, conceived not as a location of privilege but as a point of receptivity (Gregorious 2001, 139, 140). Women's work—homemaking, cooking, bearing children— once decried by some early feminists as means of patriarchal control, may be seen as ways women use material things "to interact with the larger world, a place where my values are lived out, extended out from the home into the world, as I create connections with others" (Pilardi 2010, 79).

Irina Aristarkhova goes even further. Using Luce Irigaray as a counterpoint to Derrida and Levinas, she argues that, ironically enough, the soul of hospitality can be found in the woman's role—she who traditionally owns nothing and who therefore cannot host anyone or give away anything (2012, 171). If we rethink ownership, we can recognize that the maternal (here Aristarkhova means not simply the procreative ability but also "generative, nursing, and materializing qualities" [178]) provides the site of the original home, the home of the mother, "the place of an original welcoming and hosting" (174). In acknowledging the power and role of the maternal, Aristarkhova argues, we will discover the true potential of hospitality "through acts rendered in terms of intentionality and intelligibility" (175). In sum, the maternal "will allow hospitality to be embodied as an act, to reconnect it and reactualize it" (174).

But to reassign true hospitality to the realm of women, or to label true hospitable practices as "feminist," strikes us as, well, inhospitable. It also runs the risk of associating with women the contemporary degraded versions of hospitality that kneel at the altar of money, social leverage, and friendship networking. Genuine hospitality is not the special purview of women; it is not an attribute of character or action that is feminist in nature—or masculinist, for that matter. Rather, it is a human practice that recognizes the innate dignity and promise of the guest, the stranger, the foreigner, the Other. The gendered *customs* of traditional hospitality may have dwindled over time, but its transgendered *vision* remains vital and viable. It awaits wherever strangers, good hosts and good guests (whether man or woman, teacher or student, writer or reader), understand themselves to be incomplete, "in need of ennobling growth" (Boisvert 2004, 293) and are willing to be "destabilized," jeopardized, and transformed by their mutual encounter (Sander-Staudt 2010, 42).

Perhaps the most crippling influence on traditional hospitality has been the rise of capitalism and the middle class, which has undercut that vital sense of mutual dignity and value enjoyed by host and guest. Consider how hospitable gift exchange has been debased by ostentation and consumerism. For instance, in studies of Renaissance England, Daryl Palmer argues that hospitality had already become the privilege of aristocrats and monarchs who sought to win consent or support by being, or appearing to be, beneficent (1992, 16). Reminiscent of Homeric hospitality, the politically savvy or upwardly mobile also recognized that hospitable principles of obligation and reciprocity could be used to maintain social relations with dominant groups or powerful individuals as well as foster self-promotion through "chains of access" (3, 7). Pomp and ostentation gradually excluded the lower classes.

Ironically, as hospitable practices ceased to cross class barriers and infuse common sociopolitical life, the representation of hospitality expanded in the form of pamphlets and masques. Palmer (1992) notes that the position of host was cast as the king or lord whose duty was to maintain communal order (28). Thus, with the representation rather than the genuine practice of hospitality came a mystification of economic and political dominance by the wealthy, who could claim to be virtuous because of their magnanimity. The more hospitality valorized privilege, the more it gave rise to "a mood of complaint" among commoners about the roles of hosts and guests—perhaps because the traditional exchange of gifts conflicted with the new commodification of power (29, 157).

"Responsibilité aliene. Hospitalité allege," writes Edmond Jabès (1991, 21). Under the customs of traditional hospitality, host and guest do no more than propose (*allege*) a reciprocal relationship. One stranger's gift to another stranger helps form a pathway to communication. But when hospitality is politicized and commodified, the relationship becomes asymmetrical and alienates (*aliene*), with the host taking on responsibility for the guest. This is why the current hospitality "trade" is antithetic to traditional hospitality. Missions for the moneyless and hotels for the moneyed, currently the most institutionalized forms of hospitality, send the host into the guest's homeland to draw outsiders inside the host's camp, circling us back to Homeric warrior hospitality. In the academy, what used to be called hotel and restaurant administration now bears such names as hospitality studies, hospitality business, and hospitality management (one more example of the institution appropriating populist language). "Southern hospitality" appears without fail on the lodging and dining page of town websites in every state below the Mason-Dixon line.

What these examples have in common is the reduction of hospitality to a capitalistic gambit, church promotion, or domestic grace. The "welcome" takes a range of forms: self-serving ostentation, threats of God's vengeance, or codified formulas of etiquette. This third custom reduces hospitality, as Elizabeth Telfer (1995) rightly notes, to a "minor virtue." Within the social-etiquette framework, the host seeks satisfaction by giving and receiving pleasure within a closed circle of family and friends (184). Being a good host may require skill, perhaps even attentiveness, certainly economic means, even generosity in dutiful "Good Samaritan" acts (185). There can be social and political benefits, Telfer admits. But a host may be attentive without empathy, skillful without any motive to help. Thus social entertainment is not foundational to society, where hospitality is only an "optional" virtue (191–192).

Case in point: in Western culture by the end of the nineteenth century, the pineapple had become a symbol of hospitality. Earlier, in colonial America, the hostess would set a pineapple in the center of the table when entertaining strangers, and at the end of the meal it would be shared as dessert. But such hostessing turned more and more into competitive entertainment within social ranks. Sometimes when guests were invited for dinner, a pineapple would serve as nothing but commodity and display, rented and then returned to the true owner the next day. A history of inconsequential manners? Perhaps, but cultures have been nearly destroyed by their modes of entertainment.

THE SUN'S MYTH

Witness the postcontact history of Pacific Northwest Native American tribes, some of which were destroyed by their custom of potlatch, or competitive gift exchange, when it ran amok with purely decorative European trade goods. Any application of hospitality must never forget its dark side, the way it can be and has been so readily corrupted by materialism, competition, and power seeking. Some of that dark history is unforgettably engraved in the story of "The Sun's Myth." This Kathlamet Chinook legend is discussed by Barre Toelken in *Oral Patterns of Performance: Story and Song*. In 1891 it was told by Charles Cultee, one of the last speakers of his native language, to Franz Boas. Later it was "resuscitated" by folklorist Dell Hymes from documents of the Bureau of American Ethnology (Toelken 2014, 130).

A tribal chief sets out to visit the Sun, which he has watched rise morning after morning. In the Chinook tradition, the Sun is female. After a long journey, he arrives at a large house belonging to a young girl and her grandmother. The chief marvels at the riches lining the walls, both men's property of arrows, armor, axes, clubs, and regalia, and women's property of blankets, skins, and beads. He asks the girl no fewer than thirteen times who owns this bounty, and is told each time that these items are the girl's dowry, saved for the celebration of her first menstruation when she becomes marriageable. The chief takes the girl, commands the bounty, and assumes possession of the home. So ends part 1.

In part 2, the girl and her grandmother recognize signs of the chief's emotional distress at being parted from his family and villages. He is offered anything of the women's riches for his return journey, but he demands "only one bright thing" among the grandmother's belongings. She reluctantly surrenders the shining object, a blanket, which the chief then wears. But he also takes a stone ax. As the chief nears each of his five villages—five being the number of completion— the bright object announces, "We two shall strike your town" (Toelken 2014, 127). In a mad fit, the chief slaughters the entire village. He repeats his savagery in the next four villages. Each time, the chief blames the object, but he cannot rid himself of it. Finally, after slaughtering his own family, he spies the old woman, who reclaims the blanket that is rightfully hers. The chief then builds a small house and remains there, alone.

For Toelken (2014), "The Sun's Myth" affirms the traditional values of the Chinook people, as it is a litany of grave tribal violations. The chief places himself ahead of the family as the basic social unit and abandons his social obligations in his lone quest to a remote land. He rapes a prepubescent girl. He claims her wealth, which should have been distributed to the community as part of her wedding ceremony. He steals the single most precious object in the house. And he destroys the villages he was obliged to protect. He "literally destroys the culture," says Toelken (128). The title suggests that the most important character is not the chief, whose actions dominate events, but the grandmother as Sun—wise and nurturing. In fact, it is the females in the story who provide the corrective to the "egotistical agenda" of the male (124). "It is you who choose," the grandmother tells him as he gazes upon the remains of the villages (128). As punishment, he must live by himself, alone and removed from family and community.

Alongside Toelken's compelling analysis, we would interpret "The Sun's Myth" within the frame of hospitality. In his village the chief forsakes his responsibilities as host, and as traveler and pilgrim he rejects the appropriate behavior of guest. Upon arriving at the women's house, he scorns welcome and amiable gift exchange and assumes control of the hosts' rightful domain. He is a maverick one-man colonial power, reversing the role of host and guest in order to gain power. Socially, then, the chief becomes a monster who destroys the hospitable culture that nurtured him and upon which he depends. Failing as both host and guest, the man is removed from the community as a social pariah.

This lens of hospitality might seem artificially imposed upon the story, but in fact Toelken himself offers a further interpretation that reflects the abuse we have identified as colonial hospitality. Toelken wonders what might have prompted Cultee to tell the tale to Franz Boas, since "Native people don't just recite myths for the fun of it" (2014, 129). What if the bright, shining object that so captivates the chief can be understood allegorically to describe the fascination Native American peoples felt with European goods and technology, which eventually displaced, exploited, and sometimes decimated them? But Toelken furthers the irony. What if Cultee saw a direct parallel between himself and researcher Boas, who as "a powerful man" arrives, "presents himself to a powerless Native American who possesses immense narrative riches," admires them, then covets them and says, "I will take them" (130). In the hands of the colonizer, the shining stories cannot be understood or controlled, and without native tellers and their lost languages to claim what is rightfully theirs, the cruel legacy of colonialism and genocide can never be assuaged.

For us, "The Sun's Myth" offers two lessons. First, hospitality provides a framework whereby the Chinook society could critique its practices, diagnose its spiritual illness, and pass judgment on individuals who violate the moral traditions that bind them together as a people. As Derrida has observed, hospitality is "the essence of culture" (1993, 8) because it works as a glue that holds a society together. Second, when hospitality goes wrong, the vulnerability of both hosts and guests will be disregarded. In that case, the disparity between host and guest in terms of the power they wield both corrupts and reveals the functioning of hospitality.

Today in the social sphere, a widening gap divides the wealthy and the comfortably established middle class on one side and the poor and the working class on the other. In the educational sphere, an invisible wall separates the learned and the learners. "We are at home; they are not. We are in control; they are not. We set the agenda; they do not" (Johnson 1993, 342). Hospitality does not simply demand that the haves, as some bountiful Agamemnon, occasionally feast the have-nots. Rather, hospitality addresses issues of inclusion and exclusion (Pratt and Homan 2002, 2). Inclusion is not merely an attitude or principle; if it does not translate into action, it remains only a flaccid sentiment— wherever, too often and too easily, a host, centered and secure, rejects equal terms with the stranger. Without reciprocity the host-guest relation becomes fixed, degenerating into condescension or exploitation on the part of the host, begging or parasitism on the part of the guest (Rosello 2001, 167). It is no accident that true hospitable space often is located between the interstices or on the fringes of social power, in "the margins of society, where it is offered by hosts who have a sense of their own alien status" (Pohl 1995, 136).

HOSPITALITY DEFENDED

History, clever at hindsight, is not nearly so trustworthy a guide for the future. Still, it seems safe to say that there is little chance the praxis of traditional hospitality will be resuscitated, not in its past forms, however ubiquitous they were. Indeed, there may be good reasons to hope it will not be revived. Who would want the kind of political or economic world collapse that would bring on a new need for it—impoverished crowds on the road, without home or shelter? But the notion of hospitality is alive and well, even undergoing resurgence in intellectual circles. Our question is whether a revived and re-visioned hospitality can serve as a model and impetus in the local practice of teaching college English. A defensible answer will take three steps beyond speculation based on historical examples. First, the philosophical dimensions of hospitality need study, and second, the pragmatics of its application needs scrutiny. Third, its dark sides must be remembered.

Hospitality has to be disentangled from its localized historical conditions before it can be moved to new locales, and philosophers, with their interest in ethical and phenomenological truths, will aid this extraction and transportation. In "Of Hospitality" (2000), Derrida, for instance, proposes an "unconditioned hospitality" in which hosts have no option but to accept unknown arrivants into their homes. Such a utopian hospitality cannot be lived, he admits, but the concept of it is necessary. Derrida insists that without at least the thought of this pure and unconditioned hospitality, of hospitality per se, we would have no concept of hospitality in general and would not even be able to determine any rules for conditioned hospitality, with its rituals, its legal status, its norms, its national or international conventions (Borradori 2003, 129).

Or with its educational uses? Neither unconditioned nor radical hospitality should be applied to the English classroom, argues Matthew Heard (2010), because "hospitality cannot coincide with business as usual" (327). It is a serious argument we will consider in chapters 2 and 5. Here we will only note that the disruption of business as usual may not be a bad thing, and that philosophers often posit one good end of hospitality as its resistance to authority and to other top-down power structures. For an instance that anticipates the next chapter, philosophy might warn that an effort to embed classroom hospitality within a framework of women's work will fail because, as Emmanuel Levinas would point out, such an application subverts hospitality to an act of totalization and therefore invalidates hospitality itself.

What, then, will a valid application to the English classroom look like? What happens to the utopian ideal when it is made real? Roughly drawn, the result may be not so much a utopia as a heterotopia. In a piece written early in his career but published only toward the end of it, Michel Foucault (1967) defines heterotopia as a "counter-site, a kind of effective enacted utopia in which the real sites, all the other real sites that can be found within the culture, are simultaneously represented, contested, and inverted." Heterotopias are locations, actual and functioning, where people can deviate from their society, can break the traditions of their times, can rerepresent norms, can bring together practices that elsewhere are deemed incompatible. Foucault mentions an astonishing range of these counter-sites: retirement home, psychiatric hospital, prison, cemetery, theater, cinema, formal garden, museum, library, festival, fairground, vacation site, Scandinavian sauna, Jesuit colony, brothel, boat. The list, it seems to us, could also contain the hospitable classroom. Counter, transgressive, marginal, critical, juxtapositional, and comingling, such a classroom would also have a last heterotopic trait, a custom-supported means of entry and closure: "Heterotopias always presuppose a system of opening and closing that both isolates them and makes them penetrable" (Foucault 1967).

Foucault does not mention the hospice, monastery, soup kitchen, or other continuing sites of hospitality, although he well could have. But he does mention the old colonial house-building custom, in Brazil and elsewhere in South America, of adding an isolated bedroom entered only from the outside. "These bedrooms were such that the individual who went into them never had access to the family's quarter; the visitor was absolutely the guest in transit, was not really the invited guest" (1967). While useful for wayfarers trudging the hazardous seventeenth- and eighteenth-century roads of Latin America, such ancillary rooms seem a strange model for contemporary instruction, a kind of MOOC for one student. But maybe not so odd, since they suggest accommodation of students with an honest acceptance of the fact that they are transients, passers-through—not really members of any academic family, not yet, and perhaps never will be.[2]

Indeed, returning to our three historical modes of hospitality, it is the nomadic that may offer the best model for the passing encounters of students and teachers. Disregarded by most as a desert relic of outmoded ways, more and more isolated and endangered, nomadic hospitality may, in Foucault's (1967) words, serve as an "effective enacted utopia," the heterotopic counter-site that the English classroom could well become. After all, for the contemporary learning rooms of higher education, the image of the journey is more than apt—it is constitutive. College classrooms are occupied by teachers who are guests almost as much as their students. Unlike many of their peers in the schools, they do not teach out of "home rooms." Especially if they are unladdered staff or temporary hires, they are nearly as much in transit as are the students. Of course, it is many leagues, in space and time, from carpeted tent floors to laptops on desks, but maybe not so far in mind and act. As chapter 3 will argue, the English classroom can both be *like* a hospitable space and *be* a hospitable space.

Notes

Parts of this chapter appeared in "Hospitality in College Composition Courses," *College Composition and Communication* 60(4) (2009): 707-727, an article coauthored with Glenn Blalock.

1. See, for instance, Shirley Sharon-Zisser's (1999) laudatory analysis of medieval, precolonial Europe. Her sophisticated rhetorical analysis leaves little room for sentimental generalities.

2. External rooms for wayfarers can be found in traditional housing not only in South America but throughout the world. In northern Pakistan, the guest room is called a *hujra*. In recent years, Taliban commanders moved from *hujra* to *hujra* to avoid detection. The United States knew this, and during 2009 and 2010 the majority of drone strikes in Pakistan were on *hujras*. The strikes put the families in a terrible bind. The Taliban suspected them of ratting, and the Pakistan government accused them of giving assistance to the enemy. Yet traditional hospitality laws meant they could not have refused use of their *hujra* (Coll 2014, 105). As with the Bedouin family of Habib Aqa, the traditional ways of hospitality in the Near East continue to be eroded by the West.

2

THE TOTALITY OF WAR, THE INFINITY OF HOSPITALITY

If the doors of perception were cleansed, every thing would appear to man as it is, Infinite.

—William Blake

Emmanuel Levinas (1969) begins *Totality and Infinity: An Essay on Exteriority* with possibly the two most startling sentences to open any major work of philosophy.

> Everyone will readily agree that it is of the highest importance to know whether we are not duped by morality.
>
> Does not lucidity, the mind's openness upon the true, consist in catching sight of the permanent possibility of war? (21)

How does epistemology ("to know") inquire into ethics ("morality"), and why is war so central in this inquiry? And what are morality and war doing at the start of a dense, 300-page phenomenological study of being?

Later in the book Levinas answers these questions by insisting on the primacy of ethics in any study of being and on the absolute suspension of any system of ethics during war. Another answer, however, lies already in the second sentence, with his word *openness*. "Openness" is not his word, of course, but his translator's. Levinas's (1969) word is *ouverture*. In French, *ouverture* literally means an opening to a building, usually a doorway. Only by figurative extension does the phrase *ouverture de l'esprit* mean openness or broadmindedness. So the phrase "the mind's openness upon the true" (*ouverture de l'esprit sur le vrai*) conjures up an image of hospitality, of the host standing at the door and allowing a stranger through.

In *Totality and Infinity*, hospitality is Levinas's (1969) saving grace. "This book will present subjectivity as welcoming the Other, as hospitality; in it the idea of infinity is consummated" (27). Hospitality is the act

DOI: 10.7330/9780874219883.c002

that best constitutes the process of inner being ("subjectivity"), the act allowing change in consciousness, experience, language, learning, and ethics through an openness to what lies outside the self ("exteriority"). Hospitality is the primordial act resisting social and political frames ("totality") that restrict encounters with the Other and shut the door on human change. Levinas pictures this inner being as a home, a dwelling where one can retreat from the world, and hospitality as the act that reopens that retreat toward new possibilities, or "infinity": "To exist henceforth means to dwell. To dwell . . . is a recollection, a coming to oneself, a retreat home with oneself as in a land of refuge, which answers to a hospitality, an expectancy, a human welcome" (156).

And war? What opposes hospitality is not inhospitality. Inhospitality is a degree or absence of hospitality, measured by the degradation of the phenomenological process or the social/moral practice. Nor does fear oppose hospitality, as suggested by M. Christian Green (2010), since some fear or anxiety shadows the gesture of hospitality in practically all of its acts, as serious commentary has noted for centuries. The opposite and enemy of hospitality is war.

Within the true condition of infinity, war is always a possibility, as are efforts to prevent war. But once started, war curtails open thinking, forbids conversation with strangers, and destroys public safety and private homes and other material means of hospitality. "The welcoming of the face [the Other] is peaceable from the first, for it answers to the unquenchable Desire for Infinity. War itself is but a possibility and nowise a condition for it" (Levinas 1969, 150). For Levinas, war is not only an objective reality but also a process of inner being by which objectivity itself, the self's sense of things outside the self, tricks the self into believing it must passively accept those things, that it cannot receptively face them and use them as a way to escape from them into a future they seem to deny: "We oppose to the objectivism of war a subjectivity born from the eschatological vision" (25).

In sum, for Levinas the process of war represents the iron fist of *totality*, the assumption that life is objective, calculable, codifiable, and therefore controllable. By contrast, the process of hospitality is a radical relation with the Other, a face-to-face encounter—creative, unpredictable, uncontrollable, and therefore understandable only as *infinity*. In the hospitable encounter lies the root of ethics, whereas war pursues winning by any means and thus stands outside of morality (Levinas 1969, 21). In its use of ruse, force, and spectacle, war undermines hospitality, which is open-handed, freely chosen, and receptive to critique. Within hospitality war is always a possibility, but only hospitality can prevent war. (Peace, as the current world well knows, does not necessarily oppose war.)

So it is no accident that war is the beginning topic of *Totality and Infinity* (Levinas 1969, 21–26). Of course war—actual war and the civilian displacements it caused—was the central experience of Levinas's generation. He was born in Lithuania in 1906; he moved with his family to the Ukraine during World War I, but returned with them to Lithuania in 1920 after the country had won its independence in three wars: against the Russian Bolsheviks, the anti-Bolshevik Bermontians, and Poland. He fled Lithuania with his Jewish family in 1923; he was conscripted by France in 1939, captured by the Germans in 1940, and spent six years of World War II in the Jewish barracks of a German prisoner of war camp for officers. His family was killed in the war. It is not surprising that *Totality and Infinity*, first published in 1961, seems to shed more and more light on military conflict as the decades pass.

We will resort to Levinas throughout the rest of this book, but here he serves as our authority for continuing this essay's exploration of hospitality with a study of its most absolute enemy, war. Initially in this chapter we will illustrate Levinas's observations about war and hospitality with examples from recent U.S. conflicts. Such evidence reveals the totalizing, unconscionable, even perverted use of hospitality in U.S. foreign policy, and helps explain the marginal state of hospitality in current U.S. culture, including educational institutions. The chapter will end with an introduction to Levinas's antidote to war—hospitality to the Other—in terms of its applications to U.S. classrooms.

WAR AS RUSE

Levinas (1969) distinguishes between the truth of language and the "ruse" of rhetoric, which he defines as an act of violence and injustice (70). The corruption of rhetoric during war is so total that the public is "ambushed" (225). The act of ambush, of course, is the reverse of hospitality in every way. One only has to read Arthur Ponsonby's (1940) venerable study of World War I propaganda, first published in 1928, to find support for Levinas's claim. Ponsonby identified the following rhetorical strategies employed by British authorities to mislead its own people: deliberate official lies to delude both friend and foe, statements released by officials that weren't strictly accurate but inherently probable, lies circulated to a small circle intended to spread to wider circles, heard lies not denied, mistranslations and forgeries, omissions of passages from official documents, calculated exaggerations, false personal accusations and charges, faked photographs and official secrecy, and sham official indignation. Thus were Britishers "duped by morality" (Levinas 1969, 21).

A century after World War I, and two centuries in the making, recent U.S. government rhetoric daily bombards its citizens with images calculated to dissemble war, tricking them into the belief that they are in touch with the reality of war. Some images are so diabolically perverse they appear to stage war as acts of hospitality itself. Consider the late afternoon of May 1, 2003, when George W. Bush, in the copilot's seat and wearing a flight jacket, landed on the deck of the aircraft carrier USS *Abraham Lincoln*. He was greeted with a highly contrived spectacle. Several days before the president arrived, three of his men had "embedded" themselves on the *Abraham Lincoln*: Scott Sforza, a former producer for ABC; Bob Deservi, a cameraman who had worked for NBC; and Greg Jenkins, a former Fox News producer. Sforza planned out the details of the president's arrival down to the positioning of crew members in coordinated shirt colors at Bush's right shoulder. Above his left shoulder was a huge banner reading, "Mission Accomplished." The timing was planned as well, late afternoon when the "magic hour light" would cast a "golden glow" on Bush (Engelhardt 2006; see also Pitt 2003). The stage of welcome was well counterfeited. For counterfeit it was, a production intended merely to reproduce the U.S. military construction of the war ("totality") and in no way a hospitable and enlightening encounter of strangers where truths are exchanged ("infinity").

It is perhaps a historical irony that the word *mission* was first used religiously, in the Jesuit order. In the official U.S. order, the war "mission" in Iraq was still raging three years later, and the White House was criticized for being premature in its declaration of victory accomplished. Karl Rove hastily explained that the banner reading "Mission Accomplished" may have been a White House idea but it referred to the return to port of the *Abraham Lincoln* after a ten-month tour. Later President George W. Bush contradicted Rove, saying that the crew asked for the sign and the White House staff had it made (Guardian UK 2003). Later Donald Rumsfeld contradicted his president, telling reporter Bob Woodward that Bush's speech of thanks, ghostwritten by Michael Gerson to mirror General MacArthur's remarks upon the surrender of Japan, did contain the words "mission accomplished," but at the last minute Rumsfeld had deleted the phrase as "too inclusive" and inserted "major combat operations in Iraq have ended." "They fixed the speech but not the sign" (Woodward 2006, 186–187). As Levinas says, ruse, war, corrupted rhetoric, and debased hospitality are near allied.

Another concocted propagandistic image, the toppling of Saddam Hussein's statue in Baghdad in April 2003, also reflects a debased welcome. At least President Bush, the self-declared "war president," referenced it that way: "In the images of falling statues, we have witnessed the arrival of a new era" ("President Bush Announces" 2003). The statue event was intended to be viewed not only as a moment of triumphal entrance for the American military but as a spontaneous and widespread outcry against tyranny by a liberated people. In fact the event was totally staged. U.S. tanks cordoned off the area, allowing in only a few reporters and hired Iraqi members of Ahmed Chalabi's Free Iraqi Forces Militia, recently flown into Baghdad by the Pentagon, to act out a welcome scene (Cable News Network 2003). As the image of the toppling statue was played and replayed, U.S. viewers were never given the wide-angle perspective showing U.S. tanks guarding the entrances to the square and U.S. tanks pulling the cables. And such is the rhetorically cut perspective seen when the scene is replayed on U.S. national television news to this day.

And to this day the American public has been deluged with many other faux-welcome images of the war in Iraq: a "rescued" Jessica Lynch greeted by her parents at a German hospital, a "heroic" Pat Tillman posthumously promoted and awarded the Silver Star and Purple Heart, fallen "warriors" of the day introduced to U.S. families on dinnertime national news, U.S. troops "welcomed" in Iraq as "liberators" and then "welcomed" home in the United States as "protectors." The sheer repetition of such images, false in their framing and misleading in their information, ambushes the American public with distortions that become so familiar they eventually take on the guise of objectivity.

As Levinas (1969) predicted, the totality of war treats morality not as an ongoing endeavor but as another piece of rhetoric to manipulate or deride (21). Essential to such propaganda campaigns, Paul Fussell (1989) notes, are false assumptions "about human nature and behavior, assumptions whose effect [is] to define either a world without a complicated principle of evil or one where all evil [is] easily displaced onto one simplified recipient" (288). Ethically, wartime ideology formulates a one-sided case to justify government action and situates evil solely in the enemy, instead of providing adequate ways of sorting out moral right from wrong. A government that has embarked "on the hazardous and terrible enterprise of war," Ponsonby (1940) reflected just after World War I, "must at the outset present a one-sided case in justification of its action, and cannot afford to admit in any particular whatever the smallest degree of right or reason on the part of the people it has made up its mind to fight" (15). So where hospitality is conjured up, it only reproduces "our" set of ethics congratulating itself.

Fussell and Ponsonby describe a rhetoric that fuels a self-absorbed fictionalization of history promoting the pernicious either/or binary between Us and Others, between friends of freedom (the United States and its allies) and enemies of freedom (whoever is not "with us," aka terrorists).[1] But to view the enemy as "undebatably evil" produces "a righteousness dangerous not only to the enemy but to ourselves, to countless innocent bystanders, and to future generations" (Zinn 2010, 29).[2] Fake hospitality and fake enemies, of course, go hand in hand—in neither is there the least effort to entertain the Other in Levinas's sense. War is peace. War is hospitality.

WAR AS FORCE

The war in Iraq was feigned in more ways than as welcome or hospitable act, of course. It is easy to find images of faux freedom, faux concord among parties, faux payment for work done, faux justice for rights lost, faux democratic representation, faux authority, faux sovereignty, and many other ruses. One reality of war, however, is not hidden but is in fact glorified. The public promise by the promoters of war that they will bring "shock and awe" boasts of war's essential modus operandi—brute, material force.

In Levinas's (1969) terms, war epitomizes force, and in our century "trial by force is the test of the real" (21). How does force become interchangeable with legitimacy, righteousness, and legal process? Elaine Scarry (1985) poses this question in her study *The Body in Pain: The Making and Unmaking of the World.* She observes: "The essential structure of war, its juxtaposition of the extreme facts of body and voice, resides in . . . the relation between the collective casualties that occur *within* war, and the verbal issues (freedom, national sovereignty, the right to a disputed ground, the extra-territorial authority of a particular ideology) that stand *outside* war, that are there *before* the act of war begins and *after* it ends" (63).

Each combatant nation regards physical damage as acceptable and "ideological and territorial sacrifices as unacceptable" (Scarry 1985, 89). True, dead bodies in war don't equate to disputed beliefs or ideologies, yet injury "not only provides a means of choosing between disputants but also *provides, by its massive opening of human bodies, a way of reconnecting the derealized and disembodied beliefs with the force and power of the material world*" (128). In war, superior force is spun first into ideological "fitness," then into moral superiority (105).

As we point out in chapter 1, traditional hospitality occurs when two strangers, unforced, agree to spend time entertaining one another in friendly exchange of information. Their meeting is face-to-face and unforced. Levinas (1969) calls this exchange "peaceable from the first" (150). So again hospitality proves the opposite of war. There is little of current U.S. military combat that is face-to-face. Use of pilotless drones is only the latest step toward a faceless war. In a century and a half the United States has never engaged an enemy militarily on U.S. soil. In taking the war on terror far from our own shores, perhaps the government succeeds in minimizing loss of American property and American lives. But the government also is able to control what Americans witness about the reality of war. A human face is removed from suffering and death. The number of Viet Namese, Iraqi, Afghani, and Libyan people killed by the United States is not tabulated. As Howard Zinn (2010) notes, "This suggests, to our shame, that the lives of people other than Americans are of lesser importance . . . that a Japanese child, or an Iraqi child, or an Afghani child, is worth less than an American child" (19, 63).

Even at the point of military contact on the ground, U.S. soldiers usually operate without seeing the enemy's face. In Iraq, military personnel ordered to escort convoys of private contractors roared down populated neighborhoods at sixty miles an hour, forcing civilian vehicles off the road, swerving without warning onto sidewalks and running over bystanders. Soldiers who monitored checkpoints killed whole families at a distance, often 200–500 bullets hitting a vehicle in a single minute. Between 2003 and 2006 the U.S. military paid more than $31 million in "condolence payments" to Iraqi civilians, most of them killed unseen. The commanding American officer at one street incident, in which a married couple and two small children were killed before they were recognized as such, is reported to have said, deflecting his responsibility for their deaths, "'If these fucking hajis learned to drive, this shit wouldn't happen'" (Hedges and al-Arian 2007).[3]

In contrast to the force of war, hospitality finds guest and host peaceably face-to-face, making every effort to empathize, to see into the inner workings of one another. Inside the hospitable door, nothing is forced. Levinas (1969) says that "the Other precisely reveals himself in his alterity not in a shock negating the I, but as the primordial phenomenon of gentleness" (150). "Shock and awe" lies about as far from true hospitality as human behavior can get. "Violence is corruption," Levinas concludes, "where the will is betrayed" (229).

WAR AS SPECTACLE

But whose will? Levinas answers that it is the will of the individual that is corrupted, the singular person who would stand apart from the herd. Of course, in consumer societies the will of individual citizens is under siege quite apart from war, as Guy Debord (1983) argued a half century ago in *Society of the Spectacle*. Westernized societies are drugged into passivity by the "Spectacle," comprised of images of "the totality of the commodity world," everything that can be manufactured, coveted, and consumed. The Spectacle validates the commodity as "the total occupation of social life" by convincing us that we don't work out of economic necessity, for physical survival, but for economic "growth" to fulfill our psychological "needs." Our needs, of course, are also manufactured by the Spectacle (paras. 42, 51). Citizens are valued not as individuals but as wage laborers and faithful consumers of the goods they produce. The Spectacle degrades social life into an appetite to *have*, not to *relate*, and so separates spectators from one other. It creates a society, not a community (paras. 17, 25, 193). It allows the hospitality trade but undermines any act of genuine hospitality. "It brings isolated individuals together as isolated individuals. Factories, cultural centers, tourist resorts and housing developments are specifically designed to foster this type of pseudo-community" (para. 173).

In "Spectacular Ethics: On the Television Footage of the Iraq War," Lilie Chouliaraki (2007) applies Debord's notion of spectacle in a study of the media's coverage of the "shock and awe" campaign in the first days of America's second war in Iraq. The media projects a pro-war narrative—no surprise, Chouliaraki argues, since television operates as a technology of the consumer nation (130). Coalition troops are described as benefactors, not bombers, while the sight of Iraqi suffering is masked or minimized (131). Viewed from afar, the display of bombs exploding in the Iraqi night prompts distanced and bedazzled aesthetic awe. The attack on Baghdad appears more like a video game than the occasion of hundreds of civilian deaths. The passive camera eye suggests objectivity while the reports from journalists provide the active voice of storytelling (135). Ultimately, media coverage bonds together panoramic detachment and narrative proximity into a spectacle that "suppresses the emotional, ethical and political issues that lie behind the bombardment of Baghdad" (133). "Wow!" exclaim the television reporters.

So much for the public at home. The soldier is also betrayed. Military power embodies force, force exercised by individual soldiers, trained to obey orders, trained to master weapons. But first and foremost, they are body targets controlled by the state. As such, their body is no longer a personality, source of memories and virtues, but rather "a rational sovereign subject" (Shapiro 2003, 11). Thus the body becomes a political site or exchangeable commodity, the subject of secular power and administrative control rather than a "repository of natural or divine forces" (1). Soldiers are no longer singular bodies, psyches, and souls but politicized objects, actors in a spectacle merely projecting race, class, gender, unconscious, and sexuality (2).

The soldier, of course, is not simply a target. He or she is also trained as a killer. The thinly reported cases of post-traumatic stress disorder experienced by veterans of Iraq and Afghanistan, and the acts of suicide by those veterans, speak to Levinas's (1969) argument that the worst that war violence does to people is to "interrupt their continuity." That is, the spectacle of war makes people "play roles in which they no longer recognize themselves" (21).[4] War is a spectacle that erodes the ability of surviving soldiers—as well as nonparticipant but spectating citizens—to judge themselves, to call their own knowledge into question.

This leads to the heart of Levinas's (1969) own notion of spectacle (90–98). Spectacle is an aspect of war because it is an essential function of totality, especially totality's representation of the world outside the self as objective. Levinas's notion runs very deep and encompasses not only the military but every institution in society, including education. In Levinas, the root of spectacle is the destructive belief—destructive to the essence of hospitality, among other things—that one can look at whatever lies outside the self with impunity because whatever lies outside the self cannot look back. The mythic figure illustrating spectacle is Gyges, who found a ring that made him invisible. He could see people, but people could not see him (90).[5]

It might seem that spectacle gives people power, but in fact it does the opposite. Spectacle disempowers people, says Levinas (1969), because it separates truth from justice (90–101). Spectacle projects a view of the world in which one images oneself living in such certitude and freedom that things outside the self cannot question the self. But justice is truly justice only when people believe themselves not free of it. Under spectacle, the self is free of judgment because the self is invisible to the Other. In the second book of Plato's (1997) *The Republic*, Glaucon uses the example of Gyges to argue that people prefer injustice to justice. Were they invisible and could commit injustices without fear of being caught, wouldn't they? Levinas (1969) responds that such a state of impunity would also be a state of miserable solitude (like that of the chief at the end of "The Sun's Myth"), closed off from the world, condemned to stagnancy because there is no way to judge one's own knowledge. It is the opposite of "the ethical exigency of face [the Other], which puts into question the consciousness that welcomes it" (207). The Other cannot be welcomed if the Other cannot see you.

Levinas's spectacle is everywhere in a totalizing society. In movies, television, and digital entertainment, the viewers are invisible to the entertainer. In the world of scientific objectivity, the scientists observe the subject without the subject knowing the scientists are there. On every street corner, the law enforcers invisibly surveil the potential criminal. The computer users see the advertisement but imagine (naïvely) that the advertiser cannot see them. In the school building, the parents watch the child through the one-way mirror. The readers see the author's words but the author cannot see the reader. The donors to a charitable cause do not see the recipients of their money, or see only photographs. In every case the spectators imagine themselves given power by their invisibility whereas they are only made passive vis-à-vis their own self-agency.

It is in war, however, where spectacle is embraced most unabashedly. Invisibility has been a military strategy as long as war has existed—the camouflage, the ambush, the night attack, the hidden sniper, the disguised infiltrator, the high-altitude bomber, the Stealth fighter, the long-range missile that television viewers in Kansas can see hit its foreign target from the perspective of a camera in its head. And now the unmanned drone, set on course to strike a target in Pakistan by people in a windowless room in the Nevada desert. As for the targets in Pakistan, who might turn out to be wedding guests, they see nothing.

Just as the Spectacle in Levinas (1969) poses an exteriority that can be seen but can't see, the spectacle also can be spoken to but cannot hear. Its silence, then, is especially intractable. And when it speaks it does so with a language that cannot be answered. Its language is worse than a lie, "beyond every lie," in that it cannot be refuted. As Levinas argues, "It is the inverse of language; the interlocutor has given a sign, but has declined every interpretation; this is the silence that terrifies" (91). Again, the prime example is war. What Ponsonby (1940) identified as strategies of wartime propaganda function because they are ruses, intended to be believed and not contested. Military code, battlefield orders, reports from embedded journalists, enemy mortality counts, even the initial declaration of war: all are spectacle language, unanswerable and meant to be so. As with the spectacle's invisibility, the apparent objectivity and factuality of its silence confers upon the recipient a false sense of power. Facts speak, the saying goes. Not according to Levinas (1969), who says that "the spectacle of the silent world of facts is bewitched" (91), a magic trick in which the audience participates but can't penetrate. Patriotic listeners to a war speech by political and military leaders feel possessed of freedom and certitude because they are not being asked to doubt, question, or even respond except with cheers and salutes.

And again, the opposite of wartime spectacle is hospitality, where host and guest are not free and not sure and are therefore obliged to question and respond. Levinas argues that language, dialogic or answerable language, is the only way to welcome the Other.

WAR, TOTALITY, AND INFINITY

The language of spectacle brings us to the doorstep of the English classroom. In how many ways, for instance, does the language read by students have an interlocutor who is both blind and deaf to the student? Spectacle in English teaching is not war, of course, not even warlike except in extreme examples. The English classroom, however, is familiar ground to Spectacle as well as to ruse and force, and it operates more under totality than infinity. War's extremes just help make these concepts salient.

One particular paradox of war, for instance, clarifies an underlying contradiction in spectacle. On the one hand, suffering of the body, death of the citizen-victim or soldier-victim, is fundamentally personal. "Violence can aim only at a face," as Levinas (1969, 225) says. At the same time, war destroys the subjective "I" by erasing the individual face and casting all "I"s as a totalized "we" (25). War is touted as the ultimate singular reality,[6] yet it can only take place through and as spectacle. Although an English classroom operating under the aegis of true hospitality entails paradoxes of its own, it will have no part in this particular paradox of war. It need involve no more than two individuals, face-to-face, in a scene so private that the peaceful adventures taking place there are rarely told to others. Before turning our discussion to the classroom, however, it will be wise to get a better glimpse, as Levinas puts it, of the "permanent possibility of war" (21), its implication with totality and infinity, and its enmity with hospitality.

According to Levinas, the individual has been "totalized" in Western culture, reduced to one part of a closed-off whole, which has set purposes and fixed boundaries. For Levinas, "totality" is an entity composed of countable parts that are absolutely knowable and therefore can be absolutely summed. In a totality, no part is left out but each part is lost in the sum. Totality is a matrix—economical, social, political, racial. People are seen not as singular but as identifiable bearers "of forces that command them unbeknown to themselves" (Levinas 1969, 21, 244). The totality makes puppets of us; it defines our nature and dignity in terms of causal strings and final goals (22). In the United States, the totality of society is our function as consumers and laborers for the purposes of increasing the GNP. Or, in Levinas's terms, in political life humanity is understood through works—and we comprise a humanity of interchangeable people who can do the same work (298).

In the totality of war, the goal and the work is victory, no matter what the cost in military and civilian lives. The totality is sustained by the ruse of rhetoric. U.S. citizens passively observe snippets in the evening prime-time news about a grandmother and cancer survivor wanting to serve a second tour of duty in Iraq—a benign image of war for the spectacle. As spectators, we are expected by the purveyors of war to act like children: "We decide to be entertained rather than to be citizens," writes Bill Moyers (2007). Or we are expected to function as a monolithic "we," as if millions of individual consciences merge with each other and with the motives of the state (Zinn 2010, 30). No matter what the atrocity—Dresden, Hiroshima, My Lai, Abu Ghraib—"so long as atrocities remain remotely abstract, they will be tolerated, even by decent people" (60).[7]

The individual is further totalized because his or her existence is, according to postmodern tenets, constituted in the thought of others. This sort of existence, which Levinas (1969) calls "objective," determines how each I is valued in the state, in history, in the totality. But that objective self does not *express* the I but rather *dissimulates* it (178). There is a tyranny to the politics of the spectacle, an "anarchy" or "evil genius" (90–92) that casts everything outside the self into doubt as possibly only a veil or image and therefore as something that cannot be conversed with.[8] Levinas concludes: "It deforms the I and the Other who have given rise to it, for it judges them according to universal rules, and thus as in absentia" (300). No individual can think or function distinctively; singularity is not tolerated (222). Thus totality (phenomenological violence against the individual) and war (political, economic, and military violence against the individual) go hand in glove.

Totality and war can therefore boast of alarming achievements: the dehumanization of enemies, the ambushing of citizens, the duping of soldiers, and the sustained arrogance of a foreign policy based on incomparable wealth and weapons. What can redeem the singular I in such a society?

The corrective to war and totalization is, for Levinas (1969), a twofold process. First, each person, each self or I, must be understood as "an irreducible singularity" (242), which has no place in totality (244). The I does not remain the same across time but is self-aware as it recovers its primal identity no matter what happens (36). Each self is a being responsible in such a way that "no one can replace me" and "no one can release me. To be unable to shirk: this is the I" (245). All this is to say that the self is a moral being. Identifying oneself involves "interiority," or existing at home with oneself: "Dwelling is the very mode of maintaining *oneself*" (37). Interiority—an inner life—helps to dismantle totality (118). To be at home, Levinas believes, is to be free (37).

Yet for Levinas (1969), freedom is not the ultimate good. Interiority is a dimension that is able to "await and welcome the revelation of transcendence" (150). That is, once the self is at home, in habitation, *dwelling*, she or he awaits the approach of what is *exterior* both to the self and to the totality—Levinas calls this the infinite—which is encountered only in the Other. This is the second stage of the process that corrects totality: the turn to the exterior from the position of home. For Levinas, infinity is content that overflows the container, a "surplus" that transcends the self (22, 97). Thus home-dwelling is not the end of human activity, the place one returns to after a day of "work," but its commencement (152). For at the door, inside of which the self is in possession, stands the Other, infinite to the self because Other is not contained by the self. Possession is both fulfilling and threatening to the self since possession is the destiny of the hand and "the hand is by essence groping and emprise" (159, 167). The grasp can suppress the Other like an iron fist or welcome the Other like a handshake (302).

To welcome the infinity of the Other means to be dispossessed; the self is disturbed "being at home" (Levinas 1969, 39, 210). The self, no doubt about it, takes a risk in welcoming the Other. It isn't that the self *needs* the Other as he or she needs food, drink, or dwelling; the self *desires* the Other. Desire is a condition beyond satisfaction and nonsatisfaction. The self desires to reach out, to experience infinity through "radical exteriority" that he or she must "let be" (29, 179). Hence the risk is well worth it: "It is only in approaching the Other that I attend to myself" (178).

Whether as widow, orphan, stranger, foreigner, or the "master"—the Other is equal to the self (Levinas 1969, 213). The self encounters the Other in the face (*visage*), the point of interface with a person whom the self does not contain, the concrete manifestation of infinity (196, 197). Levinas considers the face holy because it is "a living presence; it is expression" (66, 290–291). Face is the "exceptional presentation of self by self" (202). That relationship—self to Other—establishes a plurality that is the antithesis of totality, for such a plurality "is peace" (203). The face first appears to the self to be unthematicized, naked, destitute, defenseless, and "beyond rhetoric" (75), thereby requiring a nonviolent reception. The peaceful welcoming of the Other, this opening up to infinity, is what Levinas calls hospitality (27, 172, 213, 300). If totality is the basis of war, then the welcoming of the Other, or hospitality, is the basis of peace.[9]

Relating face-to-face with the Other, that "great exteriority," is also the basis for language, as opposed to rhetoric. Rhetoric is "taking the position of him who approaches his neighbor with ruse," and as such is an act of violence and injustice (Levinas 1969, 70, 296). Language, "beyond rhetoric" (75), operating as it does face-to-face and apart from the totality, reveals the Other to the self. Language is bound up with justice, since justice "consists in recognizing in the Other my master" (72).[10] In speech, the Other manifests his world, her experiences, his perceptions, her reflections. The self reciprocates, making language "an exchange of ideas about the world" (97, 202). Thus in the hospitable relation both the self and the Other retain their integrity, their singularity. They are not absorbed, assimilated, possessed, or thematicized by the Other. But they *speak truth* and thereby expand the world and experiences of each other.[11]

HOSPITALITY AND HIGHER EDUCATION

U.S. institutions of higher learning have many faults, among them a dysfunctional eagerness to take in more and more students with less and less support for them. But still, in all appearance, they remain peaceful middlemen between teachers and students, sincerely committed to the support of scholarship and the encouragement of education. Ruse, force, and spectacle run against the grain of universities in their open dissemination of knowledge, elective choice of career and coursework, and study of things-as-they-objectively-are. Every day the college teacher opens the classroom for another opportunity to guide the younger generation through unfamiliar knowledge toward a useful degree. Isn't this a kind of hospitality and the opposite of war?

But what if this appearance is part of the spectacle? What if the language of free and open knowledge is partly rhetorical ruse? What if underneath the choices allowed to students run currents that mandate much of their educational activities? What if, despite appearances, U.S. institutions of higher learning are half in league with U.S. totality? What if the peaceful demeanor of quiet walks and shaded quadrangles belies an underlying complicity with war (peace is not the opposite of war)? What if Levinas's philosophical argument is sound and an important corrective to U.S. higher education in terms of infinity and hospitality?

In a piece on hospitality and English teaching, Matthew Heard (2010) argues that hospitality is too radical a theory to sacrifice to "our present goals and objectives" (329), to the "business as usual" (327) that constitutes the totality of our university life. But we don't believe that the current U.S. academy is yet totally given over to totality, nor that the only viable hospitality is an absolute that lies beyond social laws, regulations, and morality. As the history of hospitality shows (chapter 1), those realities have always been essential to it. Hospitable praxis can change social praxis because they are part and parcel. The ways that models of hospitality can infiltrate, transgress, and improve college English teaching is very much the topic of the rest of this book, so here we will only suggests some lines of inquiry.

What role can institutions of higher learning play in hospitably resisting Levinas's ruse of rhetoric? This is an especially compelling question to professionals in the field of English, who make language and rhetoric their business. We note Chomsky's position that "the history of imperialism and of imperialist apologia . . . should be a central part of any civilized curriculum" (1966, 489). We also note Chomsky's subjunctive mood. Universities *should* contribute to society to the extent that they overcome "the temptation to conform unthinkingly to the prevailing ideology and to the existing patterns of power and privilege" (Chomsky 1973, 302). The professoriate *should* be vigilant against deceit and write history that is otherwise suppressed, not only about atrocities and injustices committed by the state but also about the documented efficacy of resistance. Unfortunately, U.S. universities and their professoriate have had a sordid history of abetting, and benefiting from, the war industry (Chomsky 1967).

Currently, how much does the nonsubjunctive "real" world of war hold sway in the U.S. academe?[12] In his examination of the National Defense Education and Innovation Initiative of 2006, Stuart Tannock (2007) warns that American institutions of higher education have, out of self-interest, resource dependency, and political opportunism, committed themselves more than ever to "promoting the interests of Americans" (3). In part as a posture of vigilance against Islamic fanatics, HR 3077 and Title VI legislation take away federal funding from campuses that deny access to military recruiters, offer fellowships for students working for U.S. intelligence agencies, provide scholarships for students going to work for the Department of Defense (once called the Department of War), and increase federal funding for the teaching and learning of "critical need languages" identified by national security dictates (4). Tannock believes that "Americans need desperately to be learning how to learn and work beyond the borders of their own limited but overpowering country, with and not against the rest of the world" (11). His closing questions cut to the core of the issue: "To whom and what precisely the academy should and should not be accountable and responsive, and how this accountability and responsiveness is to be best managed, monitored and enforced?" (7). How should we best serve the common good? (8) Or do we continue to be "the almost exclusive preserve for the children and interests of the country's most powerful and wealthy?" (8)

Such macrocosmic questions are not beyond the reach of models of hospitality, but they must be addressed first on the microcosmic level. Practices of hospitality, as we show in chapter 1, have traditionally operated at just that level, on the margins and in the niches. If we understand the act of teaching in Levinas's terms—as emerging from the encounter of the self and the Other—then the classroom is a meeting place fecund with potential. Power, influence, suppression, indoctrination, domination—all manifestations of totality—may have much materially and functionally in common with current teaching practices, but have nothing to do with the essence of teaching. Teaching introduces the self (either student or teacher) to the infinite of the Other (either student or teacher) and so breaks "the closed circle of totality" (Levinas 1969, 171). Or that is what teaching should do.

Hospitality is simply one model of that relation of the self with the Other, which cannot be imagined beforehand, for the student's world is not contained by the teacher, nor is the teacher's contained by the student. All teaching is initiated from the exterior, not the interior, says Levinas (1969), bringing to the teacher or to the student more than he or she contains (51). Only the absolutely foreign—the student different in age, gender, cultural background, experience, politics, religion, ethnicity to the teacher, and the teacher different in age, gender, cultural background, experience, politics, religion, ethnicity to the student—can instruct (73). And hospitality is one of the few intuitive social practices that fully accepts the absolutely foreign.

Levinas (1969) believes that teaching "signifies the whole infinity of exteriority" (171). Both teacher and student encounter more than they can draw from their own interiority (180). Thus teaching "is a way for truth to be produced such that it is not my work, such that I could not derive it from my own interiority" (295). For what other reason should a student go to university or a teacher go to work? For this reason, the hospitable moment and the teaching moment are intertwined. The engagement of the self with the Other requires that the self (the one at home, dwelling within his or her own interiority) understand that what is outside of the home, apart from the self, exterior and transcendent, will make richer and moral the world of experience that is already possessed.

CONCLUSIONS

Two general conclusions are readily drawn from this chapter. First, education in the English classroom would do well to move as much as it can away from a condition of totality and toward a condition of infinity. Second, much can be gained in the English classroom, for teacher and student, were instruction to shift from modes of hostility to modes of hospitality. The second conclusion, of course, will take the rest of this book to explore. The first conclusion we advocate simply because totality is a construction of education by noneducational interests for their own ends and not for educational ends, and infinity is a view of education as it actually is. "If the doors of perception were cleansed," said Blake, "every thing would appear to man as it is, Infinite" (1973, plate 14).

One can always keep the door closed, of course, stay at home and refuse to cross the threshold. Raymond Boisvert (2004) believes such resistance is endemic to our society: "The modern self is not a 'needy being' in any primal way. Its covetings have nothing to do with being an incomplete, developing creature, one ever in need of ennobling growth" (293). Still, U.S. society insists, perhaps more than any other nation's, that the eighteen-year-old citizen leave home and enter college. There is perhaps no deeper contradiction in our culture, the drive toward the infinity that college learning should represent and the drive toward the totality that college ways inculcate. Hospitality, we believe, is a practice that helps avoid that contradiction. It offers a way for teachers or students who unknowingly want to be complete, safe, and finalized instead—surprise!—to open themselves up to the incomplete, unsure, and infinite. Theologian Letty Russell had a phrase for this new world, "riotous difference," and she said it was actually not new but the world that God had created for humans (2009, 71).

Notes

1.   Howard Zinn (2010) comments on the use of the word *terrorist*: "When private bands of fanatics commit atrocities we call them 'terrorist,' which they are, and

have no trouble dismissing their reasons. But when governments do the same, and on a much larger scale, the word 'terrorism' is not used" (27). Zinn believes that the term *terrorism* has a useful meaning: "an act . . . [that is] intolerable, since it involves the indiscriminate use of violence against human beings for some political purpose" (27). But he argues that terrorism is not the act of lone-wolf fanatics but state-sponsored, official policy because weapons like napalm and atomic bombs used for the sake of "undermining of the morale" permit mass killings of civilians (38–39). See also Dower 2010, xxi–xxii.

2.   Paul Fussell's (1989) judgment remains true: Americans are a "pap-fed mass public" unable to come to "something like public maturity" in their awareness of why and how wars are waged because if they knew what war was really like, they would not tolerate citizen soldiers being deployed (267–272). Winston Churchill's words to the British Parliament in 1914 apply to current U.S. policies of self-interest: "We are not a young people with innocent record and a scanty inheritance. We have engrossed to ourselves [an] altogether disproportionate share of wealth and traffic of the world. We have got all we want in territory, and our claim to be left in the unmolested enjoyment of vast and splendid possessions, mainly acquired by violence, largely maintained by force, often seems less reasonable to others than to us" (quoted in Chomsky 2005, 119).

3.   In a form of Levinas's (1969) "ruse of rhetoric," during war racial slurs based on faces replace genuine singular faces: "towelhead" and "raghead" (from Afghanistan and Iraq), "slopehead" (from Viet Nam and Korea), "krauthead" from the European front (the French *boche* originally was *tête de boche*, or cabbagehead).

4.   Such a role, John Dower (2010) observes, involves the hubris, insularity, distancing, and delusion of using high-tech conventional warfare of maximum violence against noncombatants (xxii). Because the ignorant and propagandized members of the public still operate from the position of moral righteousness and "quasi-theological rationalization"(xxiii), they can offer no solace to veterans nor can they benefit from the re-visioned understanding of total war that veterans bring back.

5.   The French word *spectacle* goes back to the Middle Ages, where originally it meant a contrived visual entertainment. One common "spectacle" designed by authorities involved a convicted person punished by being tied to a stake in a public square in such a way that he could not protect his eyes. People threw stones and soon, literally, occupied the space Levinas (1969) calls "spectacle": they could see the convicted without the convicted being able to see them. Blindfolding prisoners before a firing squad creates this same space.

6.   In its obituary for Douglas A. Zembiec, a U.S. Marine killed in Iraq in 2007, the *Marine Corp News* reports that the "fallen warrior" had told a reporter that in battling insurgents "I never felt so alive, so exhilarated, so purposeful" (*Marine Corps News* 2007).

7.   In Andrew Jolly's (1976) forgotten but remarkable novel *A Time of Soldiers*, one of the main characters—a career military office named Jack Lear—writes a book called *War and Faith*. He draws a crucial connection: "War is an act of faith on the part of the people in their concept of the meaning of human life . . . the manner in which a people make war is heavily influenced by their common set of beliefs" (180). But when the only value operating in war is the goal of the totality, there is no room for the singular "I" or for moral principles.

8.   The term *evil genius* or *evil demon* refers to the *deus deceptor* that Descartes hypothesized in the first of his meditations, the irrefutable possibility that some god might be fooling him by fabricating the material world as well as his sense impressions of the material world. Thus, according to Levinas (1969), does the spectacle create "the possibility of universal doubt" with no way of resolving that doubt (90).

9.   Jacques Derrida called *Totality and Infinity* "an immense treatise on hospitality" (1999, 21). In his analysis of war, George Lakoff comes to a similar conclusion about what he calls "nurturant morality": "It is a view of ethical behavior that centers on (a) empathy and (b) responsibility (for both yourself and others needing your help). Many things follow from these central principles: fairness, minimal violence (for example, justice without vengeance), an ethic of care, protection of those needing it, a recognition of interdependence, cooperation for the common good, the building of community, mutual respect" (2001).

10.   Levinas (1969) refers to the Other in the act of speech as the interlocutor who "is not a Thou, he is a You; he reveals himself in his lordship. Thus exteriority coincides with a mastery. My freedom is thus challenged by a Master who can invest it" (101).

11.   Many scholars share Levinas's belief that truth-in-language is a necessary antidote to our warring society. One of the most notable is Noam Chomsky, who urges: "Instead of repeating ideological fanaticism, dismantle it, try to find out the truth, and tell the truth. It's something any one of us can do . . . How complicated is it to understand the truth or to know how to act?" (2005, 63–64).

12.   The Bush doctrine of preemptive war, of course, eliminates the subjunctive. Contingent or hypothetical conditions are dismissed and the cruise missiles launched. When asked by Diane Sawyer to address the disjunction between his prewar claims and his postwar discoveries, a disjunction between conditional or rhetorical desires and actual capabilities, President Bush only laughed: "What's the difference?" (Alterman 2004, 296, 300). He was not a "fact-checker," according to his spokesmen. But then neither were they. When asked in January 2011 by NBC newscaster Brian Williams about the administration's false claims arguing for the invasion of Iraq, Bush's chief of staff James Baker said, "You know, I think it was appropriate to use all the arguments . . . use them all, because we were doing the right thing" (*NBC Nightly News*, January 20, 2011). In October 2004 independent journalist Ron Suskind asked an unnamed senior advisor to the president about the facts as they are known and the preinvasion "facts" as the White House had positioned them, and the advisor replied that journalists are in "the reality-based community" and "believe that solutions emerge from your judicious study of discernible reality." "That's not the way the world really works anymore," the aide continued. "We're an empire now, and when we act, we create our own reality" (quoted in Lapham 2005, 8). Thus does totality talk and act. The United States can and will control world events now and deal with the future conditional later.

3
HOSPITALITY IN THE CLASSROOM

*The alchemists have a saying, Tertium non data. The third is not
given. That is, the transformation from one element into another, from
waste matter into best gold is a process that cannot be documented. It is
fully mysterious.*

—Jeanette Winterson

It is in *Just Hospitality*, published after her death in 2007, where Letty
Russell (2009) writes that God "created a world of riotous difference in
which creation and creature alike show forth a rainbow variety of God's
goodness" (71). The only way to welcome and respect this difference,
says Russell, is through hospitality, which she describes as "an expression of unity without uniformity" (80). Her phrase recalls the African
concept of ubuntu, as we will see, which imagines "a person through
other persons." The phrase also parallels Levinas's notion of the face
first appearing to the self "beyond rhetoric" (1969, 75) and Agamben's
futuristic vision in *The Coming Community* of a society where "*singularities form a community without affirming an identity*" (1993, 86), a group of
people always willing to make hospitable and easeful space for others to
develop everyone's own different potentialities (see chapter 11).

Levinas (1969) would call Agamben's vision "eschatological" (25).
Levinas says that when the self is genuinely hospitable to the difference of the Other, the effect is a "traumatism of astonishment" (73).
Traditional hospitality is not a shoo-in. As Jeanette Winterson (1998)
puts it, "Tertium non data. The third is not given." As in the alchemist's
hope of lead transformed into gold, the outcome of the mixture of
Same and Other, host and guest, is unpredictable and unaccountable,
"fully mysterious."

So when we recommend that English teachers convert their classrooms into venues for hospitality, we are asking for not a little. We are
asking that teachers stop depending upon given expectations of uniformity and given constructions of identity and fully accept difference, an
ungiven transformation—mysterious or not, documented or not—that

DOI: 10.7330/9780874219883.c003

could be traumatic indeed. Especially traumatic for scholar-teachers who make their living in the current academia of accountability, predictive testing, uniform conduct codes, total quality management, fixation on performance, syllabuses with grade standards preposted publicly online, tenure files with exhaustively documented paper trails, and classrooms with seating packed for efficiency like an airline cabin or a military barracks. We are rashly asking that employees hired for totality work for infinity. With good reason many intellectuals hesitate on the doorstep of traditional hospitality.

To its credit, much of the English professoriate have resisted the inhospitable and sometimes hostile climate of their own institutions, valorizing pedagogies clearly related to traditional hospitality, pedagogies variously called "student-centered," "caring," "dialogic," "reciprocal," "transformative," and "liberatory" (for a synthesis of these pedagogies, see Irene Ward 1994; and Wallace and Ewald 2000). But invisibly the institutional totality acts like a magnetic force field, and far too often when teachers and students do enter into a host-guest relationship, they soon drift toward ways that are the antithesis of hospitable engagement. Consider three familiar scenarios.

Scenario 1

A teacher wants to host students by welcoming them into the academy and offering to share his or her own training and expertise. Many students, however, are not cooperative, gift-reciprocating guests. Since they or their parents have already paid tuition, they assume that the credit for the course has already been bought and they shouldn't have to earn it. They view the course as another consumer function of our society. The college belongs to the hospitality trade, the classroom serves as a hotel room, and learning becomes secondary to accumulating credits that supposedly add up, as advertised, to the credentials for employment. At odds, teacher and student battle all semester, and more often than not the teacher loses.

Scenario 2

The teacher wants, hostlike, to facilitate learning, to usher students through the strange chambers of academic lore. But too much of education is erected, both literally and figuratively, as "a long endless row of obligations to be fulfilled" (Nouwen 1966, 84). The teacher is forced to act more like a demanding sergeant in a boot camp than

a maieutic guide in a collaborative search for knowledge and understanding. Solutions are identified before students have conceived of the
problems, answers "offered without the existence of a question" (85). As
Mary Rose O'Reilley laments, too many students end up recalling school
"as a long process of humiliation" (O'Reilley 1984, 107). Through "academic brutalization" young people learn by being "insulted, bullied,
turned into objects" (110). If we use violence, O'Reilley notes, our students will imitate us in their turn. If we destroy students' confidence and
self-respect, we can stunt "the very reflective powers that alone make the
individual able to resist the dominion of force" (1993, 30).

In a gentler form of this scenario, or perhaps a more ironic form, a
teacher reduces hospitality to responsibility for others. The teacher is
responsible for getting the students to learn. Brighter students are given
the task of helping less bright students. All students find themselves
demoted to objects of responsibility. Feminists are acutely aware of this
dynamic. The hospitable college morphs into a hospital and the classroom into a patient's recovery room where the student-guest can only
respond with passive thanks.

Scenario 3

A teacher wants to host stranger-students by showing them the terrain.
But unconsciously the teacher excludes other voices in the profession
and proselytizes only his or her paradigm, views, insights, understanding. The teacher joins the kind of hosts who, unaware, take themselves
to be the controlling source of knowledge or the only site of epistemic
privilege (see Groome 1988, 17). Such host-scholars use their training
and status first to allow in and then to distance and exclude others, colleagues and students alike. Devouring-host teachers reduce students and
fellow teachers to versions of themselves, or ascribe only a subservient
and resistant role to them.[1] As Julie Kristeva characterizes the type, "'I
speak to you, you listen, therefore I am. Listen to me in order that I may
exist'" (quoted in Bennett 2000a). Spider-parlor classrooms keep the
students in their powerless place by reminding them of what they don't
know and haven't mastered, thereby sucking them of their self-esteem
(McAvoy 1998). In a Blakean or Levinian narrative, hospitality trans-
forms into its opposite. Hospitality becomes hostility.[2]

Insofar as these scenarios describe failed hospitality, they also show
a form of teaching that resorts to something like human traffick-
ing. Students are represented as slaves, transients, beggars, clients, or
apprentices to be charmed, corralled, trained, examined, and certified.

They are not excluded from the academic community per se. Instead, they are in a state of *relegation*—excluded not as outsiders but as marginal insiders. As Mireille Rosello (2001) explains, relegated individuals are "expected to be set aside . . . banned from the community" as guests too fragile to be absorbed (159). So between host and guest an exclusionary asymmetrical relationship is established. As we have seen in chapter 1, a sign that hospitality has lost its ethical core is the inability of host and guest to change roles: "If the guest is always the guest, if the host is always the host," insists Rosello, "something has probably gone very wrong; hospitality has somehow been replaced by parasitism or charity" (167).

How, then, does ethical or just hospitality get a permanent start in the classroom? How can a teacher make a worthy hospitality work? We suggest three attitudes—postures, dispositions, or inner values—that energize distinct social, cultural, pedagogical practices: *intellectual* hospitality, *transformative* hospitality, and *ubuntu* hospitality. The three postures stand as an operational taxonomy for English teaching, cutting across the historical taxonomy we called Homeric, biblical, and nomadic traditions in chapter 1 (for a third taxonomy of hospitality, see chapter 5).

The term *intellectual hospitality* comes from John B. Bennett, one of many scholars who have championed the presence of hospitality in higher education. Intellectual hospitality assumes that true inquiry involves welcoming novel understanding, and so the scholar's life must be open to constant mutual exchanges of experiences, perspectives, and insights. Intellectual hospitality is not simple courtesy or civility, since such attitudes fortify rather than dismantle boundaries between expert and learner. Rather, it incorporates what Bennett calls the spirit of "collegium." Teachers seek neither to isolate themselves from other learners nor to assimilate others into their sphere of influence or way of thinking. Instead, through mutual respect, interaction, and reciprocity, they invite students to help one another with personal intellectual projects (Bennett 2000a). Hospitable considerateness of strange perspectives, says Bennett, "could validate, supplement, or correct one's own work." He adds that "in both sharing and receiving, learning and knowledge are treated not as possessions to be hoarded but gifts to be given" (2000b, 92–93). These gifts are impossible to predict. Host-teachers, for instance, should assume that the guest-student has stories to tell, as in composition-course "literacy narratives," but should never assume what those stories will be. Teachers can give in return since they often recognize meanings to the stories that the student-teller may not see, and thus offer a new insight.

Through such reciprocal respect and gift giving, intellectual hospitality may cross over into our second form or manifestation, *transformative* hospitality (Pohl 1995, 136; see also Winslow 1999, 185; and Bennett 2000b, 93). There is no doubt that intellectual prowess may conflict with any kind of hospitality. As Henri Nouwen rightly says, "Someone who is filled with ideas, concepts, opinions and convictions cannot be a good host. There is no inner space to listen, no openness to discover the gift of the other" (1966, 103). We all know the scholar giant who relentlessly defends her or his castle of scholarship, switching back and forth from eagle-eyed lookout for possible rivals to prideful complacency over laurels won. But intellectual walls can be breached when teacher-scholars decenter themselves and invite in the student-guest. In a Levinian switch from inner dwelling to exteriority, a new worldview and self-understanding can be discerned with an awareness of "the relativity and finitude of our own worldview and self-understanding" (Johnson 1993, 346–347). The student-guest promises news from a different world—the world of a different generation, age, gender, class, or ethnicity, and the world of that singular person's experiences, hopes, mullings, insights, and interpretations. The stage is set for change.

We assume that learners change, but if teachers are hosts they are also learners and change as well. "If we ourselves are not changing," Mary Rose O'Reilley observes, "I suspect we are not permitting ourselves to be put at risk by our students" (1993, 30). The first of such risks entails true dialogue. As host, the teacher has the authority and skill to create a free and nonhostile space where intellectual, ethical, and emotional development can take place. The way is through easeful communication that allows students' "respective life experiences to be their primary and most valuable source of growth and maturation" (Nouwen 1966, 85). English teachers may have objections against "personal writing" in college courses, but how else can unique life experiences be expressed? If students understand they have something to offer, they will realize they have something to give. At this point the teacher must become the guest, allowing the host-students to explore their teacher's experiences and knowledge. What strange patterns are there? What strange values?

For student-guests to become student-hosts, English teachers must give up their habitual dominance and become like the stranger. We are, after all, as transient as our students. We, too, move from class to class, semester by semester, moving to and from groups of students, *peregrine* in nature (Pratt and Homan 2002, 12; see also Kristeva 1991, 88), not yet giving up entirely the professional mode of the wandering scholars of the Middle Ages. It is a risk, for teachers as for students, to walk into a new classroom and welcome the other or be welcomed by the other. It is even a peril, for, as Rosello notes, if hospitality requires a willingness to be changed by the other, it requires a willingness to live with fear (2001, 176). Possibly only on such emotional cliffs will the transformation from host to guest and from guest to host prefigure the transformation that lasts after the hospitable instructional encounter ends.

Embracing intellectual and transformation leads to our final attitude or posture, which in truth is both the foundation and end point of the other two. Ubuntu is rooted in African traditions.[3] Standing for inner values such as compassion, respect, and generosity, ubuntu requires an openness and availability to others because "my humanity is caught up, is inextricably bound up, in yours" (Tutu 1999, 31). I am uplifted when you are uplifted, advanced when you are advanced. Similarly, what dehumanizes you dehumanizes me. I am diminished by your suffering. Anger and hatred, selfishness and competition, envy and jealousy reduce my ubuntu because such emotions separate us. My identity and yours are bound to a greater whole, and I find assurance and security in that bond.[4]

The value of ubuntu describes not only relations within a community but those between communities and cultures as well. As social frame enabling strangers to meet and act, ubuntu is, in a fundamental sense, hospitality in action; it acknowledges "a complicity, a folded-togetherness of human-beings." As Mark Sanders details, ubuntu is "a relation to the stranger, to the one not one's own, to the one not *of* one's own, to the one who has come to be treated as one not one's own. Hospitality is called for when the ties that make an other one's own do not exist or have fallen away. Hospitality is a way of owning—in a limited sense, through artifice of convention—the one who is not one's own, the one through whom one owns oneself and becomes who one is" (Sanders 2002, 125).

In effect, ubuntu is as uncompromising as the Christian ethic of caritas, which once underwrote traditional European hospitality. Encountering the Other produces a shock, Levinas's (1969, 73) "traumatism of astonishment," as one realizes the depth of the self-absorption in one's own self. Thus does the guest serve the needs of the host and vice versa. Stranger and host give and accept the hospitality that transcends self and provides a unity without uniformity, a community without identity.

English teaching in college, of course, has long promoted attitudes that are ubuntu like. For instance, in *Mutuality in the Rhetoric and Composition Classroom*, David L. Wallace and Helen Rothschild Ewald argue for equality of teacher and student, dialogic interaction, and sharing of classroom goals, all directed toward "transformative" ends. They isolate three means through which such "mutuality" may take effect: the reconstitution of speech genres in the classroom, the redesigning of the syllabus, and the revaluing of the students' "interpretive agency." So far, so good, from our point of view. What seems missing are cultural practices that would serve as vehicles for these learning changes. Wallace and Ewald mention neither hospitality nor any other social praxis other than profession-centered activities such as "teacher student dialogue" and "classroom conversation." Late in the book they seem to recognize this need: "One critical challenge faced by teachers striving for mutuality is enabling situations in which students must confront the ways in which cultural forces have contributed to the construction of their subjectivities" (Wallace and Ewald 2000, 141). For years now, critical pedagogy in English studies has produced numerous calls for transformation, teacher-student equality, open dialogue, and other changes that we are recommending, too, but this critical pedagogy has produced few socially rooted "enabling situations" to help bring those changes about.

Here the importance of precise rhetorical framing becomes clear. A social practice that looks to be hospitality in fact may be its near opposite. As we have seen, an instructional posture that advertises itself as recognizing the dignity of students can in fact objectify or disempower them. The idea of hospitality is easily fetishized, since it can be akin to many cultural-geopolitical actions—enculturation, assimilation, naturalization, initiation, absorption, resettlement—all with a public face of good intentions and all with a subtext, usually more real than the face, of capturing and devouring. Indeed, when there is no personal risk or internal change for the host, then the host has merely assimilated, or relegated, the guest into his or her own world. The just hospitable classroom can turn into any of the failed hospitable classrooms in a flick of the wrist. It may be something as minute as the way the teacher keys in a command on a student's computer, with its unsaid "I had better do this for you."

For instance, actions resembling ubuntu can hide a sort of cannibalism. Take, for instance, Levinas's (1969) critique of Martin Buber's "I-Thou" relationship. I-Thou is not a Same-Other relationship because it is not truly reciprocal, says Levinas. It treats the Other as an object, not allowing the Other the Other's singular voice. The I-Thou relationship lacks "the interpellation, the vocative," that is, will not let the Other speak in any way that the Same cannot absorb, devour, and remain the Same (68–69). Levinas's argument runs parallel to Thomas W. Ogletree's questioning of Paul Tillich. In *Love, Power, and Justice: Ontological Analyses and Ethical Applications,* Tillich (1954) argues that self-agency ("power") is actualized only through encounters with others. Initially this sounds very Levinian and a brief for hospitality. But Ogletree argues that Tillich's belief may be unethical since it does not ask the self to recognize in others "a center of meaning and value which cannot legitimately be reduced in significance to our own drives for self-actualization" (1991, 42). Without that moral imperative, the Other is there only to be used for one's own ends. Tillich's power play lacks any motive to decenter the self's perspective.[5]

Or consider Brian White's critique of Nel Noddings's (1984) much admired *Caring: A Feminine Approach to Ethics and Moral Education.* Noddings's sense of care is founded on two fixed subject positions: the students as recipients or objects of caring (the "cared-for") and the teacher as the dispenser of caring (the "one-caring"). Noddings, in company with many liberatory educators, believes that literacy is transformative in its power to help people *care* about others. Such caring promotes respect for diversity, the argument goes. It instills an openness to others and brings people together. But the cruel truth, White argues, is that the cared-for are thus rendered dangerously powerless (White 2003, 296). What looks like an apparent welcoming again in fact is a kind of devouring. Behind the rhetoric about community, compassion, and safety, beyond Noddings's emphasis on fairness (guaranteeing inclusion) and intense interest (more productive than empathy) is Noddings's flawed belief that "if the cared-for does not respond to the one-caring's efforts at inclusion, the relationship cannot be considered a caring relationship" (White 2003, 305). The one-caring demands that the cared-for respond by freely and spontaneously disclosing him- or herself. But how can one be both obliged and free, White wonders. It is the teacher, not the student, who is thus the ultimate beneficiary of an ethic of care.

White is aware of the way the student's potentiality enters into this dynamic of caring. He points out that appreciation on the part of students may be muted, unexpressed, or in other ways unactualized. The sign that the one-caring waits for may be long in coming. In self-defense the teacher may feel no obligation to act as one-caring if she or he sees no possibility of completion in the other. Thus the ethic of caring suffers from "potentially destructive self-centeredness" (White 2003, 307–314). White argues that our caring should not be linked to the student's reciprocation but rather should be freely given simply because each student is worthy. His ideal pedagogy comes close to the mixture of the potential, the singular, and the hospitable that this book recommends: what is needed is "relentless attentiveness to all students in their unique circumstances; faith that sees beyond their (and our) immediate reactions and responses; a principled, ethical foundation to guide, guard, and support relationship with each student" (325).

Just hospitality in the classroom is a precarious adventure. Rosello calls it a "precarious equilibrium" (2001, 167). We have noted how host and guest must exchange roles; if not, openness and sharing shift into mutual devouring, the guest assimilated or the host exploited. But equilibrium has its own dangers, especially in the form of that time-honored feature of hospitality legends: gift exchange. Generosity that is equally reciprocated between host and guest, teacher and student, to the point of constant escalation, can inflate through a desire to impress into an addictive, self-serving competition, a mutually destructive potlatch relationship. As the hospitality legends all seem to say, in hospitality mutual and reciprocal gift giving may not be the same thing as perfect symmetry.[6] This applies directly to the classroom. If the teacher is truly open to the student's world of meaning, the teacher will let the student teach that world; the stranger-student is thus the teacher's teacher. Giving students the chance to write what they truly feel about a famous work of literature may turn into an occasion when teachers learn, once again, that they receive more than they give.

Then again it may not. A final precarious point is for the teacher who, versed in hospitality theory, may happily exchange roles with the student-guest but retains a sense of metamastery over the relationship. Among other inequalities, teacher and student are never equally free. Students can grade each other's compositions, but it is the teacher who gives the final course grade. What teacher doesn't need, psychologically, that knowledge of ultimate control? The hospitable classroom, if it is just, must be out of control. One group of students will enter into the host-guest relation differently than a previous group. Of this new group, each individual guest will reciprocate in an unforeseen and perhaps unrecognized way. Each classroom, each new learning room, each new novel or paper topic assigned, each new occasion of reciprocity between singular persons requires a new interpretation. Each encounter, each context requires a rethinking of who is free to give enough, who is free to receive enough and, most important, "who has enough power to define freedom" (Rosello 2001, 174). The only certainty in this complex, asymmetrical, risky, peregrine, marginalized space is host and guest sharing the same intuitions about hospitality itself.

A NEW SET OF RS

From the theoretical and modal we have gleaned four basic characteristics that allow us to touch back to those two attributes of authoring
described in our introduction, potentiality and singularity, and look
ahead to further chapters about concrete classroom practices, models
and means, in literature and composition. The four characteristics are
restlessness, resistance, risk taking, and *retreat* from the center.

Restlessness

All three modes of hospitality—Homeric, biblical, and nomadic—are
characterized by changefulness. This applies to potentiality in its final
end as continued potentiality rather than some end-stopping actualization. It also applies to singularity in its human form as unfinished life history. In terms of social praxis, hospitality is a custom that allows strangers
in transit to pause and learn from each other (note that from the perspective of the guest, it is the host who is on the move). Hospitality has to
accept the transitory nature of its own modus. Even in the Bedouin tent
the host has the right to kick the guest out after three days. The "ease,"
the elbow room that Agamben says is the secret of true hospitality and
true community, is simply the room that each singular one of us offers
to each singular one of us to continue freely on our way, pursuing "what
we may be" (1993, 23–25; see our chapter 11).

Resistance

To be hospitable is to resist. All three historical modes of hospitality
resist naming or totalizing in every guise: categorizing, identifying, sub-
jectifying, relegating to ethnic group or sexual orientation or social class
or cultural region or family history. Potential conserves itself as potential to the extent that it remains open to possibilities, to infinity, does
not trap and deplete itself inside the fixed boundaries of some actuality. By definition, the singular resists generalization or essentialization,
and in human lives maintains itself by preserving potential. Singularity,
says Agamben, is "the simple fact of one's own existence as possibility or
potentiality" (1993, 43). And as all serious students of hospitality insist,
most especially Levinas, the door of welcome opens to a stranger who,
if truly entertained, will not be naturalized through totalities familiar to
the host. In the nomad's tent it is a blunder to even ask the guest's name.

This is one meaning of *theoxenia,* the god disguised in the form of a
stranger. There is always the possibility that the host may be entertaining

an angel unawares, someone of a different order, even a human whose singularity provides difference enough. "Le dieu n'est autre qu'autrui, c'est-à-dire l'autre," says Joachim Manzi, "The god is nothing other than neighbor, that is to say, other" (1999, 338). Manzi remembers his own naturalization as a French citizen, his complete conversion from guest (*hôte invité*) to host (*hôte invitant*). Or rather his always almost (*presque*) complete conversion. He is never fully identified as *sang de France*. It is the *presque* that Manzi decides lies at the true center of hospitality. In that slippage (*décalage*) lies our "reality as an excess or a transgression" (325–326), that is, our inalienable condition of being stranger to others, in which lies our singularity, our potential, and our worth. The hospitable welcome, says, Levinas, is the recognition of a "incessant surplus" that is nothing less than infinity (1969, 218). Only in totality is a person useful because that person is exactly like another person. This is the condition that in essence hospitality resists.

Risk Taking

Hosts and guests must both take risks. To live one's potential means ever to be venturing out of the safety of actualities. To live one's singularity means ever to challenge the normative ethos of social groupings. To live hospitality means to open the door of oneself and welcome in an unknown person or to cross the threshold, without defenses, into an unknown parlor. In the intersection of the potential, the singular, and the truly hospitable, there is no escape from risk. "Hospitality is the crossroads," says Edmond Jabès (1991, 46). There is no way to choose a road without peril—even the way back will have changed and possibly become more dangerous.

Risk is the *deferens* that distinguishes true hospitality from institutionalized versions of it. The "hospitality trade" is hedged about with safeties, and the guest is "guaranteed" a quiet night or his or her money back while the innkeeper is protected by state regulations tacked to the inside door of the rooms (not to mention by the credit-card imprint at the "reception" desk in the lobby). Packaged tours of foreign lands now all include "hospitality," that is, reservations at restaurants deemed sanitary and hotels deemed secure. And nothing can be more free of risk than the official state reception for visiting foreign dignitaries, with preapproved host-guest protocols, vetted toasts, and bodyguards on every balcony.[7]

Retreat

The term is meant not in the military sense but in the religious: retreat to the margins. Potentiality operates in the edgy, permanently moving boundary between capability and deed. As it is usually constructed, singularity occupies the outlier ranges of frequency distributions for every human parameter as well as the wallflower fringe of social groups. And all three historical modes of hospitality involved marginalization. In the traditional literature, from folk tale to Wordsworth (1800) (for example, "The Ruined Cottage"), hospitality is offered by marginal figures—the isolated cottage couple, the elderly, the widower, the recluse, and the poor. Above all the poor.

Today, as it is usually practiced, true hospitality, the hospitality that earns Derrida's epithet "ethical" as opposed to "political," operates away from the centers of power. Even in urban centers, true hospitality settles in the margins. René Schérer (1993) describes an "urban nomadism" formed of transitional or transitory groups such as students, the unemployed, street people, and undocumented immigrants, a largely dispossessed stratum of society, which nonetheless could have as its motto the title of an underground French film, *Viens chez moi, j'habite chez un copine* (Stay with me, I'm living with a buddy). Schérer qualifies this city hospitality as "semi-clandestine, without being proscribed . . . bordering on illegality" (34), in a word, relegated. It may approach a hostless state, where host-guest roles are exchangeable to the point that "each may call oneself host/guest of the host/guest" (*l'hôte de l'hôte*) (183). Clearly this sort of hobo hospitality is a threat to the possessed. It is that marginal practice, that shadow work, that can't be recorded and acted upon by all those institutionalized totalities that want to control us, from the IRS to the college admissions and testing office.[8] The triangulation of potentiality, singularity, and hospitality locates an outlandish place where there are greater chances for people to free themselves from the establishment, the *stable*, in order to change.[9]

These four basic attributes—restlessness, resistance, risk taking, and retreat—need the same willingness to be open to the Other. We will be exploring that willingness throughout the rest of this book. With potentiality, Other is the different self each of us might or might not construct out of our current self so that "what we may be" can always emerge from "what we are." With singularity, Other is the difference our own difference encourages us to look for outside our self. With just hospitality, Other takes on a parallel but more social dynamic. Other becomes the stranger whom we truly welcome in, that is, to whom we truly open out. In the ancient tales, Other is figured as a god bearing the gift of altered life. Theoxenia overcomes xenophobia.[10] In secular literature, the Other is often literally a stranger who mysteriously appears at the beginning and disappears at the end, leaving transformed Coleridge's wedding guest, Crane's frontier town, Conrad's novice sea captain and, in Lionel Trilling's unsetting tale "Of This Time, Of That Place" (about a singular and disturbing student), the English teacher.

Notes

Parts of this chapter appeared in "Hospitality in College Composition Courses," *College Composition and Communication* 60(4) (2009): 707–727, an article coauthored with Glenn Blalock. This piece was published after but was written before Jacobs 2008, which makes many of the same points about hospitality and the English profession. Our essay received some very hostile reviews from readers and editors. Some members of the profession did not much welcome the idea of professional welcoming.

1.   In his satiric theogony, "The Marriage of Heaven and Hell," Blake (1973) divides humankind into Devourer and Prolific, but he is wise enough to know that one depends on the other: "The Prolific would cease to be Prolific unless the Devourer, as a sea, received the excess of his delights." That, of course, does not keep Blake from accusing the Devourers of exercising their "power to resist energy" (that is, Aristotle's *energeia* or the shaping imagination that actualizes potentiality) and using their cunning to keep the Prolific in chains. Nor does it keep Blake from putting his allegiance with the Prolific, as do we. The classic representation of the Devourer can be found in the character of Dr. Bradshaw in Virginia Woolf's (1981) *Mrs. Dalloway*. Woolf associates Bradshaw with his modus operandi of conversion, disguised as brotherly love, offering help but desiring power. Whether in his role of mental health specialist or husband, Bradshaw cloaks his actions with venerable words like "love," "duty," and "self-sacrifice." But the converter "feasts most subtly on the human will" (100). No wonder Septimus Smith thinks of Bradshaw as the "brute with the red nostrils," swooping in, devouring (102, 147).

2.   A student of Henri Nouwen told of being a guest in the house of a family while he was studying at the university. The husband and wife had become estranged from one another and used the student-guest as a surrogate for their lack of affection and eventually forced him to take sides—are you with me or with my spouse? As Nouwen puts it, the story "illustrates how difficult it is to create free space for a stranger when there is no solitude in our lives" (1966, 102). Parker Palmer (1998) speaks of teachers who function as divided selves that bully and swagger, inflicting wounds because they themselves have been wounded (14–15). Both host and guest, or teacher and student, need room to be themselves, that is, to follow their potential. As we have noted, in *The Coming Community* Agamben (1993) calls Nouwen's free space "ease," or elbow room, and names it as the central practice of the ideal sociopolitical community (33–35; see our chapter 11).

3.   Ubuntu was most widely manifested to the West with the dismantlement of the apartheid regime in South Africa and the mandate of the Truth and Reconciliation Commission. The new South Africa faced a crucial decision in how to come to terms with the evils of apartheid. It could, for instance, pursue retributive justice as enacted by the victorious Allies at Nuremberg after World War II. This would involve juridical proceedings based on forensic, "factual truth." The cost would

have broken the economic back of the new democracy, since the state would have had to pay for legal representation of the defendants, who were, for the most part, former government employees. And there was a more fundamental problem. Once issues of justice and punishment were pronounced at Nuremberg, the Allies could (in the words of Desmond Tutu) "pick up and go home." But white and black South Africans had to find a way to live with one another (Tutu 1999, 21). A second option was blanket amnesty for members and minions of the previous government. But this was unthinkable, amounting as it did to national amnesia, which would only silence and violate victims yet again (30). Rather than deliberations in the courts or executive decree, the third option of restorative justice was pursued through the Truth and Reconciliation Commission, wherein the "truth of wounded memories" could be narrated (26). Restorative justice is based on the spiritual principle called *botho* in Sotho languages or, more commonly, *ubuntu* in Nguni languages.

4.   An excellent source for the relationship between ubuntu and the Truth and Reconciliation hearings is Antjie Krog's (1988) *Country of My Skull.* Her definition of ubuntu is a model of concision: "a person is a person through other persons" (344).

5.   Ogletree (1991) finds a counter to Tillich in Seyla Benhabib's notion of the "concrete other." Benhabib's formulation also approaches our own sense of potential, singularity, and hospitality: It "enjoins us to view every moral person as a unique individual, with a certain life history, disposition, and endowment, as well as need and limitations" (1992, 10). Benhabib contrasts her notion of the concrete other with the "generalized other," "a rational being entitled to the same rights and duties we would want to ascribe to ourselves"—what we have in common, which is formal equality and reciprocity (1987, 87). Acting upon a generalized sense of the other entails a loss. "To recognize the generalized other, we must abstract from the individuality and concrete identity of the other . . . what constitutes his or her moral dignity is not what differentiates us from each other, but rather what we, as speaking and acting rational agents, have in common" (Benhabib 1992, 158–159). The loss, in short, is on both sides. I have lost a sense of the diversity and richness of humankind, which may be potentially useful to me, and the other has lost the possible gains from any traits or experiences not included in my gaze. In a truly hospitable relationship, both host and guest do not merely recognize in the other a fellow human being (that is, their commonality) but also recognize their human individuality.

6.   Rosello (2001) reflects that "asymmetry may not be the opposite of hospitality" (171). In tales of hospitality that date before imperial Rome, the gift exchange is usually present, but the gifts are rarely equivalent. Sarah and Abraham, centenarians both, give the two *elohim* (angels in disguise) oaten cakes and receive in turn the promise of a son. Lot gives two strangers shelter and protection from the xenophobic Sodomites, but the two strangers, angels in disguise, save Lot and his family from the destruction of Sodom. Philomon and Baucis offer two strangers a simple country meal, but the two strangers, Jupiter and Mercury in disguise, give the rustic couple a pitcher that is never empty and safety from a flood that destroys their town. Saint Julian gives a mendicant leper all he has, bread and wine to stave off hunger and thirst and an embrace to stave off the cold, but the leper, Jesus in disguise, then raises Julian to heaven. The beggar-prince is given a match and bestows a kingdom on the generous daughter. Behind the themes of unequal gift exchange and theoxenia (god/royalty-as-stranger) lies hospitality's commitment to singularity and potentiality. Because of the social situation that underwrites an act of hospitality, host and guest can never be equals, so why should the gifts be equivalent? It is, in fact, upon the given of unequal status that the aporia of hospitality forever twists. Offerer and devourer finally cannot be distinguished. But it does make clear that the mode of the hospitable act involves reversible roles and

unequal exchanges. In the Zen koan, the head monk says to the merchant donor, who wants to be thanked for his gift of money to the monastery, "It is the giver who should be thankful."

7. See Marin Allen (1985) for the "guest-host archetype" as it has functioned in U.S. presidencies.

8. It was popular demand that forced the U.S. Census Bureau to allow checking of multiple boxes under "race and ethnicity" in the 2000 forms. Despite pressure, the bureau did not include a box labeled "multiracial."

9. Tracy McNulty (1999) provides a thorough and fascinating analysis of the role nomadic or marginal hospitality plays in challenging identity constructions in Old Testament narratives. Her study provides another meld of potentiality, singularity, and hospitality. In the Bible, hospitality tales are conversion narratives and therefore often take place in wilderness borderlands: "At the limits of mankind, and at the limits of the knowable, religious hospitality stages the encounter with pure alterity: what can neither be identified with a sign nor inscribed within a common measure" (para. 3).

10. Openness to the Other is the key to Luce Irigaray's (1999) recent explorations into singularity, potentiality, hospitality, and gender. She argues that healthy personal change will occur only when we are open to others fully, that is, when we understand that the Other is never completely assimilable by us. In an age of globalization, immigration, and mixing of cultures, says Irigaray, it is essential to accept that "the other remains unknowable to us," "beyond all that we can predicate of him or her" (123–124). Such a Levinian position goes against Western ideology and educational practices, which value appropriation or understanding of things outside us: "This opening of a world of one's own, experienced as familiar, in order to welcome the stranger, while remaining oneself and letting the stranger be other, do not correspond to our mental habits, to our Western logic" (125). Irigaray further argues that the essential I/Other pair is the married couple. For the role of openness to the stranger (the *atopon*) in modern hermeneutics or personal development theory, see R. Haswell 1991, 126–135.

4

INHOSPITABLE RECEPTION
The Critic as Host

Tyranny, face it, fears very few literary critics.
—Mary Rose O'Reilley

One of Jan's students, struggling with the prospect of leaving coastal Texas for graduate school, explained why moving was so unappealing to him. "Outside of South Texas," Adrian said, "I am not brown enough."

How can a person be not brown enough? Adrian wasn't innocent of the plight of the marginalized in Texas. Growing up in Corpus Christi barrios, he had experienced racism, injustice, poverty. He had dealt with gangs of white teenagers on the prowl to teach "Mexicans" their place because they weren't white enough. But he had managed to develop a clear sense of his own unique personhood and the value of the cultural heritage that he thought was his. After high school, he had lived for a few months in New Mexico, where he felt alienated and belittled by the Hispanics he met. Perhaps because of his refusal to associate only with "acceptable" people, perhaps because of his belief in empathy rather than violence as a means of social change, perhaps because of his refusal to reduce issues of justice to racial terms alone, he was not well received by his own ethnic group. Adrian wasn't brown enough because he wasn't political enough.

THE READER AS HOST

Adrian's new acquaintances in New Mexico may have forgotten the first crucial step in a hospitable relationship, which is an act of self-restraint. The host must hold back the impulse to categorize before knowing— more exactly, the impulse to categorize in order to begin knowing. The good host resists pigeonholing the guest as "brown," "old," "foreigner," "Mexican," "Texan," "odd," "badly dressed," or as any other of

DOI: 10.7330/9780874219883.c004

the endless uniform traits and identities by which people size up and sort other people before they can begin seriously interacting with them. Instead the hospitable host begins with soaking in. How does this particular guest talk and gesture? How does the guest feel? What does the guest know that the host does not? Hospitality begins with a charitable absorption of all that information that brings people closer together not by assignment to cubbyholes but by appreciation as unique. The host has to relish the shock of difference.

To the immature adolescent, the act may seem counterintuitive. Don't you get closer to a stranger by finding out the groups you both belong to? But that would be to bond through shared totalities and to shut out Agamben's community without identity or Russell's unity without uniformity. It might be a way to embrace the Other as Us, but it is also a way to reject the Other as Them, to cast Them as different from Us and then to cast them out. It is hospitality as social friendship, being generous and sharing with one's group or the friends of one's group. It is not hospitality as the act of opening up to the strange in the stranger.

It goes without saying that the hospitable guest also resists prematurely categorizing the host, but in this chapter we will focus on the host's reception of the guest. We will also treat one of the two primordial literacy acts in English studies, the reception of a piece of writing new to the reader. The writing may be deemed "fiction" or "nonfiction"—it is of no import to our analysis. (The other primordial act, of course, is the authoring of a piece of writing new to the reader.)

And we will focus on that peculiar act of literary criticism, the reception of a smart, successful literary author by a smart, well-read literary scholar. There are plenty in the profession who believe that this act lies at the very core of English studies. Perhaps they are right, though it might depend upon how one interprets "smart," "successful," and "literary."

We are assuming that the social act of hospitality models and, to a degree, inheres in the act of reading, that the reader receives into his or her house of intellect a new piece of discourse much as the host receives the arrivant. Note, however, that this trope or extension of hospitality reverses tradition, in which it is the literary work that is the host who embraces the guest-reader, the ends of the scroll or the facing pages of the book opening like welcoming arms. That is the old trope beloved of writers, but our switch, we trust, will make as much sense. Ultimately, in the act of authoring and perusing, writers and readers must switch roles just as host and guest do in the act of hospitality.

We warn that the reader as host is a necessary but perilous role to play. It is easier, always easier, for the reader to give a new work an inhospitable reception. That applies not only to the experienced critic-scholar but to the student-scholar as well.

COLONIAL CRITICISM

Adrian discovered what published authors have always known, that a person's politics can be as important as his or her skin color—or work very much like it. The same kinds of judgments, for instance, not being brown or black or native or multicultural enough, are habitually made about authors of ethnic and postcolonial texts. This chapter will plumb one perversion of the writer-as-host and reader-as-guest inversion, when the guest invades the text and takes control of it as host. That is what we mean by colonial criticism.

As we have said, inversion of host-guest roles is natural in traditional hospitality, and the same is true with reader-writer roles in critical reading. Where is the perversion? Sometimes it can start with the temptation of the critic or theorist to act as a host controlling the gateway to academic or scholarly acceptance. If the temptation includes premature categorization, criticism can revert to colonialism and violate the kind of intellectual hospitality that should characterize scholarship. Most unfortunate both for English teachers and students is when this colonial criticism degenerates into high-handed, even arrogant attacks by scholars upon writers at the very point where affirmation of human dignity is most needed. That point is the threshold where host first meets guest.

The mandate for exploitive reading of all kinds sometimes is laid, incorrectly, on the doorstep of Roland Barthes and Michel Foucault, who speak of the death of the author. Barthes and Foucault are understood to argue against contaminating a text with an autonomous subject-writer and to argue for instating the reader or "scriptor" as the only authority. Reception theorists vary in the kind of spending spree they allow readers with the inheritance of the dead author. Probably most would qualify Donald Pease's (1990) bald assertion that "the critic is free to reconstitute the text according to his own terms" as one of the most profligate (113). But even halfway surrendering the reins of authority into the hands of the reader-critic too early in the reading process can have disastrous consequences. Literature can become the pawn of a factional argumentative game, a puppet or a straw dog for academic ideologues who, however subtly and eruditely, end up alone on the threshold converting the artwork into their own politics.

We mark our words when we call this abuse colonial criticism. Forgive us if occasionally we refer to it in more heated language, such as "critical imperialism." Analysis that denies the author's presence, totalizes the author's singular vision, or consigns the author to some cardboard political identity repeats the gestures of first world domination of third world resources. In short, it repeats Adrian's experiences, albeit on paper. It also parallels a history that we recount in chapter 1, the modern commercialization of traditional hospitality into colonial hospitality. Colonial criticism betrays the ethic of hospitality not because the role of host and guest are inverted but because once the foreign guest, the reader-critic, becomes established as host, there is little opportunity for participants to exchange gifts or to define their own roles. Inevitably the occupier host devours and cannibalizes the native writer, once host and now perpetual and powerless guest (Rosello 2001, 28–30).

ONDAATJE'S *RUNNING IN THE FAMILY*

By way of example, we turn to recent criticism of Michael Ondaatje's (1982) *Running in the Family*, a multisided text that has been referred to as an example of biography, travel literature, pastoral, personal history, memoir, life writing, and autobiographical metafiction. Ondaatje wrote *Running in the Family* after two trips, in 1978 and 1980, to Sri Lanka, his birthplace.[1] The narrative reads like a quest. The speaker seeks to unveil the mystery of his parents' marriage, understand the enigma of his father's taciturn personality, and reexperience this location of heat and lush vegetation that contrasts so starkly with Toronto, his home at the time.

Readers familiar with Ondaatje's prose will be comfortable with the fragmented, circular, and anecdotal sequence of memories and experiences that comprise this family history. While the narrator faithfully undertakes the historian's work (researching archives, interviewing witnesses, absorbing folk history), it becomes obvious that a simple, clear, or "true" sense of his father, Mervyn Ondaatje, or of Sri Lanka and its people, is nearly impossible to write. Both public and private history require interpretation. Interpretation involves the subjectivities of the historian writer, who in this case is at once foreigner and native son, hôte invité and hôte invitant.

Ondaatje calls himself a "prodigal"—either fleeing his family's house or running back to it. His relationship to the family remains ambivalent throughout. The gerund in the title can indicate the author is "in" (as a genetic strain *runs* in a family) or "with" (as a member of the pack *runs* with the pack) or perhaps "against" (as a family member *runs* against its grain). Though estranged from his past, the narrator discerns that the theatricality of his mother, the secrecy of his father, and the need, it seems, of everyone to abuse alcohol, also "run" in the family. Whether pointing to action or character, the title ultimately speaks not to a present condition (*runs*) and not to a past condition (*ran*) but to an ongoing condition (*running*). We might call it a condition of potentiality, though that seems far from the interpretation of some of the book's critics.

AN UNFRIENDLY RECEPTION: ARUN P. MUKHERJEE

Generally, critical reaction to *Running in the Family* has been favorable, with a few exceptions, including Arun P. Mukherjee's (1985) "The Poetry of Michael Ondaatje and Cyril Dabydeen: Two Responses to Otherness" and Sangeeta Ray's (1993) "Memory, Identity, Patriarchy: Projecting a Past in the Memoirs of Sara Suleri and Michael Ondaatje." We take up these exceptions and make a good-faith effort to understand their differences.

Mukherjee (1985) believes Ondaatje has betrayed his ethnic hybridity. His success as a Canadian writer is won "largely through a sacrifice of his [Sri Lankan] regionality," to the point that his relationship with "his country of origin is highly problematic" (50). Basing her case on Ondaatje's early poetry and on *Running in the Family*, Mukherjee finds little evidence of the trauma that should have accompanied his cultural uprooting. She denounces his brand of metapoetry as reminiscent of Wallace Stevens—poems about writing poems from a position of the "unmediated present" (51). Far preferable, she believes, is verse situated historically, culturally, and politically so that the "question of otherness" is addressed (54). Ondaatje, it seems, is not Sri Lankan enough.

According to Mukherjee (1985), in *Running in the Family* Ondaatje's view from an unsituated, universalist aestheticism marks him as a person "who does not want to come to terms with the multiplicity and diversity of cultural modes as well as differences of race and class" (55). Ondaatje is in denial about his family's complicity in colonial Ceylon. He appears unable "to place his family in a network of social relationships" (57). In fact, argues Mukherjee, if there is any political position in *Running in the Family*, it involves the writer taking sides with the colonizer (56). As a corrective to Ondaatje, Mukherjee notes the work of Cyril Dabydeen, who "sings of the history of his community rather than of the naked individual in converse with the universe" (58). Authentic ethnic language speaks to oppression, victimization, and resistance, while universalists like Ondaatje "retreat from the questions of ideology, power, race and class" (65).

In sum, Mukherjee believes Ondaatje proves false to the ethnic emigrant, the hybrid subject uprooted and exposed, who can neither reclaim his homeland nor masquerade in his adopted home as an entirely assimilated individual. A few critics have accepted her view.[2] But other scholars have mustered to Ondaatje's defense, arguing that the very elements Mukherjee believes crucial to the postcolonial experience—a consciousness of his own colonial heritage, a sense of an identity situated in a specific culture and history, an understanding of the evils of empire, and a critique of history written through the eyes of the colonizer—actually are exhibited by *Running in the Family* in a self-reflective and insightful way.

For instance, critics have noted that the design of Ondaatje's memoir—the multivocal narrative structure, with numerous storytellers interweaving their views with the narrator's—demonstrates that the author insists on a polycentric viewpoint and rejects both the conventional egocentric or Eurocentric perspective of the colonizer and the Asia-centric perspective of the colonized. Rather than marginalizing the local and indigenous, Ondaatje recenters them through his emphasis on subjectivity and multivocality. Through his interlaced choir of voices, he gradually understands the communal nature of his own self. As Levinas (1969) would put it, Ondaatje has allowed the shock of the Other to "recollect" himself (150). Ondaatje values the intensity of artistic inspiration because it welcomes in the public, collective, social, interpretive, and constructed nature of all of history. With his father's inaccessibility and his country's complexity, he shows how elusive knowledge of the past is and how inadequate are the very sort of totalizing narratives that Mukherjee condemns.[3]

Other responses also call into question the ideological assumptions that underpin Mukherjee's attack. Ajay Heble (1994), for instance, sees her assumption that it is possible to represent ethnic authenticity as an essentialist distortion of ethnicity itself (187). Josef Pesch (1998) notes that Mukherjee speaks as though the eleven years of Ondaatje's life in Ceylon signify his "true" self, rendering twenty-five years in England and Canada irrelevant, as if cultural and ethnic identities are determined by birth alone (67). More scathing is Suwanda Sugunasiri's attack on Mukherjee's inability to grasp Ondaatje's message because of "an understandable unfamiliarity with Sri Lankan society, generalized and extended from her own Indian society, [having] fallen into the trap of being ahistorical and acontextual" (1992, 64)—exactly Mukherjee's accusation of Ondaatje.

Rarely can such debate be resolved. It reduces down to one identity versus another, always a draw. We'd rather not ask, for instance, what is more essentialist, whiteness or brownness, Europeanness or Asianness, coloniality or postcoloniality, ethnicity or multiethnicity. We are more concerned with missteps in initial reception that may lead to such impasses. Why should a reader feel the need in the first place to start interpreting *Running in the Family* as a white or brown narrative, or as a colonial or postcolonial one, or as a Eurocentric or Asia-centric or even polycentric one? What is this immediate need for centricity? Mukherjee's (1985) interpretation, it is clear, begins with the individual Michael Ondaatje already placed in relation to such categories. Her very first mention of Ondaatje reads, "Michael Ondaatje is one of the very few South Asian poets [in Canada] to have been heard by the white audience" (49). In Levinas's terms, this reception by the host-reader sees the arrivant author through the lens of familiar totalities rather than the lens of the infinite Other. If this is a misstep in critical reading, how do we propose the reader better proceed?

ANOTHER UNFRIENDLY RECEPTION: SANGEETA RAY

It might seem that a better way is shown by a second major critique of *Running in the Family*, Sangeeta Ray's (1993) "Memory, Identity, Patriarchy: Projecting a Past in the Memoirs of Sara Suleri and Michael Ondaatje." In fact Ray begins her essay by questioning the essentialism of the term *postcolonial*. It is too imprecise for her needs as a reader because of its erasure of "crucial differences between various countries too easily included under the all-encompassing rubric" (38). It would finally render many geographical spaces, literary traditions, and political views as more similar than different. Ray illustrates the limitations of the term and dangers in the reading strategy that adopts it wholesale by comparing two memoirs published by previous residents of the Indian subcontinent, Ondaatje's (1982) *Running in the Family* and Sara Suleri's *Meatless Days* (1991).

Ray (1993) continues in a way that will hearten anyone who distrusts centricities or totalities. In both Suleri and Ondaatje she finds a highly self-conscious, paradoxical, and indeterminate version of the bildungs-roman, filled with anecdotes that cross geographic spaces and generational time. Both texts ask how one establishes links between self-identity and cultural home when home is plural and identity is multilayered. Ray's approach to cultural hybridity illuminates for the reader the rich, reflexive, material, nonlinear, and ever-shifting identities of two individuals, one female and one male, whose lives travel from one culture to another. Ondaatje, part Dutch and part Sri Lankan, lived in Ceylon,

England, then Canada. Suleri (now Sara Suleri Goodyear), part Welsh and part Pakistani, lived in Pakistan and then the United States.

But Ray's friendly reception turns almost instantly into a reception like Mukherjee's. Indeed Ray's (1993) sentence that first welcomes Ondaatje and Suleri to her house of critique begins by saying that they "recognize the provisionality of the nature of personal, cultural, and geopolitical identifications" but continues, without a break, with the assertion that they "delineate a symbolic cartography that in its allegorical and referential sweep is never entirely detached from the Sri Lanka and Pakistan on a map" (38–39). As her essay proceeds, it becomes clear that "map" will take precedence over "provisionality" in her reception of Ondaatje.

Ray (1993) argues that Suleri's memoir is superior to Ondaatje's on three levels. First, Ondaatje is colonialist, siding with his Dutch heritage, whereas Suleri identifies with her Pakistani side (Suleri's mother is Welsh, her father Pakistani). Second, Ondaatje is elitist, referring to members of the subaltern working poor or servant class as anonymous types rather than named individuals, a failing that Suleri avoids. Third, Ondaatje is masculinist, mainly seeking to discover his father, whom he had not seen since he left Ceylon at the age of eleven, whereas Suleri places the women in her family as those most valued. In terms of Ray's opening issue—defining the valid parameters of the term *postcolonial*—she concedes that both memoirs display "the rhetoric of disembodiment, dislocation, and displacement" appropriate to what postcolonial literature should entail and what postcolonial theory valorizes. But she warns against the first world "liberal pluralist agenda of multicultural education" that would posit equal value when the political and social locations treated by Suleri and Ondaatje are disparate and divided (55). She decides that only Suleri's text can properly be called postcolonial.

Ray's (1993) condemnation of *Running in the Family* concentrates upon the sequence of poems in the section "Don't Talk to Me about Matisse," located at the center of the memoir. At the very core of this center is the "powerful and angry" poem of Sri Lankan Lakdasa Wikkramasinha, which refers to the brutal repression of the Marxist insurrection of 1971.

> Don't talk to me about Matisse . . .
> the European style of 1900, the tradition of the studio
> where the nude woman reclines forever
> on a sheet of blood. (Ondaatje 1982, 86)

Following this poem are four written by Ondaatje, as if he seeks to insinuate his voice within the same choir of Sri Lankan culture. But

Ondaatje's own verse is devoid of what Ray calls the language of accountability that is found in Wikkramasinha's poem.

The reason, Ray asserts, is that rather than acknowledging the role of his Dutch ancestors as foreign conquerors, Ondaatje believes his own family members are superior to the cold and reserved British, who refused to integrate themselves into Ceylonese culture. In Ray's words, Ondaatje makes his own ancestors "palatable invaders" (1993, 45). Rather than admit to the imperialist role of his family as members of the Burgher community,[4] Ondaatje orchestrates his stories so that while privileged, landed, and extravagant, his parents' generation is represented as eccentric, creative, educated, and charming. As for the present generation, Ondaatje's family is often described as dispossessed, with hands unbloodied from the 1971 insurrection.

Even as Ondaatje insists on the fluid identities of his parents, so, Ray (1993) argues, he constructs a static identity of the native subaltern, indulging in a "repression of class and gender differences" (46). Just as the poor, servant class was exploited by his ancestors, Ondaatje now exploits the native subaltern in his series of poems. In "High Flowers," for instance, Ondaatje notices "the woman my ancestors ignored" but identifies her only by her work. Because she remains unnamed and hidden from history by shadow, she is depersonalized, anonymous, and undifferentiated (1982, 45). Ondaatje depersonalizes and disempowers the native Other, and thus is guilty of enacting cultural violence through the art of this memoir (as did the paintings of Matisse).

While the poem "The Cinnamon Peeler" might call attention to Ceylon's most important export and to the virile peeler workers, Ray (1993) continues, Ondaatje renders the peeler's wife submissive and inconsequential compared to her husband (46). Although the stories recounted in *Running in the Family* are told predominately by women, those women do not enjoy the author's attention; rather, they are subordinated to a "recuperation of the wild, misunderstood, alcoholic father" (47).[5] Through Ondaatje's mystification and romanticization of his father (47, 53), he reifies a Ceylonese fantasy, a fantasy founded on the metaphor of his father's life as pages of an uncut book; this metaphor essentializes the name of the father that the son has sought throughout his journey at the expense of crucial gender differences (53, 55).

In some ways Ray's reception of Ondaatje is the reverse of Mukherjee's. Mukherjee sees him as not participating in Sri Lanka's issues of class, race, and colonial oppression. Ray sees him as participating in these issues but on the wrong side. Yet Mukherjee and Ray follow the same interpretive strategy of judging Ondaatje in terms of those categories.

For both Ray (1993) and Mukherjee (1985), Ondaatje is just "not brown enough." Both have a nuanced conception of these categories as complex and fluid, with Mukherjee talking about "the multiplicity and diversity of cultural modes" (55) and Ray about the postcolonial themes of "disembodiment, dislocation, and displacement" (55). Yet both their receptions seem to run counter (and in the end prove disloyal) to that complexity and fluidity.

Though both would fiercely deny it, there is kind of colonial appropriation underlying their hermeneutic tactic: my centricity is better than yours. Theirs is power of a kind—the censorship of tyranny by literary critics who have little power against tyranny itself, as Mary Rose O'Reilley (1993) notes. But critical practice can also erect a pseudo-tyranny. The power of the critic may be used to circumscribe group membership, defining that membership not on grounds of hybridity or nativism but on a fabricated sense of "purism" based on the writer's political views as enacted in the aesthetic work. In such critical maneuvers, there is only one acceptable view of postcolonized people, one metanarrative (however layered or fragmented) that passes muster. It's as if while "tyranny fears very few literary critics" (61), the critics themselves are tempted by tyranny. Of all literary theories, shouldn't it be postcolonialism to abhor colonial attitudes within its own ranks?

THE HOSPITABLE READER OF *RUNNING IN THE FAMILY*

How can the postcolonial critic welcome Ondaatje's singular hybridity? There are plenty of models or metaphors for reading, as we will see in the next chapter, ranging from oral conversation to travel to biochemical catalytic reaction. As we have said, our model, traditional hospitality, advises that the reader postpone fitting Ondaatje into normalized personal traits, habitualized political identities, or naturalized cultural uniformities. Instead the reader will look for opportunities to create a community or unity with Ondaatje that recognizes, embraces, and finally safeguards the ways he does not fit, the ways he is singular.[6] Both traditional and philosophical hospitality insist that the first step for the host is be open to the otherness of the guest. A reader receptive to the unique gestures of *Running in the Family* will recognize many opportunities for this othering precisely because Ondaatje is a cultural hybrid.

The most obvious opportunity is on the doorstep, the way Ondaatje first presents himself. In the opening paragraph of the book, he tells us of a dream he had of his father surrounded by barking dogs. The dream wakes him, in tears, and for a minute he is simultaneously in the past and in the present, at his father's house in Sri Lanka and on his friend's couch in Toronto with a glowing fish tank in the corner: "in a jungle, hot, sweating. Street lights bounced off the snow" (Ondaatje 1982, 21). Ondaatje doesn't represent himself as pro- or anti-Asian, pro- or anticolonial, pro- or antifemale, pro- or antiworker, but merely as someone who has unexpectedly dreamed of his past and his father in another land. In the rest of the paragraph, he doesn't come across as seriously male, Canadian, Sri Lankan, a writer, rich, or any other politicized identity. He comes across as an odd show-off, one who is sure of himself only when drunk and when drunk one who can fall down, twist around, and get up again—all with a wineglass balanced on his head. His impulse to return to the place of his upbringing and write about it he calls "a perverse and solitary desire" (22). How singular, how human!

At this point, a hospitable reception can proceed in an infinite number of ways. We will stick to one quirk in the writer's self-presentation, his fondness for the doubling of reality. The dream about his father reveals his desire to "journey back" to his family, "those relations from my parents' generation who stood in my memory . . . I wanted to touch them into words" (Ondaatje 1982, 22). Memory and memoir, of course, always entail a mental doubling, at least two consciousnesses.[7] But Ondaatje complicates things because his reminiscence often articulates two disparate views at once and thus creates a liminal interpretive space for readers that a monolithic account would suppress. In this first chapter, Asia for Ondaatje is not a parceled and politicized uniformity: "*Asia* . . . An ancient word that had to be whispered, would never be used as a battle cry. The word sprawled" (22). If the reader is the host, Ondaatje is a double-faced stranger who resists quick categorization.

The reader soon begins to notice the strange obsession and range of Ondaatje's doublings, of the auditor (listening to and taping the sounds of Ceylon, replaying the tape in Canada), of the author (both archivist/interviewer and character in the history being researched), of the narrator (the child and the man), of narrative consciousness (dreamer and runner), of geography (Sri Lanka and Canada), of historical place (colonial Ceylon and independent Sri Lanka), of race (Dutch and native Sri Lankan), of nativeness (Sinhalese and Tamil), of temporality (past situated as present-telling moment with present seeming to be future), of personal past (the narrator's own and his parents'), of story (none told just once or the same), of habit (Mervyn Ondaatje's drinking and his son's). The pairings never stop.[8]

For the receptive reader, such doubling leads in several interpretive directions. For one, it emphasizes the tension within Ondaatje's family, generated between his histrionic mother and secretive father, so that the children felt their job was "to keep peace with enemy camps" (Ondaatje 1982, 179). Since Ondaatje refuses to resolve any of these contradictions, as host-readers, we, too, must weigh perceptions, facts, and confused accounts. Totalizing is blocked in every direction. How can we run intercept, for instance, between Ceylon's history and the figure of Mervyn Ondaatje, a man torn (at least in the imaginative eye of his son) between depression and a sense of humor, between sacredness of life and the "poison" that oozed up from the ground to threaten his family and friends? Taken at face value, as Ondaatje presents him and as he first should be read, he can't be singly labeled by *any* historical generalization, political front, or cultural centricity.

The reader aware of Ondaatje's doubling will also be alert to the way memoir works as a metanarrative establishing aporetic links between history and text. Given his initial purpose—to touch his parents' generation "into words," not into facts or memories—the reader can only guess at the multiple purposes of the book. Ondaatje is not merely recuperating his family's history or the history of his birthplace. He is enacting the process whereby history is written, from collecting stories of witnesses, stimulating and testing memories, locating archival materials, and so on, to juxtaposing those often contradictory pieces together into a passing text, all the while painfully conscious of the fragility of text that may seem as if etched in stone (Ondaatje 1982, 65) but over time washes from the hands in the form of paper dust (68). In the only words in the book spoken directly from the child/adult to his father, Ondaatje admits, "I am writing this book about you at a time when I am least sure about such words" (180). The most unsettling instance of this textual-historical aporia happens when the reader reaches page 189, which describes Mervyn watching ants carry away page 189 of the novel that he has tossed on the lavatory floor. How could Ondaatje have achieved this effect except by altering the history he is recounting, changing the page number in Mervyn's book after he had seen page proofs of *Running in the Family*? Mervyn Ondaatje ends up a double paradox: he is both untold history and unwritten text: "He is still one of those books we long to read whose pages remain uncut" (200). Is *Running in the Family* history or fiction? As reader-host, initially we can only accept what our writer-guest tells us.

In the same way, we must accept a final point this author-stranger makes about the very stories he is telling us and his propensity to double: "No story is ever told just once" (Ondaatje 1982, 26). The disavowal will take center stage in his next novel, *In the Skin of the Lion* (Ondaatje

1987), which has as epigraph a quote from John Berger: "Never again will a single story be told as though it were the only one."[9] To the degree that politics broadcasts itself as univocal, Ondaatje does not appear to operate politically, although his story might lend itself to such an approach, given a different writer. "I am not interested in politics *on the public level,*" he said in an interview (quoted in Bok 1992, 111). We have emphasized the last phrase. With *Running in the Family,* odds are the stranger in the book in our hands is withholding his personal commitments to particular political agendas, as is customary in traditional host-guest meetings.

How do you talk about your own family to a stranger? In facing the risk of betraying members of his family, of writing about people he knew and cared about but who are unknown to the reader, Ondaatje prefers a measuring rod that is not political. In the "exchange of gift and character" (Ondaatje 1982, 54), Ondaatje seeks a certain kind of shadow, the shade of another's presence that we call love. As he said in an interview, "I just had to say to myself that I thought I was writing the book with enough love" (quoted in Solecki 1985, 331—the interview, by the way, is the genre of literary criticism with the most affinity to the hospitable mode). In the same way, the narrator in *Running* might long to sit down "with someone and talk with utter directness, want to talk to all the lost history like that deserving lover" (54). Who would dialogue with him— his father, his mother, his grandmother, people he never knew? Does the reader replace that impossible auditor?

At this point it is insightful to ask how a hospitable first reading might see differently the concerns brought by Mukherjee and Ray to *Running in the Family.* Ray sees a patri-focal drive. Mervyn Ondaatje is the dominant vehicle of the author's misunderstanding, guilt, emptiness, confusion, and longing, and all the other members of his nuclear family follow in Mervyn's wake. But with an initial tolerant disposition toward everything the narrator offers, the reader would find an equal attention to various storytelling aunts or to various storied women (like grandmother Lalla). *Running* would more likely appear a balanced and caring narrative that does not take family necessarily as the privileged territory of the male nor deny women their place in personal and public histories. If Ondaatje seems more interested in tracking his father's character than his mother's, that simply makes sense in terms of individual oddities, such as his father's habitual taciturnity. But this does not automatically make the author guilty of relegating women back into the shadows from which postcolonial critics have liberated them or of dismissing "crucial gender differences" (Ray 1993, 53).[10]

A hospitable reception reads very differently from Ray's complaint that Ondaatje keeps nameless the subaltern—the toddy tappers, the cinnamon peeler and his wife, the ladies of the mountain. Does this mean that all natives are the same to Ondaatje, or that the native subjects of his poems are stripped of their dignity and individuality? As we have said, traditions of hospitality forbid the host from asking the guest's name, a custom that in fact lends dignity to the stranger-guest. In turn, the guest has the right to withhold the names of people he or she mentions to the stranger-host, a dignity (and perhaps protection) that the guest extends to his or her friends and acquaintances. And if we imagine Ondaatje as our guest, telling us about the people he has casually met on his trip to Sri Lanka, do we expect him to know their names? Would a respectful traveler go up to "subalterns" seen on the street and ask their name? As Ondaatje discovers in his next novels, *In the Skin of the Lion* (1987) and *The English Patient* (1992), naming can be a form of owning, labeling, mastering, and not-naming exactly the opposite of Ray's charge: a form of respect for others. Not-naming can be a way to escape totalities.

Not-naming does not necessarily deprive the not-named of individuality. Ondaatje's poems in *Running in the Family* record once-only moments in a traveler's day, and the people described in them are thereby singularized. Read with a host's openness to a guest traveler's reminiscence, the first impression the poems give is not of colonial distancing but of imaginative connectedness. "The Cinnamon Peeler," for instance, would not come across as depicting a passive, "receptive" woman, as Ray projects. Rather, it seems imaginatively to enter a way of life new and strange to the viewer. He imagines the woman's body taking in her husband's cinnamon scent with the touch of his hands; so marked, she becomes a sensuous explorer, aware of her own body and celebrating the unique scent of her skin traced "in the act of love" (1982, 96). Instead of exoticizing the native, Ondaatje is trying to defamiliarize her, to create a sensuous, joyous, and vibrant life that exists and carries on away from the Westerner's shadow. As Cynthia Carey argues, the poems in *Running* function as a microcosm of the larger text, decolonizing both imagination and language (2001, 47, 50).

What the hospitable reader might find exotic is Mukherjee's accusation that Ondaatje speaks to a generalized audience and not to Sri Lankans. A reader who simply takes in the narrator's stories without attempting to fit them into racist or colonialist packages will find an observer alert to an astonishing variety of people living in Sri Lanka, now and in the past. If this observer is estranged from any native, it would be the fanciful "native" who exists in a pure ethnic state, pure

Ceylonese, blood without some mix of Indian Tamil, Sri Lankan Tamil, Sinhalese, Moorish, Portuguese, Dutch, British, German, Swedish, Kaffir, Austronesians, or aboriginal Vedda.[11] One of the virtues of the hospitable mode of reading is its fidelity to hybridity.

Discourse from hybrid or liminal spaces *should* work to dismantle ethnic, cultural, national, or professional insistence on purity and superiority.[12] Ray pits "Burgher blood" (the Eurasian mixed community in Sri Lanka to which Ondaatje legally belongs) against "native blood," communities that culturally are hardly less hybrid (1993, 41). Hers may be a losing battle. The insistence that someone is not white enough is the classic sign of colonial racism. Isn't the insistence that someone is not brown enough the current sign of postcolonial racism? No doubt the increasingly mixed world will reach a point when there will be an insistence in some quarters that someone is not hybrid enough. Hospitality will still be there to resist that moment.

EMBRACING HYBRIDITY, EMBRACING THE SINGULAR

How should a reader receive a strange text? There is no question that little, if anything, escapes the brush of politics. Certainly the political paradigms of postmodern literary criticism have been a powerful tool in challenging inflexible canons, narrow standards of literary excellence, and formalist or gender-blind ways of reading. Even so, the scholar-theorist and the artist-writer may march to a different drumbeat, calling for critics to exercise the kind of "enlarged thinking" that Seyla Benhabib advocates, wherein "I" come out of my domain to converse with other "I"s until an agreement is reached (1990, 362; see also Benhabib 1992, 9). There must be room in postcolonial discourse for serious and penetrating inquiry that does not fall into the trap of purism. If ethnic identity is founded on sociocultural differences but also on interpretive, imaginative work (Sennett 1990, 198), the academic world must allow hybrid individual writers (and readers) to define what that hybridity means; to define it *for* them is to perpetuate anew the colonial mindset. If the true postcolonial condition is one of transition, instability, hybridity, and singularity, scholars will need to look to authors for help in defining it.

So what can a hospitable reception of a writer like Michael Ondaatje offer to critics (and other readers, including student readers) about personal identity, family relations, and cultural interaction? Or put another way, *what does traditional hospitality do with art that current theory does not?* From Ondaatje's point of view, art does not ape ideology. Mukherjee's attempt to fashion him into "an ideological conscript" (Huggan 1996, 118) violates the singularity and potentiality that Ondaatje's authoring conveys. "The trouble with ideology is that it hates the private. You must make it human," Ondaatje said to an interviewer (quoted in Bok 1992, 112). From the perspective of the "private" and "human," the narrator of *Running in the Family* inserts himself into a web of memories and conversations, an ongoing stream of conversation that "runs" in his family and that he is still running with. From the perspective of hospitality, the host-reader resists initially taking in the narrator of *Running in the Family* as a Canadian, male, Sri Lankan Burgher, postcolonialist, aesthete, emigrant, liberal—but instead takes in the narrator as this unique someone returning to Sri Lanka after many years, someone who likes listening to stories, someone who wants to understand better his dead father, someone who watches people, someone who suffers from the tropical heat.

We are aware, of course, that there is no pure reception, as the hermeneuticists long ago insisted, that people take in the singular and the strange only through presuppositions and forestructures with preset gendered, historical, political, and cultural frames. Probably no reader can posit the "someone" narrating *Running in the Family* as anything but "male." Nor are literary scholars forbidden from applying their theoretical political agendas or from sounding out and charting the gendered, racist, or colonialist undercurrents hidden beneath the literary surface, hidden perhaps from the authors themselves. This is how scholar-critics make their living. Ultimately hospitality itself, as will become clear in the next chapter, must tolerate the guest's politics along with any other individual oddities the guest brings.

But there are degrees of emphasis. Critic host-readers can start the hermeneutic circle closer to the point of singularity or, as we might put it, closer to the point of hospitality. That subsequently might make the theory and the critique a little more human and a little more open to the author. There is a world of difference between thinking "male" and thinking "a man," between thinking "Canadian" and thinking "someone living in Canada." And that might help spiral the criticism, as it is being applied, back to the point of singularity. Kenneth Burke wrote, "just as no two leaves are exactly alike," the terministic screens applied by critics should eventually "provide a route into inquiries about the unique nature of an *individual*" (1966, 77). A reading route that begins with singularity, proceeds through critical application, and ends with singularity strikes us as a reasonable method for scholar-critics, and a hospitable goal that they might teach the apprentice readers in their literature courses. That may ask English teachers to teach love, as Ondaatje suggests. But also to teach courage. In *Letters to a Young Poet*, Rilke speaks of the only thing life demands of us in the end: "to have courage for the most strange, the most singular and the most inexplicable that we may encounter. That mankind has in this sense been cowardly has done life endless harm" (1962, 67).

That might change the criticism. As Ajay Heble (1994) reminds us, the potential for art is to effect change, not through its political message but through an imaginative restoration, a power with which the author can span cultural divides so that the "I" of the "Cinnamon Peeler" will include the narrator and the native (199). What Heble calls the "agency of imaginative intervention" (197) we call hospitable reception, which (as Levinas would put it) allows the Same to change through the surplus of the Other or, as Blake put it, allows the Devourer to receive the excess of the Prolific's delights. Only if we as readers-critics are willing, in Samira Kawash's (1997) words, to enter the "disorder, excess, nonidentity, inassimilable difference" of the artist's singularity will we be able to experience "the unique, the unrepeatable, the unknowable, the irreducible otherness of the other" (213, 214). Nothing becomes real that is not first imagined.[13]

For his part, Ondaatje seeks readers who initially are willing to imagine and accept rather than categorize and politicize the personal and the historical. Maybe we should heed Mary Rose O'Reilley's call for "some sort of just-war theory to govern the excesses of criticism" (1993, 92). What becomes of theory if the theorist condemns rather than celebrates a text that asks for readers who, along with the author, linger over the telling? What becomes of reading if readers cannot "honor the passion of the writer" (Sennett 1990, 195)? If reading is a hospitable ritual in which author and reader form a microcommunity, readers can cross the boundaries of identity politics and identity criticism and remap a new "we." That may be what is gained most through the writer-reader, guest-host relationship.

BROWN ENOUGH

Once Rich drove his family into the foothills of the Idaho panhandle for a Sunday picnic. It was 1979. Where a farm track dwindled out beside a stream trickling under cottonwoods and shrub willows, they sat eating pickle loaf sandwiches and drinking hot cocoa. A dusty Impala came slowly up the track, stopped, and a man stepped out. They said howdy. He said howdy. Come have a bite, they said. Don't mind if I do, he said. He sat on a silvered cottonwood round eating a sandwich with a styrofoam cup on his knee, talking about the weather, the state of the woods, the wheat crop, and the spot. He grew up here, he said, right over that hill. Every once in a while he comes back to see the homestead, though nothing is left but the stone chimney and some rolls of barbed wire. Found a darning needle last time, he said, and everybody laughed. I'll be off, he said. Thanks for the hospitality. Rich believes it was the first time he ever heard someone speak the word. Then, amazingly, the man drove his car, bouncing and swaying, up and over the meadowy hill, following faint tire tracks in the grass that Rich had not noticed before.

Was the man host or guest, rancher or hired hand, Idahoan or Montanan, Republican or Democrat, white enough, brown enough? Rich doesn't remember. Maybe it didn't matter.

Notes

1. Historically called Ceylon, the island officially became Sri Lanka in 1972 when it ceased being a British dominion and became a Commonwealth nation. So Ondaatje was born in Ceylon and returned to Sri Lanka.

2. See Chelva Kanaganynkani (1992), for instance, who agrees that Ondaatje should deal with the burning issues of Sri Lanka's history and exhibit impassioned involvement with its politics.

3. We are summarizing Ganapathy-Dore 1997, 125; Coleman 1993, 73; Leahy 1992, 69; Matthews 2000, 358; Bok 1992, 122; and Snelling 1997, 22.

4. Suwanda H. J. Sugunasiri (1992) identifies the Burgher community in Ceylon as offspring of colonizing Portuguese (1505–1656), Dutch (1656–1815), and British (1815–1948). The British East India Company wrested control of the coastal regions from the Dutch in 1796, and in 1802 these areas were declared a crown colony with a governor appointed by the queen. According to Sugunasiri, all but the British intermarried with the native population (61), although no doubt some British males had their *bibis* (mistresses).

5. To clarify Ray's (1993) position about Ondaatje, we should point out that while Ray finds Suleri's family equally elite, she does not detect any "latent desire" in *Meatless Days* "to hypostatize the subaltern at the site of an irreproachable and irrecuperable authenticity" (49). Unlike Ondaatje, Ray argues, Suleri valorizes the role of her community of women by privileging the presence of grandmother, mother, sisters, and friends "in a textual celebration of hegemonic heterogeneity" (52). Rather than anonymous, the subalterns (in the form of household cooks) are known as individuals named (and sometimes misnamed) by their masters (50). It is difficult to understand why Ray does not react to such misnaming as conditions of shaming the native Other.

6. Technically, the process by which authors and readers pursue this critical course is sometimes called defamiliarization or disautomatization. Interest in defamiliarization has a long history, from Coleridge's (1983) hope, as expressed in the *Biographia Literaria*, that certain kinds of poetry will dissolve the "film of familiarity" and the "lethargy of custom" and charm the reader with the "interest of novelty" (2:7), to the Russian formalists' notion of *ostranenie*, or making strange, to current cognitive science's studies of natural language (for a synopsis, see Renan 1984; and Crawford 1984).

7.   See Wordsworth's (1800) much-analyzed lines in *The Prelude* about remembering his childhood: "So wide appears / The vacancy between me and those days / Which yet have such self-presence in my mind, / That, musing on them, often do I seem / Two consciousnesses, conscious of myself / And of some other Being" (II: 28–33).

8.   Other doublings: of chapter ("Kegalle i" and "Kegalle ii"; "Monsoon Notebooks" i, ii, and iii; "Tongue" and "Father's Tongue"), of image (Mervyn Ondaatje surrounded by dogs in his son's dream; Mervyn Ondaatje surrounded by dogs in Archer Jayawardene's story), of accidental death (Lalla's near drowning with David Grenier; her death in Nuwara Eliya), of parental imagery (their photograph detailed in narrative, then provided visually), of family clan (groups of siblings and stepsiblings), of childhood (a wonder, a nightmare), of authoring (aunts knit the story together; ants tear the story apart). See the illuminating analysis by Giltrow and Stouck (1992) of Ondaatje's syntax and grammar, which work to double possible meanings in the text (167–177). John Russell (1991) astutely describes how the six sections of the memoir work in pairs, with the odd-numbered sections having a stabilizing effect, the even-numbered then destabilizing the insights from the previous section (27–28).

9.   In an interview with William Dafoe, Ondaatje comments, "I just recently realized that each book is a rewriting of what you didn't quite get to in the previous book" (Dafoe 1997, 16). In that spirit, it seems appropriate to examine subsequent publications, even though Mukherjee couldn't have been aware of these texts at the time she published her analysis. Obviously, the issue of Ondaatje's position in relation to the history and politics of postcolonial Sri Lanka will be addressed in an entirely new light with Ondaatje's 2000 publication of *Anil's Ghost.*

10. Several critics comment on what they see as Ondaatje's decidedly masculinist discourse. See Daniel Coleman (1993) as an example. Even so, Coleman was personally affected by Ondaatje's narrative, finding his own displacement from his Ethiopian childhood reflected in *Running.* As a consequence, he elected to travel back to Ethiopia for the first time and face his own ghosts. In so doing, Coleman recognized yet another purpose of Ondaatje's quest: "There is yet a kind of health, a kind of self-creation, to be found in examining and acknowledging the traces of its [the past's] passing" (75).

11. "Ethnicity is not a natural but a socially constructed category," Graham Huggan (1996) correctly observes: "Whether ethnicity is adversarial or assimilative, whether it articulates diversity or divisiveness, whether it protects the status quo or promotes the need for social change: all of this depends on the influence, as well as the effectiveness, of those who represent it" (116).

12. Neluka Silva (2002) argues that Ondaatje's enactment of a hybrid narrator resists "facile attempts at classification" (71) and in doing so may reflect the kind of personal political agenda that he disowns. There can be hybridities of historiography and literary genre, too, of course. Daniel Coleman (1993) argues that *Running* offers a set of self-representations that "destabilizes a whole range of hegemonic technologies of the subject" (71).

13. With thanks to William Blake's (2008) *Proverbs of Hell* ("What is now proved was once only imagined") but also to Le Ly Hayslip's (1989) memoir, *When Heaven and Earth Changed Places.* In describing her decision to find a way to move herself and her son from war-torn Viet Nam to the United States, she makes clear that her first step was "speaking positively" so that she half believed in the possibility (311).

5

HOSPITABLE RECEPTION
Reading in Student Writing

*What in fact does language name, the so-called mother tongue, the
language you carry with you, the one that also carries us from birth to
death? Doesn't it figure the home that never leaves us?*
                                                    —Jacques Derrida

*Life is love of life, a relation with contents that are not my being but
more dear than my being: thinking, eating, sleeping, reading, working,
warming oneself in the sun.*
                                                    —Emmanuel Levinas

There is a riddle hidden in the title of this chapter. How does reading
get *in* writing? For that matter, how does writing get in reading? How do
writing and reading get inside each other? The "in" is like the "in" of the
old joke about the boy who discovers that he is locked out of his house,
so he runs around and around it until he is all in. We English teachers
run around and around the problematic of the reading-writing connection until we are all in—either exhausted by the topic or mysteriously
inside it. Either way, we can then forget about it. No doubt it is easy to
forget about literacy in our own tongue, so natural a thing we seem to
have been born in it, "the home that never leaves us," as Derrida says
(2000, 89).

So the riddle stands. One answer, for a long time dogmatic in
American education, is that reading and writing are not inside each
other but are alongside each other. They are like two months of the year.
First you get to February and then you get to March. First you learn to
read and then you learn to write. Reading and writing become curricular sequence. And curricular turf. More than one English teacher has
proposed a new English department course, to be called The Reading-
Writing Connection, only to be told by the university curriculum com-
mittee that the topic is unacceptable since reading is the province of

DOI: 10.7330/9780874219883.c005

the School of Education. Historically in the United States, the syntactic sequence of readin' 'n' writin' was honored by institutional sequence as well. Reading instruction started early and ended early in the schools, and in college writing instruction carried on without it. In practice the 'n' was a contraction of "and then."

During the late 1960s English studies started interpreting the 'n' as "in" when they joined the trend to treat "literacy" not as a regulated standard but as an acquired ability. How were literate people able to write without some competence in reading or able to read without some competence in writing? Somehow the two abilities must really be inside each other. The next two decades saw a proliferation of research and speculation concerning the interdependency or interactivity of the reading-writing connection.[1]

The sacred quest was to discover the exact mechanisms allowing the connection. Xs on theoretical maps depended upon discipline. At first, educationists and cognitive scientists favored cognitive monitoring, metacognitive awareness, linguistic competence, Piagetian and other developmental operations, context sharing, goal sharing, communal or social frames, and disciplinarity itself. English scholars tended to fix on mechanisms they were familiar with: invention, intention, implication, prediction, anticipation, conversation, shared discursive purpose, conventions of interpretation, imagination. For instance, they proposed that authors in the act of composing invent the reader who will be reading their words in the future, and readers in the act of reading those words invent the author who has composed them in the past. The "implied reader" plays a necessary role in the composing of text, and the "implied author" plays an equally necessary role in the reading of text.

(By way of aside, we note that currently *imagination* is not the first word that occurs to most people when they try to describe the reading-writing connection. Twenty or more years ago, when imagination had clout as a cognitive process, when it was seen as necessary to the work of everyone, including scientists and mathematicians, language experts with major clout of their own singled out imagination as a central means through which readers and writers connect, for example, Emig 1983; Smith 1984; Haas 1993. For a recent voice, see Sirc 2011).

Later, there was much disciplinary swapping of theories. Chronologically across fields, cognitive mechanisms connecting reading and writing are of older vintage: meaning making, language processing, dual coding, electromyographic activity, foreshadowing, interpreting, constructing of mental schema. Social mechanisms are more recent: principles of cooperative communication, collaboration, community or group membership, coproduction, genre sense, inner speech, custom protocols, and shared prior knowledge. All along, everyone agreed that however separated over time, space, and background, readers and writers somehow bridge, or else neither the act of authoring nor the act of comprehending will ever take place.

All scholars agreed that the reading-writing rapprochement of bodies and social minds is tacit—silent, imageless. Understandably, abstractions and metaphors proliferated. Besides *relationship, connection,* and *interaction,* the most common abstractions have been *complementarity, convergence, engagement, matrix, negotiation, nexus, reciprocality,* and *transaction.* Clearly the profession wants to imagine this meeting as taking place on a two-way street. As for metaphor, besides *two-way street,* we find *bond, pact, bridge, catalyst, crossroads, crossover, conversation, dialogue, joint action, game playing, ecology, landscape, marriage, travel, voice,* and *yin-yang.*

And *hospitality?* Although today the most common mechanism proposed by English studies is social framing, and that is where the most common metaphors are rooted, *hospitality* is absent. One reason, as we will see, is that hospitality—praxis and symbol and their implications—proposes changes to customary instruction in reading and writing, radical changes.

EFFECT OF THE READER-WRITER CONNECTION ON ENGLISH CLASSROOM PRACTICES

This is not to say that the other proposed mechanisms allowing readers and writers to translate one another don't have radical implications of their own for instruction. For instance, by 1970 *interpretation* was understood as no slavish extraction of the "correct" meaning of a text but as an open-ended play of experience, knowledge, and creativity in which the writer shapes gaps for readers to fill and refill with their unique readings.

But knowledge of these game-changing mechanisms did little to change the traditional pedagogy of the English classroom. A few classroom tactics emerged. There were in-class writing exercises that asked students to reflect on writer tactics in the material they were reading (Salvatori 1996). There was some focus on mining of strategies such as framing or synopsizing in one mode and using them in the other. There was some classroom staging of student response to peer writing and of student writing for peer response, and some efforts in placement to assess skill level in reading with skill level in writing. Largely, though, teachers who have not shelved the reader-writer connection have been willing to connect readers and writers in theory but reluctant to do so in practice.

In some ways the situation has reenacted the old saga of the split English department. Application in the classroom has largely been uni- lateral, with readers in the literature classroom focused on the author's "meaning" and writers in the composition classroom focused on the readers' "needs." The divide can be seen early and especially clearly in Edward M. White, who with a doctorate in literature and an expertise in composition might have been expected to circumnavigate it. In 1970 White prefaced an anthology of readings for composition students with some words of advice about "the reader-writer relationship." The advice, however, turns out to be directed only at the writer and concerned only with the writer's "responsibility to his reader." The writer has an "obliga- tion to say something which someone else will want to hear," to organize so readers can "follow what the writer is trying to say," to create the tone that will encourage readers to "hear him out." In gist, the worst student writing happens when students "imagine no audience" (1970, viii–xi). Nowhere does White suggest that, in a truly interactive "reader-writer relationship," the student writer might expect a reader with a reciprocal obligation to imagine the writer.

In all fairness, White was giving advice to writers, and student writers to boot. Yet fifteen years later, in *Teaching and Assessing Writing*, when White (1985) turns his attention to the responsibilities of teachers as readers of student writing, the message has not changed very much. During those years the phrase "reading-writing connection" had become so much a touchstone that it was being used to title textbooks. By then the major post-structuralist works in interpretation, reception, and deconstruction had been published and widely debated; their theory radically valorized the reader's side. Indeed, in a chapter of *Teaching and Assessing Writing*, "How Theories of Reading Affect Responses to Student Writing," White summarizes the reader-response scholarship with considerable lucidity. Yet his conclusion does not champion the freedom of readers. Quite the contrary. When teachers assess student writing, White says, they should become readers who have confined their response to the evalu- ative framework of their "interpretive community," and that framework decides what is of value and what is not.

So student writers obey teacher frames and teacher-readers obey teacher community frames. Totality reigns, Levinas might say. The inter- pretive scheme of the community can be changed, of course, and should be. "One way to think of what this book is trying to do," says White, "is to shake up an out-of-date interpretive community, to revise what we ask for—and thus what we get—from student writing" (1985, 97). It seems the obligation is still on composition students to fulfill the needs of their audience. Teachers should tell student writers what they want, to make clear, as White succinctly puts it, "what we ask for—and thus what we get." Unthinkable is the reverse, in tune with a truly reciprocal reader-writer relationship: that the student writer might ask something of the teacher-reader, and even get it.

HOSPITALITY, LITERACY, AND READER-WRITER TRUST

White is addressing the composition profession, where the phrase *audience awareness* operates as a shibboleth and the phrase *writer awareness* sounds like a translation from a foreign language.[2] As Sartre and others have long pointed out, communication imposes more constraints on conversers who are face-to-face than it does on writers and readers distant from one another. Yet it is precisely into a spoken conversation that for years now the profession has been at some pains to mold the discourse their students emulate and write. Historically most of the profession was willing to consign oral instruction to communications departments, yet in recent decades it has turned the student writer's audience into response-group classmates sitting across the table or across cyberspace, and it thinks of its own scholarship as a "Burkean parlor" or open-ended sociable chatter of peers. Regardless of the reasons given and the benefits proposed, and there are many of both, one upshot has been to deprive students and teachers of some of the freedom that elsewhere writers and readers enjoy. What the scholarly profession still calls the "reading-writing connection" and still imagines to be wide as the open seas with communication potentials, the teaching profession has narrowed for students to a shoal-ridden strait.

We believe the connection could use some two-way channel widening, and for that hospitality may well serve.

The traditional practice of hospitality relies on face-to-face conversation yet allows freedoms in it that socially are barred elsewhere. One freedom is the license to speak openly. In an English classroom, comparable would be the freedom for students to write what students want to write and for teachers to welcome what they read of it. If to the status quo this expansion of educational writing-reading protocol seems threatening, it is. As we have already said, the gentle art of hospitality can assume a razor-like edge.

What activity best connects both host and guest and reader and writer: comprehension, bond, pact, compact, duty, shared frames? In this chapter, we will examine *trust*, as currently do many other scholars.[3] Chapter 1 notes that in a hospitable encounter between strangers, the inherent risk can be countered only by trust. Similarly, readers trust the writer in a multitude of ways, some beneath their awareness. They trust that the book was written by the named author, or that the murder will be solved at the end. For their part, writers also trust: for instance, that the reader will carry on to the end and appreciate clever turns of phrase. In the English classroom, students trust the teacher to be fair in the grading of their papers; the teacher trusts students to be honest about their authoring.

But in all these situations nothing is guaranteed. On entering the house, the stranger-guest has no guarantees that the host will remain friendly. The host has no guarantees that the guest is not disguised, in reality a thief or an angel. And the same with readers and writers. On entering a book, the reader has no guarantees that it will turn out as expected. In a murder mystery, the trusty speaker may be the murderer, as in Agatha Christie's notorious experiment. There is no absolute certainty that a geology report will be based on accurately reported data or that a romance will not end up a parody. On entering a writing project, the author trusts that there will be readers who will enjoy and benefit from the words, but that trust also is only a wager. From the student writer's point of view, the teacher-reader may be bored with the topic, her rubric spotty, his grading uneven. And from the teacher-reader's point of view (the focus of this chapter), the student essayist may turn out a trickster, scofflaw, expert, or even someone other than the named author of the essay. In our fallen world, trust always comes in degrees.

Degrees of trust can be matched across different activities. Any activity, including trusting, will be a continuum, of course, but it will help to construct a rough three-part homology of little trust, partial trust, and complete trust.

In some material situations, trust can be *guaranteed*, perhaps with insurance or legal backing. Thus is a buyer protected against ending up with a lemon from a car dealer. More often the trust we have in people is *conditioned* by an infinite and unstable set of future events. We can't totally trust the weather forecaster. Sometimes we take precautions, driving the high road, sometimes not. Most of our life, however, proceeds in *open* trust, and we motor across highway bridges without doubting or even thinking about the engineer, the builders, or the bridge inspector. (Is this last degree of trust, mindless and automatic, something other than trust?)

The hospitable encounter runs the same gamut. In commercial hospitality, owners of motels, stores, and casinos hardly need trust the

Table 5.1

Trust	Materiality	Hospitality	Reading
little	guaranteed	regulated	critical
partial	conditioned	reciprocal	receptive
complete	open	unconditional	surrendered

customer since they are protected by insurance, law, "house rules," sometimes a gun under the counter—the trust is *regulated*. With *reciprocal* social hospitality and with many acts of private hospitality, trust is a risk but one partially safeguarded by mutual obligation and other quid pro quo expectations. The dinner host has some certainty that the guest will not steal the bric-a-brac, in part because the guest is a friend who has brought a house gift and who, by courtesy, will eventually return the invitation. In the traditional hospitable encounter between strangers, mutual trust is also conditioned by duties, customs, and cultural laws. The nomad host knows he may be the nomad guest in the future. However, in the extreme form of hospitality that Derrida calls *unconditional* or "hyperbolic" (1999, 99; 2000, 75), the host expects nothing of and nothing from the stranger arrivant. No one is turned away from the monastery door. The hospitable act is totally gratuitous, performed "before any determination, before any anticipation, before any identification" (Derrida 2000, 76). (Is this an act of total trust or one in which trust plays no part? Is it an act that exceeds or transgresses trust, as Derrida's word "hyperbolic" suggests?)

These questions bear on our modes of reader trust. In certain job-circumscribed situations, the *critical* reader approaches the text with no trust in the author. This is the mindset of a code breaker, text editor, or critical discourse analyst—or perhaps a holistic scorer following a rubric, or a writing teacher reading a student submission only to nab solecisms. Pure *critical* reading, however, is rare if not impossible in humans, although humans have manufactured it in computer programs such as Turnitin.com. By contrast, ordinary reading is reader friendly or *receptive* in that it begins with trust and departs from it only when the text arouses suspicions. The business card has a telephone number with an outdated area code, the environmental assessment document uses boilerplate language, the historical novel betrays anachronisms.

When it comes to student texts, suspicion arrives quickly. English teachers are jumpy as troop pickets at night. They are trained in Peter Elbow's (2008) doubting game, and any and every signal will awaken their distrust—a misspelling, a cliché, an adolescent sentiment, a digression from the set topic, a too-sophisticated word, a lack of expected improvement: the list is endless. The last thing an English teacher will do in reading student writing is wholly *surrender* to it. Yet that is exactly what we recommend to English teachers.

Surrendering to a text, absolutely trusting it, is not an impossible mode of reading. Indeed, it may be the original mode in our growth as readers. Can't we all remember getting "lost" in a book? In the act of reading, surrendering is analogous to welcoming in Levinas's (1969) act of hospitality. In *Totality and Infinity* the word translated as "welcome" is *accueillir.* It means not only to welcome or receive a guest warmly but also to accede to a request, to honor a treaty, or to accept a doctrine. So it contains a sense of giving in to, of trusting or surrendering to a higher authority. The availability of the Other to the welcoming of the self, Levinas says, is "a surrender in radiation" (45). Surrendering to a text is more than Coleridge's "suspension of disbelief." It is an act of reception that precedes belief and perhaps, as Derrida suggests, precedes any anticipation or determination. Levinas would say it precedes "thematization." The unconditional host does not believe or disbelieve the stranger before opening the door; the surrendered reader does not judge the text before responding to it. In both cases, the act of reception is unpremeditated.

This is why in exploring hospitality and reading we have chosen to explore trusting and distrusting rather than Elbow's believing and doubting. In his latest discussion of the believing game, Elbow (2008, 7) says that it "teaches us to welcome." So belief precedes welcome. Yet in Levinas, the hospitable host "welcomes" before anything else. In fact, Levinas, who suffered much under the totalitarian ideologies of World War II, had a deep distrust of the act of believing. In *Totality and Infinity,* he says that an atheist can become so separated from Being that eventually he will be "capable of adhering to it by belief" (1969, 58). What is missing from belief and present in welcome is pleasure and direct physical contact. Levinas says that reading is "love of life," a relation with something "more dear than my being," like eating or warming oneself in the sun (112). True, Elbow's believing game moves in the same direction as hospitality. He says that in the act of reading, "the believing game helps us enter more fully into texts that we find difficult or alien—and also helps us discover and understand a wider range of interpretations. We want to teach students critical thinking, but we also want them to enter into texts that feel alien to them—to dwell in them and experience them—not just criticize them" (9).

Still, there is an essential difference between believing and trusting. It is the difference between open reception of a text and open reception of an author. In traditional hospitality, all it takes is a knock. The host welcomes the guest before hearing the guest, trusting the person before trusting the person's language. So surrendering to the student may be asking English teachers to reverse two of their deepest mindsets: oblivion of the student as bona fide author and reverence of the student text as the only arena for learning. Isn't it asking teachers to give up their central strength, critique of deficient student texts? Yet, as we say, it is precisely surrendering to the student that we suggest English teachers try. And we argue that, sometimes, surrendering to a person will lead to better critique of text. Examples can help make this clear.[4]

AN EXAMPLE: THE NUMINOUS IN LITERACY

Imagine a reverse spelling test. From the student's spelling, you must infer the target word. This may not always be easy. During Cromwell's time, a British justice of the peace in Ireland famously once penned the word "yowzitch," which has none of the letters in his target word, "usage."[5] If this case appears outré, consider the student whose misspelling was "hare." The target word must have been "hair," or perhaps "hear," right? Wrong. The student was spelling "cherry." Given the illogic of English orthography, there is some sense to "yowzitch." But "hare" for "cherry"?

In fact, the student's spelling is more reasonable than the magistrate's. Imagine a first-grade student who has already been taught to recite the alphabet, that is, to recite the names of the letters of the alphabet. Then imagine a teacher giving a spelling test and saying, "Spell *cherry*" and then explaining, "A cherry, as in 'I ate a cherry.'" Now imagine the student mentally sounding the letters H-A-R-E and getting a decent hit on the sound of "a cherry."

This is a *receptive* reading of the student's spelling since it seeks the conditions that might have understandably or humanly led to it. It discovers not a stupid speller but one following a logical system. As such, it expands in a hospitable way a purely *critical* reading that would have recorded the student's spelling as merely incorrect. *Surrendering* to the student, however, goes further.

Imagine yourself a first-grade student again. You have memorized the names of the letters of the alphabet but have had nothing but trouble and frustration in applying them to reading and spelling. The word "cut," which you comprehend perfectly well, is pronounced with no letter names you have been taught, and the sound of its spelling, "see-youtee," bears little relationship with its pronunciation. Indeed, you have found rare as hen's teeth words spelled using the *names* of the letters of the alphabet. You know of only one: "easy" as E-Z. Suddenly, here is a word, "a cherry," that you can make work: H-A-R-E. The different worlds of literacy—alphabet, reading, speaking, spelling—cleanly converge. It is a magical moment. The mysteries of language, your own discovery, your own cleverness all synchronize.

We have said that genuine hospitality is a site for learning and that one essential motivation for it is gaining new experience and new knowledge. In reading a new piece of student writing, hospitable teachers always look for what the student can teach them. Any teacher would welcome this first-grader's experience. Or maybe welcome again. As literate adults, we all must have had such moments when the dark mechanics of language suddenly clicked. Rich still remembers one such moment. He was eleven years old and reading Booth Tarkington's *Penrod*. On page 181 he came to the phrase "left to the haphazard vignettist of Grub Street" and proceeded to look up *vignettist* in Webster's Third New International Dictionary. (This 3,350-page compendium of literacy his father had salvaged from a pile his college's library had set out for pulping.) Rich read Webster's definition of *vignettist* and then was astonished to see that the example provided was the very sentence from Tarkington he had just read. Astonished is the wrong word. It was more an electric numinosity. In an act of prestidigitation he had performed but couldn't explain, his reading and the infinitely elevated world of adult literacy were suddenly and mysteriously connected.

In *Totality and Infinity*, Levinas (1969) takes pains to show that the safe, in-dwelling personal world shut off from the Other is still not opposed to encounter with the Other. *Recueillir* (to gather in) is always prepared for *accueillir* (to welcome).[6] As teachers we may have forgotten our first personal face-to-face receptions of the alien world of literacy, but we can reharvest those moments if we surrender to our students. Then the host-guest switch takes place and they are our teachers.

TWO MORE EXAMPLES: THE RICH WORLD OF SENSE DEPRIVATION

A teaching assistant once brought his writing-program administrator (Rich) a student essay as evidence that the writer, a Yakima Indian, should be transferred to an ESL class. The teacher had highlighted a particularly telling sentence, about the student's uncle: "He know the two river like the back of his hand." Rich had enough sense to consult the secretary of the department of Native American studies. She laughed and said the student and his parents speak nothing but English and added that the student is hearing impaired, a fact he tries to keep secret. With loss of hearing, of course, sibilants such as the "s" at the end of "knows" and "rivers" are the first to go. Again, a *receptive* reading avoids a *critical* misreading by trusting circumstantial facts. But reception is not yet surrender.

Let's *surrender* a bit to the author. "He know the two river like the back of his hand." It's only one short sentence, but it comes intimately from a world new to most readers, the world of growing up half deaf on the Yakima Indian Reservation in Washington State. The "two river" are the Yakima and the Columbia—powerful and treacherous torrents of water that must be handled more by feel and sight than by sound. Reading the sentence, the teacher focuses just as the nephew once must have focused on the back of his uncle's hand as it grasps fishing pole or paddle or outboard-motor tiller. The back of the hand, of course, is especially sensitive to temperature or texture. A parent tests the child's forehead for fever with the back of the hand. A textile buyer runs the back of the hand over the sample for nap and softness. The "know" of the sentence, then, emerges from an outdoor world not dominated by hearing. The writer has transferred to the surrendered reader the experience of a unique and alien sensory life.[7]

Jan's student was also born and raised in the United States, but she wrote English as a true second language since she had been totally deaf from birth. Her mother tongue was American Sign Language. In a world literature course, for a classroom essay-exam question that asked how male characters regard and treat women, the student wrote,

> In *Iliad,* Gods treats women very well. Zues respects Thetis, a goddess because he owes her a big favor. Also Zues is very concerned about his wife, Hera. He told her to be quiet. Zues is being fair to decide for godess women. Hephaestus (Smith) treats the women very well because the women have a beauty.

Imagine trying to write academic English without ever having *heard* English. The incomplete experience in English speech helps explain most of the surface errors in the student's paragraph. For instance, it is from speech that hearing people, probably very young, have learned the distinction between "be quiet" and "keep quiet." Or consider the odd spelling of Zeus. The class signer whom the student relied on for lectures had established novel signs for literary characters so the signer would not have to spell them out every time. When the student had to spell "Zeus," lip reading would not have helped. Reliance on sign language also partly explains the missing "the" in the phrase "In *Iliad*," since articles are not in the ASL lexicon. We English teachers have heard "in *The Iliad*," with the article, hundreds of times and so without the article it sounds wrong, even though when referring to works of literature the articleless phrase is many times more common: in *Antigone*, in *Paradise Lost*, in Dante's *Inferno*, in Homer's *Iliad*, and so on.

But imagine further. The student, perhaps against her wishes, is opening up the world of deaf writing to hearing readers. It's a terrifying world where the writer knows many of her ideas will be overlooked because of problems in expression she cannot recognize as problems. The perfect logic and syntax of "being fair to decide for" and "have a beauty" will be dismissed, yet the writer has little way of knowing that "being reluctant to decide for" or "have a demeanor," for instance, are acceptable just because speakers have used them and therefore they sound better to writers and readers. In this student's silent world, the knowledge is there; she knows about Zeus's past debt to Thetis. But her act of expressing that knowledge, and her awareness that she was scribing only the most simplistic scraps of it, must have been a frustration, like trying to spell using only letter names for sounds, or trying to converse in a second language learned only from books. Risking academic English is hard enough for students who have both heard and read some of it, as we will see in a minute. But think of attempting it without that intuitive, experiential sound of people speaking it. Surrendering to Jan's student reveals a text written with a kind of desperate courage.

A LAST EXAMPLE: WRITER AWARENESS

Before "interpretive community" became a byword, Levinas (1969) exposed its limitations as an explanation of the reader-writer connection. He points out that "the community of thought ought to have made language as a relation between beings impossible." A shocking statement, but perfectly sensible. If two people belong to the same interpretive community, then they have no reason to communicate, except maybe to celebrate the Same: "A universal thought dispenses with communication." Theirs is the language of totality. But when two strangers meet, then language comes into its own. There universal thought, which Levinas calls "reason," will not serve: "How can a reason be an I or an Other, since its very being consists in renouncing singularity?" (72).

How, then, should a teacher read a student text that is trying to enter an interpretive community? Contradictions surface. For instance, does the teacher treat the student's language as novice attempts to express the Same, or as a stranger's voice at the door expressing singularity?

For a junior-level agricultural course in soils management, a student submitted a documented paper called "DDT: Friend or Foe?" The paper begins,

> From the very beginning of its existence DDT was thought to be the miracle chemical of the century, and it was. DDT saved millions of lives. DDT is an acronym for dichloro-diphenyl-tricholroethane. It controlled insects that transmitted diseases such as malaria, typhus, yellow fever, and bubonic plague which were responsible for killing hundreds of thousands of people worldwide. It is hard to understand or believe that a chemical that accomplished so much came under so much criticism. How can this chemical be so bad if it saved so many lives, and what was the reason for all the controversy, was it plausible?

By way of commentary, the teacher has deleted "of its existence," moved the third sentence up before the second sentence, and corrected the comma splice at the end. The teacher does not correct the misspelling of the chemical compound, point out the misuse of the word "acronym," or add the "every year" that would make the fourth sentence jibe with the second.

The teacher knows the hazard of continuing to rewrite the paragraph until it matches the accepted style of a learned discipline. Beside the effort needed by the teacher, imagine the dampening impact on the student. The student simply does not have, cannot be expected to have, the enormous knowledge that informs professional choice of words and syntax. An *Environmental Defense Fund Newsletter* piece, "Ospreys and the DDT Ban," begins,

> In the colorful history of DDT, a significant incident occurred in a Riverhead, New York courtroom in late 1966. In six days of testimony, a small group of scientists and conservationists convinced a judge that DDT was adversely affecting many non-target organisms and should therefore not be used for local mosquito control (Puleston 1976).

How to explain to an undergraduate student the professional rightness of "history of DDT" and the wrongness of "existence of DDT"? How to explain why it is professional to say that DDT was "used for local mosquito control" and not professional to say that DDT "controlled insects" (although "helped control" would be permissible)? How would this student be expected to understand the disciplinary rightness of "colorful," "significant," "convinced," "adversely," "non-target," and other vocabulary here? As more than one English scholar has noted, undergraduates discursively entering upper-division courses in their majors are strangers in a strange land. It would seem all a *receptive* reading can tell this student writer is to be aware of and to trust his audience.

But what happens if the at-home teacher *surrenders* to the stranger-student? The communicative happening switches from a novice trying to tell an expert what the expert already knows (which, according to Levinas, is not communication at all) to a stranger conveying something new, his singularity. Now it is the teacher-reader who is being aware of and trusting the student writer. To the sentence "It is hard to understand or believe that a chemical that accomplished so much came under so much criticism," the reader responds not with skepticism (part of what DDT accomplished was the killing of nearly every insect it came in contact with) but with a glimpse inside the mind of person new to the evidence and the history. In his introduction to the paper, the student mentions he had worked as an assistant to a golf-course superintendent who had used pesticides liberally, and that in reading for this paper he had his "awareness raised." If at the end of the paper he concludes that DDT can be used "under strict regulations where there is no other solution," he may have arrived at exactly Rachel Carson's position four decades years earlier in *Silent Spring*, but it is a position new to him. Part of what he reveals to the hospitable reader is a young adult of goodwill gradually loosening the hold of adolescent durable categories (Kegan 1994). Imagine again young-adult unself-conscious mixture of unqualified and qualified abstractions in the paragraph: DDT's existence, insect control, responsibility for killing versus "thought to be," "so much criticism," "so many lives," plausibility. Or imagine yourself at one time writing the unprofessional "bad" tempered with the qualifier "so." What reader will not find that appealing?

SURRENDER AND PEDAGOGY

The face of the Other, says Levinas, *is* an appeal, an expressiveness that demands response, and in that response lies responsibility. To surrender to a student is to trust the text as written by an author, that is, by someone other and singular. This chapter is not just an exercise in reading student writing. It is an exposure of the reading that lies axiomatic in all writing. It recommends that teachers read in student writing much as they would read in science fiction, Victorian biology, or contemporary philosophy. That means trusting the student author more than usual. Or perhaps it means going beyond trust and welcoming what the student has written with openness and pleasure and no more, much as you might welcome a perfect stranger to your table.

But will surrendering to the student promote student writing in English classes? For one, surrendering, even upon occasion, will help teachers see *disconstraints* fostered by their teaching. You won't find this word in the 3,350 pages of Webster's Third Unabridged.[8] We mean by disconstraints false limits set by teachers to what students can write. It is parallel but distinct from *misconstraints*, which Martin Nystrand (1989) defines as ways that immature writers simplify and otherwise misunderstand the needs of their audience. By contrast, *dis*constraints are ways writing teachers misunderstand the needs of their student authors. Usually there is a professional or ideological intent behind disconstraints. Students are not allowed as much time or space to write as they would like because the teachers would like less to read (or because machine-scoring algorithms can handle only simplistic organizations). Or, less obviously, students are discouraged from writing out of their unique background because teachers can't empathize with it or impose alien language standards on it. Just as *dis*information spread by civic leaders becomes *mis*formation among the public, so *dis*constraints spread by teachers become *mis*constraints among students, false notions that impoverish their writing. Students come to think that teachers want logically simple organizations, or dislike reading about nonmainstream backgrounds.

Disconstraints produce a kind of pedagogical rarefaction.[9] Whereas an infinity of verbal expressions are possible, the totalized rhetorical universe of teachers restricts the student to only a few. Surrendering helps teachers see what students haven't done and can't do on their own. It doesn't ask students to be better aware of audience but to read their own writing and become aware of what *they* have been unaware of. The responsibility in the response of the teacher-reader is to ask, truly ask, the student what the student doesn't know. Advance in writing will come when the teacher and the student locate what neither knows.

This may seem unduly complicated or even casuistical. But it is no more than instinct for good hosts and good guests. So where are you coming from? Philadelphia? I've never taken much to Philadelphia— what have I been missing? Therefore another pedagogical benefit from surrendering to the student is the fruitful responses it gives teachers. How can you know a river like the back of your hand? Do you think you could tell me more about your understanding of *The Iliad* by signing? Do you remember which facts about DDT helped change your mind about it?

Risky response, and neither the teacher nor the student knows where such questions will lead. They are vastly different from teacher response that emerges from teacher totality systems ("You should review the rules of subject-verb agreement"). But risky response is one of the deepest and most ordinary facts about the reading-writing connection. In actuality, the author writes and the reader reads with neither knowing what the other does or does not know. Both are a venture. Both exercise potential—never a sure thing—rather than test achievement.

Risky response also lies at the heart of traditional hospitality, which is also never a sure thing. "The deep meaning of hospitality," say Pratt and Homan, "involves our entrance into the mess of things; it means we run right into the chaos if that's what it takes" (2002, 113). And as Levinas well knew, risky response founds learning itself. Learning is not limited to transferring an idea from one person to another. Nor is it limited to maieutics, the Socratic method by which a teacher awakens in the learner ideas that the teacher already knows and that lie already in the learner. Levinas disliked the notion of maieutics (1969, 204, 219). True learning happens when Self welcomes the Other in an open-ended conversation within which ideas "overflow" from the Other—a "surplus" or "radiation in surrender" (45)—ideas that are new to the Self. "Teaching is not reducible to maieutics; it comes from the exterior and brings me more than I contain" (51). And further still: "Ideas instruct me coming from the master who *presents* them to me, who puts them in question" (69). In sum, neither the teacher nor the student knows exactly when learning will occur. They can only imagine. That means asking questions of one another and trusting.

And that means bucking the current educational current. Colleges and universities call themselves "institutions of learning," yet—it is a most pitiful irony—more and more they are shaping themselves as places instilling bogus learning, learning that ends up forgotten. More and more their preferred modes and methods of instruction, impelled and lured by material, economic, and political values, gravitate toward a future classroom that looks not much different than Duke's MOOC. The hospitable English classroom resists this gravitational pull. More and more the resistance will be treated as transgressive by the institution, the hospitable teacher treated as subversive. Compositionist Matthew Heard (2010), who stands nearly alone in his field to consider the worsening plight of hospitality as applied to English teaching, argues that the solution is to make a "distinction between generosity as a limited practice and hospitality as a more radical, open-ended ideal" (322) and then to remove the latter from the classroom. The danger that Heard sees is that attempts to incorporate radical, or what Derrida calls "unconditional" hospitality, into the current university will only debase hospitality as a fructifying ideal. "My worry here is that by moving hospitality into the economy of value that structures our practical work as writing scholars we stand to contain and manage all aspects of hospitality that do not fit into the current matrix of composition practice" (325). Heard concludes by hoping that "hospitality will not become useful to our field, at least not in a way that allows the business of writing to proceed as usual" (330).

We understand Heard's concerns but do not accept his assumption that the only hospitality is radical hospitality. As we have tried to make clear, hospitality, even traditional hospitality, comes in all stripes and can be adapted to many situations. Is hospitality such a feared name that we have to rename some of its activities as "generosity"? Let teachers and scholars choose. Some of hospitality's gestures in the classroom will not cause institutional waves, though they will help stem the institutional flow toward bogus learning. Let's leave it the right of teachers to risk, if they want, the wrath of the institutional gods by adapting or adopting the more radical of hospitable pedagogies, such as the "multiple common space" that we will explore in chapter 11 or the kind of "surrendered reading" we promote in this chapter.

Regardless, for students surrendered reading answers the riddle of the reading-writing connection in a very human way. It shows that reading and writing are inside each other to the degree that reader and writer are outside each other, when both the reader and the writer are truly master to the other, Other to the Other. On this relationship depend all the mechanisms that have been proposed to explain the reading-writing connection: metacognition, goal sharing, conventions of interpretation, and the like. And preliminary to the mechanisms and the connection itself stands welcoming. As so often, Levinas puts it succinctly and memorably. Welcoming is "to receive from the Other beyond the capacity of the I, which means exactly: to have the idea of infinity. But this also means to be taught" (1969, 51).

Notes

Parts of this chapter are based on talks Richard Haswell gave at the Writing Program Administration Regional Conference, Longbeach, CA (October 1997) and at Carleton College, Northfield, MN (October 2001).

1. Scholarship on the reading-writing connection is voluminous. In composition studies, the first review of research was in 1986 (Bishop and Davis 1986). In education, two superb overviews are Nelson and Calfee's 1998 edited collection; and Langer and Flihan 2000.

2. A search of 105,267 titles in writing studies, from 1939 to 2014, found 36 using the phrase "audience awareness" and none using "writer awareness" or "author

awareness." Yet the reader's awareness of the author is a much-studied issue in scholarship of the reading-writing connection (see Shanahan 1998).

3.   Recently and foremost, Miller 2007. But the notion that trust is integral to any kind of communication between humans goes far back, for instance, to the trust that underlies H. Paul Grice's (1975) cooperative principles of truthfulness, relevance, adequacy, etc., or further back to Michael Polanyi's (1958) fiduciary or postcritical position that both reader and writer know more than they know and therefore must trust that tacit knowledge, or —why not?—to St. Augustine's mantra, *Crede ut intelligas* (Believe in order to understand).

4.   Our idea of surrendering to the student writer should not be confused with Sven Birkerts's (1995) notion of "deep reading" in *The Gutenberg Elegies*. For Birkerts, deep reading involves using the words to explore the self, a "slow and meditative possession of a book" (146). This would be profoundly disturbing to Levinas, who always imagined that it was the Other who mastered the self. The thought of teachers "possessing" student writing doesn't much appeal to us. More to our liking is Patricia F. Carini's (1994) method of reading the writing of schoolchildren. She and her coteachers held "codes, conventions, and judgments at bay" in order to see "how the writing might be recognized and valued back to an author in ways that would nurture growth" (53).

5.   Later the magistrate blamed his misspelling on quills made from Irish geese (Taylor 1831, 80). Even later, *Ripley's Believe It or Not* attributed the misspelling to a Nebraska schoolboy.

6.   In French, *recueillir* has as rich a meaning as *accueillir* and well rewards Levinas in his opposing of the two terms. *Recueillir* can mean to catch (as rainwater), to select (from a range of choices), to harvest or set by, to inherit, to succeed (to a throne), to gather (news), to write out (thoughts), to count (votes). Phenomenologically, *recueillir* follows *accueillir*. It is what one does, often immediately, with the new experience that welcoming allows in. (In *Totality and Infinity* the translation of Levinas's *recueillir* as "to recollect" often will mislead the reader.)

7.   Perhaps a *surrendered* reading not only excuses the absence of the esses but even relishes them. Where two rivers converge, as the Yakima and the Columbia do on the Yakima Reservation, don't we have "two river," two rivers that are one?

8.   Although "disconstraint" is now a psychological trait on the Minnesota Multiphasic Personality Inventory. Persons high on the DISC scale are impulsives, risk takers, dislikers of routine, and skeptics of moral limits. So teachers who are discontrainers (in the MMPI sense) may tend to avoid imposing disconstraints (in our sense) upon students.

9.   Foucault's (1972) "Discourse on Language" first offered the notion of rarefaction.

6

TEN STUDENTS REFLECT ON THEIR INDEPENDENT AUTHORING

Both in life and in literature it is necessary to have some means of bridging the gulf between the hostess and her unknown guest on one hand, the writer and his unknown reader on the other.

—Virginia Woolf

In the fall of 2010 we arranged to have ten student authors interviewed. These were students distinguished by the fact that they habitually wrote on their own in ways unconnected with academic courses. Six undergraduate English majors, one undergraduate history major, and three English master's candidates—what was there to know about their independent composing lives? What motivates them, what fulfills them, what frustrates them as writers? We also wanted to know if at any point in the composing process they envision a recipient of their authoring—someone who would engage with them in the shared undertaking of reading their texts. Finally, we asked them if hospitality fit their experience of independent authoring in any way.

We first interviewed Rebecca, an honors student majoring in English, and then as part of an internship she interviewed the other nine. Both we and Rebecca followed a protocol of questions:

Why is writing important to you? What motivates you to write?

What do you get out of writing? What does writing provide for *you*?

How does it feel when you are in the act of writing? What is your inner sense when you are writing? How do you feel when writing in different genres, academic or self-sponsored?

Do you envision your reader? At what point? Do you seek a relationship with your reader? What kind?

A fifth and last question, explicitly on hospitality, we will discuss later.[1] The taped and transcribed responses to these four questions surprised us on a number of levels. First, the extracurricular writing of the

DOI: 10.7330/9780874219883.c006

ten student authors occupied much of their time and entailed a variety of genres: blog, poetry, prose fiction, journal, editorial. This authoring was not done for classes, not even for creative-writing courses. It was off the institutional map, out of bounds, subterranean, private, even secret. Yet it was fundamental to their lives. Second, the majority of our participants far prefer their personal writing to their academic writing. They find assignments not of their own making uncreative and unmotivating, are disinterested and uninvested in institutionally required writing. They judge reader feedback, conveyed through peer response or teacher evaluation, as irrelevant, coercive, and sometimes punitive. Most believed that the writing they produce in the classroom is a far cry from their best writing, the kind *they* value. Third, they were surprised to be asked about their extracurricular authoring selves. No one had asked before.

And fourth, they expressed a tenuous and conflicted sense of themselves as writers who are actively seeking a relationship with readers. As we will see, thinking about this relationship in terms of hospitality was a new and elusive prospect for them.

JASON: "TO WRITE EXACTLY WHAT I WANT TO WRITE"

A senior English major, Jason thinks he would go crazy without a creative outlet such as writing. There is a lot going on in the world that he hates, hates passionately, and through writing he can escape to a world entirely different. Not surprisingly, science fiction is his preferred genre, since it "is supposed to make commentaries about the way we're heading or the way we could head." The act of writing itself is both therapeutic and frustrating. "I have so many ideas and they change all the time." He calls himself a self-propelled writer, someone figuring out in the act of writing what he wants to say and how he wants to say it.

For Jason, academic writing is another sort of animal. In fact, it is among those things he hates because it isn't his choice—neither the subject matter nor the urge to write about it. As a member of an independent writing group, Jason gathers with fellow student authors, blocking out a three-hour period of time during which they talk, write, talk some more, write again. We find it interesting that the act of writing is therefore semicommunal for Jason, yet he never thinks about his reader. Never. He doesn't want to end up catering to readers as he has to cater to teachers, since "that would just change what you exactly wanted to do . . . I want to write exactly what I want to write and not think about what anyone's going to think about it."

JUSTIN: "YOU KIND OF SEE WHO YOU ARE"

For Justin, a junior English major, writing is compelling and rewarding. As a young child, he could entertain himself by writing from his "lucid imagination." He began writing "seriously" six years ago and practices every week "just for fun." As he gets better and better, he feels more motivated to continue. Fiction writing has helped Justin know himself better, especially when it is unconstrained writing with no set direction. "You kind of see who you are really—you can see what your morals are and just what kind of personality you have." He learns about himself in the act of writing. He learns what he sees and what he values. The more he writes, the more developed his personality becomes.

How does it feel to write? "Good and terrible." Sometimes the outcome is "really bad," sometimes "really good." Growth is not inevitable for Justin. It is "what you write that makes you better." Some days he deletes everything he has composed, perhaps because he was distracted by his surroundings or because he couldn't make his mind jump to another world or another time period (he calls the mind "a conflicting agent"). He prefers writing fiction that has no limits, not even definite beginning and end points—elements that make the process of writing "forced." The quintessential forced writing is academic assignments with their requirements about length, subject, style, content, all defined by teacher expectations and standards. To meet these requirements, Justin often has to "dumb down" what he wants to say and how he wants to say it.

But this doesn't mean that Justin discredits the reader. The reader, after all, can often see things the writer himself cannot. "You have to see a reader so you can, it almost grounds you, puts you down to earth." Without readers, Justin's writing would be more abstract; with them in mind, his texts are more realistic.

MATT: "I ENVISION WHAT I WOULD WANT TO READ"

A junior English major, Matt recognizes the utility of writing, since it is a basic form of communication. But as a guitarist, a composer, and a poet, he writes to express himself and paint a picture of what is going on in his life. His motivation to write is generated by specific feelings (happiness, anger) or experiences (a beautiful sunset). It can be frustrating, he admits, when the text deviates from its original purpose. Still, his personal writing is more fulfilling than academic writing, which often forces him to stay "inside the box." Course assignments just need to be finished. Personal writing needs to be perfected. There's skill in the second.

A prospective reader doesn't figure into Matt's authoring. "I envision what I would want to read." That might mean, of course, that someone else might want to read his work. Someone like him: politically liberal, more creative than book smart, carefree, relaxed. But a writer shouldn't cater to a reader. "I'm just writing for myself and if someone else likes it, that's awesome."

MARC: "WHAT I WAS THINKING AT THAT VERY MOMENT"

Marc writes in order to think through his own thoughts, which can flow too quickly or "clump up" all at once. A junior English major, he values academic as well as personal writing. The former allows him to remember what he thinks about; the latter enables him to show people what he is thinking. In both cases, Marc writes to discover: "I don't know exactly what I'm going to write until I—get there." Writing is a practiced art. "You have to learn it," he believes, and gradually you can master the craft. It is difficult work, since the inner critic often silences him. There are outer critics as well. "The act of pleasing everybody or pleasing yourself is stressful to balance, to find the good balance in between." He feels most free as a writer contributing to his online blog, which he runs under a pseudonym.

First and foremost, Marc believes, the writer must envision himself or herself as the reader. "If I write something today, ten years from now I want to understand what I was thinking at that very moment." Details need to be explained, even if only his eyes see the final product. But the outside reader adds a new dimension, perhaps helping him to become inspired, perhaps critiquing, but certainly wanting to discuss ideas. "I want them to feel the same emotion, to spark something in them that they can relate to."

SARAH: "WHATEVER MEMORY IT WAS WITH ME"

A senior history major, Sarah is the author of a 1,500-page unfinished autobiography. Sarah knows exactly why she writes: to figure out what is going on in her life, to map out issues, experiences, and reflections. She doesn't expect that in the act of writing she will clearly understand the how or why of an event, but six months down the line, she will have the tools to reflect back and then, perhaps, find some meaning in it. For her, writing is different than just talking something through with a friend or family member because she doesn't have to deal with another opinion. Putting pen to paper relieves stress, provides an emotional outlet, and allows anger or frustration to dissipate.

The freedom Sarah finds in personal writing isn't available to her in academic writing. You can't just write in that context, she explains. You have to consult the rubric, figure out what the professor wants, check quotes and documentation, monitor your language. "You have to take a lot more into consideration," and thus everything changes for her. Certainly in academic writing the readers loom large, and the challenge is "to make sure they're going to interpret exactly what I wrote out, the way I want it to be interpreted."

Initially in her personal writing, it seemed that her audience was solely herself. But recently, after the death of her grandmother, she started to wonder "if someone did ever read this. And I started kind of describing things more—so that way you can sort of feel like you were there, and not just for me to, you know, write out." She wanted to include little things, the sorts of things that disappear over time, and in twenty years she wants to know and feel what was clear to her now. "When I started working on that project I started thinking about, okay, if I wasn't the only one reading it, like maybe my little sister, my little brother, you know, at the time they were six and eight, so they don't know that much . . . I want them to be able to feel like they were there experiencing whatever memory it was with me." Writing is a way for Sarah to give back her grandmother to family members.

TRACY: "IF I HAD TO STOP WRITING, I WOULD JUST STOP LIVING"

A senior English major, Tracy was our only creative-writing minor. Whether for therapy, entertainment, or personal expression, Tracy considers writing vital to her life. "It's like, writing is like eating and drinking and breathing for me." "I think if I had to stop writing I would just stop living, because it's a major part of my life." If she is writing a spiritual poem, then she begins to feel the tranquility or connection she is describing. If she is writing a poem about current experiences and frustrations, then she is able to work through situations stressful for her. If she wants to imagine a better social or political world, she writes science fiction. Writing affords her as many avenues as she needs. Academic writing is as rewarding as personal writing. But she tends to "pull my hair out" when working on a paper for class. "I get really excited and my roommate laughs at me because I talk to myself and I talk to my paper. And I'll yell at my paper because it's not behaving. When I really like a phrase that I come up with, I'll sit there and go, 'Ooh, I really like that.'"

For Tracy, reading and writing are bound together. "I read a lot and so for me writing is like . . . turning the reading upside down and . . . creating the characters and the scenes myself. Besides just reading a book, now I'm kind of living a book." It isn't surprising, then, that she often thinks of her reader. She needs the reader to be open-minded, since her recent fiction has addressed controversial ideas such as homosexuality and the death penalty. She has her own point of view, which not every reader will accept. But she also hopes that people who can relate to her views and experiences would have that "Oh, I'm not alone" kind of feeling. Her conservative readers might become more open-minded: "I would hope that some of my writing would at least kind of educate and—even if they don't completely change their mind, at least suddenly go, well, maybe that's more valid than I thought, and so maybe they could go and explore."

REBECCA: "THIS IS MY OWN WRITING, THIS IS ME, WRITING"

Rebecca was a junior double majoring in English and history, and our partner interviewer. She was homeschooled by her mother, an English teacher by profession, who instilled in her daughter a love for writing, partly by sharing her own fiction she wrote years ago in college, partly by doing the English exercises she assigned and then sharing her efforts with her students. So Rebecca was not only required to write but encouraged to write even outside of her school day, keeping a journal, writing "creatively." She grew up with someone who loved to write and who modeled a writer's life.

During her own college career, Rebecca has carried over that motivation in both academic and independent writing. For required assignments, she enjoys learning and feels affirmed by her high grades. She sometimes feels constrained, however, by deadlines or by topics too narrowly defined. Outside of classes, Rebecca exercises the freedom to write what she wants to write. In writing fiction she also finds a way to "escape," escape in the Tolkien sense of fitting real-life experiences into fictional settings. But she resists drawing a clear line between her academic and creative work. "Writing is writing" even when the purpose of one text differs from another. She can stand back from a research paper and say, "Wow, I learned a lot" and from a short story and say, "Wow, that's a good sentence."

In the act of writing, Rebecca feels

> at peace, I feel—like myself, feel like this is where I'm supposed to be, this is what I'm supposed to be doing. I'd feel like this inner joy. And I always

believed, "Oh, okay, this comes from God." Like this must be some kind of gift that he's given me and so this is, this is going to sound corny, but Tolkien writes about this too, the idea of your subcreating so you're close to the creator. And so I always, I still experience that, I experience it more when I'm creatively writing than when I'm writing for school. But even when I'm writing for school there is that, like I am writing and I am making something and I am—not proving, but I am showing that I, you know, have this ability to correlate what I want to say.

As writer and subcreator, at times Rebecca is haunted by the thought that there's nothing new under the sun. The more she reads, the more challenging it is to be original. Oddly, there appears more room for her ideas and insights in academic writing: so-and-so has argued this about a text, but here is what I think.

Then there is the awkwardness of putting so much of herself in her writing. "I've always had trouble disconnecting myself from my work." Creative texts feel overwhelmingly personal and everyone is a critic. But even in writing about Oscar Wilde, for instance, "This is my own writing, this is me, writing." So if someone doesn't like Rebecca's paper, it is almost like that person doesn't like Rebecca. "Of course it's not like that at all, but for some reason there's always been that connection with me to my writing."

So does she write for anyone apart from herself? Does she envision a reader? In her personal writing, she consciously writes only for herself, but in the back of her mind she is thinking, I hope so-and-so likes this, or I hope so-and-so can find herself in this. The so-and-so is first and foremost her mother, her role model. Then there is the teacher—an endless series of teachers with different expectations—who need pleasing and who are for the most part affirming and encouraging.

DARCY: THE "GOLDEN MOMENT"

An English teaching assistant, Darcy applied to the master's program after working for several years in the "real world," where it is "more and more important . . . that people be able to articulate themselves well, be able to communicate well, not only succinctly but also professionally." Writing provides a means of expression and an avenue of personal fulfillment. When she writes creatively, she feels something "release" in her, like a pressure valve. "When you write, you can kind of let off some steam and you can come back to being normal again. It's a normalizing thing for me." She has volumes of journals full of poems but no desire to make this material public. They are "just for me."

Whereas creative writing stimulates "your soul," academic writing stimulates the mind.

> I may not articulate myself well in person, but having the moment to sit there and think about what you want to say before you say it—find the perfect word, to have the time to put it together in a very meaningful way—it makes you feel that much more emboldened and empowered.

Since academic writing allows her to join the scholarly "conversation," Darcy understands that there is a larger audience for her work (larger as in beyond the teacher). As she becomes more and more immersed in critical theory, she resists the kind of professional writing that proves inaccessible, so unreadable it is "painful." Darcy wants her academic papers to be "readable."

How does writing make her feel? Like a good workout. It may hurt while you are doing it, but as your ideas solidify, clarify what you are thinking and what you believe, "you feel so much better." She also reflects on the value of writing in her own classroom. Watching her students open up, "or for lack of a better word, blossom, in the ability to express themselves, it's very fulfilling for me to watch that happen with them." Finally escaping from high-stakes testing in the schools, her students "take flight" because they can finally write about things they are interested in. Her role is to guide them in the revision process so that their essays are not "totally conversational" but more appropriate for an academic audience. But their voice is still there. For her, combining academic purposes with voice is the "golden moment."

MICHELLE: "YOU CAN GET CREATIVE WITH ACADEMIC PAPERS"

Now an MA student, Michelle became an English major because she loves to write. Academic writing may feel "forced" at times, but it has helped her become more confident as a person and a member of society. She selects topics of interest to her, like cultural identity and cross-cultural interactions, to better understand her world. Once she has completed an assignment, she enjoys the resulting sense of accomplishment. Certainly creative and academic writing are different, but "they kind of bleed into each other because you can get creative with academic papers," at least as long as she is free to select the focus and the approach of the paper.

The reader isn't present to Michelle until her revision stage. Throughout the drafting process, her primary concern is "what do I have to say and how am I going to say it?" But in revising, she considers the particular community she is addressing. Fellow graduate students or faculty will want to "hear certain lingo," so she will have to incorporate scholarly language she doesn't necessarily incorporate in her early drafts. What worked in undergraduate courses—personal anecdotes, numerous quotes, epigraphs—are often eliminated as she envisions a more sophisticated audience. In this way, writing in graduate courses is much more demanding.

VICKIE: "YOU SCRATCH AN ITCH, I WRITE"

An English MA student, Vickie has been writing "ever since I could put letters together into words." "It's like what I am—I write, that's what I do. You know, it's sort of like brushing your teeth, or you know, things that you do habitually, things you do instinctively, you know. You scratch an itch, I write."

With the support of her parents, who fostered her love of reading, and the encouragement of teachers, who have advanced her creative and academic skills, Vickie is aware of what writing provides for her: catharsis, stimulation, escape, a way to cope, a way to deal with sadness. "It helps you set a frame around something that's hard to deal with, and then it's something you can deal with, at least to the extent you're able to write about it." Mother-daughter issues are important to her, and writing allows her to deal with them "in safety." When she writes fiction, she creates a world she can control. Characters and situations come "from somewhere inside you." With academic writing, she enjoys picking an issue and figuring out its causes and effects and how it connects with other things she has studied. She feels like a detective, going into history and context and pulling out meaning.

The act of writing is for Vickie like being "in the zone": "I'm really sort of on a roll—everything else sort of stops mattering." Sometimes she is surprised by what comes out.

> You think, "Wow, where did that come from?" Or you write something and you think, "Geez, that's depraved. I'm not like that." But it's in there somewhere! So you can learn a lot about yourself by just letting yourself write, letting yourself get into that groove.

She isn't a disciplined writer. She doesn't have a routine of composing a certain number of pages at a certain time each day. She doesn't keep a daily journal. The mood has to be there, which makes academic writing a challenge since someone else is setting the deadlines, the purpose, the subject matter.

Even when she is in the zone, Vickie thinks of her reader. In terms of scholarly writing, she seeks mastery of the concepts and vocabulary, but she also wants to be readable. "Throwing a bunch of big fat words in there just because I know them isn't necessarily good writing." Her sense of academic audience has changed since enrolling in the graduate program because the expectations have changed. So, too, has her own need for feedback: "You want the good grade, you want it to be something that other people want to read." Similarly, when she writes fiction for young adults, she consciously pitches her style to that audience. In exchange, she needs to know if her readers enjoy her stories.

STUDENT SELF-SPONSORED AUTHORING
AND ENGLISH TEACHING

Self-sponsored authoring among undergraduates puts some unsettling questions to standard undergraduate English instruction. Why do most of these ten students characterize academic writing assignments as constraining and noncreative? By contrast, they see self-sponsored authoring as open, creative, compulsive, therapeutic, voiced, pleasureful, and ripe with discovery and growth. Generally their description of nonacademic composing fits that of published writers (see Haswell and Haswell 2010, 13–22). By comparison, they judge writing promoted by English instruction as secondary, artificial, and insular. Although the authorly motives of these ten students are sometimes encouraged in the abstract by English pedagogy, they are discouraged in practice by classroom teachers, who usually teach writing as an academic or professional nicety and necessity, not as a compelling personal need.

And why do most of these ten students regard audience in such a tenuous, mixed, or dismissive way? Most of them say they completely disregard the reader as they compose. Matt writes "for myself," Darcy "just for me." Jason does not "think about what anyone's going to think." Marc writes for an older self who is reading years in the future. So does Sarah, or else she writes for someone close and intimate such as a little sister or brother, just as Rebecca addresses a guiding soul such as her mother. For most of these students, attention to a broader audience comes only with academic tasks. Even so, academic readership is pictured as circumscribed, partial, and sympathetic, people who will agree with their views (Tracy) and find their writing readable (Darcy and Vickie) or insightful (Rebecca). Most often the academic audience is simply the teacher who gave the assignment and looks to see how well it was followed. Only the graduate student Michelle seems to reflect the conventional English-profession view that the writer must know and satisfy the demands and knowledge of a discipline-wide audience, and she applies that view only at the revising stage. Nowhere in the interviews can be found the dogma of the field, expressed so well by Edward White (see chapter 5), that good writers learn what readers want and then give it to them.

Most disturbing about these interviews is the position that there is no bridge between independent and academic writing. Sarah expresses the consensus.

> When I'm doing it just for me, my emotions are in it. You can tell in any-thing that I've written—whether you start from the very, very beginning or just jump into it—you can tell, you can kind of feel what I was feeling at the moment, because the emotions are in there, of course. When I write academically, though, you can't just write just to write. You have to take into consideration what your—okay, am I following the rubric, am I mak-ing sure I'm doing what so-and-so wants, do I have this, do I have that, did I quote right, did I—you know.

Sarah doesn't wonder if academic writing might have space for emo-tions, or whether personal writing doesn't follow rubrics of its own. Only Darcy brings up the possibility that sometimes an individual "voice" can be heard in academic writing and that this might be something a teacher would welcome.

HOSPITALITY AND STUDENT SELF-SPONSORED AUTHORING

So it is both surprising and unsurprising that these English students had not connected authoring with hospitality. Not once did the notion arise spontaneously in their responses to the first four interview questions. And the ten reacted with initial befuddlement to our fifth and last ques-tion, which forced the issue.

> What if I were to suggest that the writer-reader relation is one of hospitality—that the writer hosts the reader-guest. Would that fit your experience?

After thinking about the question, they responded with curiosity and then with major reservations.

One reason for this cautious reception is that all these students con-ceived of hospitality in contemporary terms, as social or business eti-quette. Jason and Matt initially don't like the idea of the writer obliged to "entertain" a guest. Tracy sees it as the author "drawing in" read-ers, getting their attention and arousing their desires. Marc says that it depends "on what I had in store for my guest—I'd want them to feel comfortable when I wanted them to feel comfortable." Matt, who understands the "one-on-one" nature of hospitality, also sees it as the author "writing directly to the individual" in order to make her or him feel "comfortable." Rebecca (as Virginia Woolf before her) stresses the hospitable act of sharing food, the writer allowing the reader to make "some sort of communion with me." Sarah thinks of Nicholas Sparks as a writer who "welcomes" the reader, not in his later novels where "he's just writing to make his paycheck" but in his earlier ones where he was helping "the reader to find a place to escape to." This is hospitality as drawing attention, making comfortable, offering entertainment, sharing food, providing escape—nowhere do we get the traditional sense of engaging in dialogue, a two-way street where the host may learn as much as the guest. Despite their avowed independence from academic authoring, these ten students seemed to have absorbed the teacher dictum that writers are responsible to their readers but not the other way around.

Thus emerges the strange position—strange to our eyes—that only academic authoring has anything to do with hospitality. At least school writing demands a respect for an audience, although, as Michelle notes, to make it hospitable will require a "sufficient command of scholarly content to help readers feel welcome." Sarah sees the academic writer as communal, expressing what "everybody does think about but they're unwilling to admit." Some of the students disagree. Darcy and Marc see academic language as "inhospitable," since hospitality is about a person talking to others, a voice speaking to others, a person on the other side of the text who welcomes readers seeking such contact. According to Tracy, hospitable writing puts "a little nice mat out to draw the reader in," whereas school writing always finds the writer "trying to get a point across" and that "might make people take a step back." It seems even in their disagreement about the virtues of academic writing tasks, these students can't get away from the contemporary notion of hospitality as mere entertainment. Vickie says of graduate papers, "You have to find a way to engage the reader. Everything has to be tasty enough so that they'll stay to the end." By contrast, self-sponsored authoring hardly fits any definition of hospitality since it is self-focused, written for only the author.

There is a more fundamental reason, however, why these students shy away from hospitality as underlying their personal authoring. It is a reason that attaches to the most powerful dynamic projected by these interviews, the clash between self-sponsored writing as "creative" and academic writing as "noncreative." Deep down, what these authors want for their authoring is protection. They want it safe from unfriendly hands. They want to remain free as writers, to begin and carry on as they please and as the writing leads. Freedom of authoring is an ineluctable motive. So Marc publishes his online blog under a pseudonym. Darcy will not show her volumes of poem manuscripts to the public because they are "just for me." No one but Sarah has seen her 1,500-page journal.

Some of the fear is of readers who will misread. Sarah says that if there is a future audience for her journal, the challenge will be "to make sure they're going to interpret exactly what I wrote out, the way I want it to be interpreted." Jason says, "I want to write exactly what I want to write and not think about what anyone's going to think about it." And some of the fear is attached to writing that is highly personal and compulsive, writing often therapeutic at base, "stress reliever" (Sarah) or "straight catharsis" (Vickie). So Vickie chooses to write privately about sensitive issues, such as her relationship with her mother, because she can do so "in safety." Perhaps justified is Rebecca's worry that if a reader doesn't like her writing, the reader won't like Rebecca, justified because of the revealing nature of the writing. Interestingly enough, these students never express a concern that readers would find their writing bad.

The essential anxiety in protecting their freedom, however, concerns not only continuing a piece the way they want. It is to keep *authoring* in their lives, as that activity will grow and develop naturally. This is why one of their synonyms for "creative" is "organic." Vickie pens fiction because "it's a world you can create and you can control; you have control over what the characters do." It's also an arena where you have to let characters "mushroom—you have to be open to that, you have to be able to free yourself to let things happen." Marc keeps his blog pseudonymous because "it allows me to be more free—it's not so confining." Sarah, who writes to "map out" and "make sense" of her life, sums up for the other nine student authors: "It's, you can do it, nobody's going to mess with it, it's going to go just like that."

Herein lies a main source of the dislike of academic writing. Teachers take possession of a student text in many ways, sometimes starting before the student composes it. They limit the topic, the length, the attitude, the language. Darcy's words for it are "stringent" and "tunnel-visioned," Michelle's is "constrictive," Sarah's is "monitoring." Sometimes, as with paper corrections, teachers themselves will take over the text. Worse, through their directives, teachers will force the student to alter it. The academic ethos has a presence that invades the students in the very act of authoring, forcing them to ask, as we have heard Sarah put it, "Am I following the rubric, am I making sure I'm doing what so-and-so wants, do I have this, do I have that, did I quote right, did I—you know." Teachers impose the mindset, so Michelle observes, of "just let me get it done and let me do it well enough to pass the bar, whatever the bar is."

So these students do not mean "creative" as "fictional or "undisciplined." Their contrast between "creative" and "academic" is not between unschooled and schooled, or personal and communal, or private and public. By "creative" they mean "not-yet-possessed." Authoring is "creative" (or "organic" or "unstructured") when readers have not yet got a hold of it and made it their own, not yet found ways to make the author do this or do that to it, above all, not yet found ways to shape it, to make the author shape it, into something that has not grown out of the author's free druthers. Jason puts it in the raw when he says that as a writer you should never have to be hospitable to readers, "to cater to them, because I feel like that would just change what you exactly wanted to do."

In *Totality and Infinity*, a book these student authors have never read and probably never heard of, Levinas (1969) puts their position as concisely and profoundly as possible, as philosophers are wont to do. "Possession masters, suspends, postpones the unforeseeable future of the element—its independence, its being" (158). Levinas means that once something is owned, taken as belonging to someone, then its inherent potential is suddenly and severely curtailed. In the case of a wildflower, his meaning is obvious. Compare the unknowable future of a flower in the field—for instance, where its seeds might blow or be carried by animals—to its meager future as a countertop ornament: cut, trimmed, dried, stuck in a vase. In the case of other "elements," Levinas's point may come less readily. Teachers might think that taking over and critiquing a student-authored essay augments its potential future. On the other hand, students could well think of academic assignments (the more circumscribed, the better, according to some teacher lore) as "mastering, suspending, and postponing" the potential outcome of any essay they might start.

Jason's "catering" to the reader reflects a kind of hospitality that Levinas would not call hospitality, of course. The hospitality that Levinas (1969) describes as welcoming the Other entails a different kind of possession: "To possess by enjoying is also to be possessed and to be delivered to the fathomless depth, the disquieting future of the element" (158). What if teachers welcomed, "possessed," the student essay in that way? We have explored that question in the previous chapter. If Jason had envisioned just that sort of hospitable academic reception, he might have been happier with teacher-assigned writing tasks. That would require, it goes without saying, teachers who would look at student authoring not under the constrictive systems of totality but under the opening light of infinity.

A RECOMMENDATION FOR STUDENTS AND TEACHERS

It is too easy to say that these ten student authors simply want teachers who ask what can the student do, not how well the student has done. Teachers can reasonably counter that learning requires students to attempt things they have never done before and likely, without teachers, would never think to do. We imagine that hospitality, true hospitality, opens up a way through this impasse. If students could only risk thinking of their teacher-readers as guests-hosts open to the Other . . . if teachers could only risk thinking of their student-authors as guests-hosts pregnant with the New. . . . Sad it would be if these talented students left college with the image of English teachers only as possessive taskmasters, or if English teachers left this chapter with the image of these ten students as a cantankerous, stubborn, self-willed, anomalous splinter group.

These interviews surprised us—and not because the students had never before thought of their writing in terms of hosting a guest. They reveal a side of our students that teachers rarely see. These ten students show us that writing isn't onerous or foreign to what they value. They compose voluntarily, even naturally. They have a drive to author, a hunger to articulate their insights and express their views. *They* know when their writing is successful, when their skills develop, when they learn as thinkers and change as writers. Are they anomalous? Are they a tiny fraction of English students? If so, we would be left with a terrible irony. For the ten have something that English teachers have always wished they could find or cultivate in their students: a love of writing.

Note

1.   In no way was the selection of these ten students random. Four had been Jan's students and she knew they wrote independently. The other six heard about the project by word of mouth and asked to be included. The ten participants gave us permission to use real first names and to quote from their interviews.

7

THE NOVEL AS MORAL DIALOGUE

Authors depend a great deal for well-being and peace of mind on the unconscious courtesy of strangers.

—Paul Scott

If an ethic of hospitality allows a more conscious reciprocity in the writer-reader bond, it is because in a true hospitable relationship, the host-guest function changes hands. When an author is intellectually hospitable, he or she is open to mutual and constant exchanges of views, perspectives, and experiences, and so functions both as host (of the text) and guest (of readers' reception, perspectives, and insights upon engaging with the text). As we have noted in chapter 3, intellectual hospitality is not simple courtesy or civility but a refusal to remain isolated from other learners or to assimilate others into our sphere of influence or way of thinking. Recall Henri Nouwen's observation: "Someone who is filled with ideas, concepts, opinions and convictions cannot be a good host. There is no inner space to listen, no openness to discover the gift of the other" (1966, 103).

In previous chapters, we advocate for a different way of reading, a mode that is open to respecting and fostering the potentiality of each singular writer, whether master or student. In this chapter we will examine an author who was politically impassioned and yet a model of the hospitable author: Paul Mark Scott (1920–1978), author of the Raj Quartet. For Scott, the act of authoring is a dialogic one wherein writer and reader "face" each other to consider together an image, a character, an event; both engage with the narrative, weigh perspectives, and work toward difficult and hard-earned conclusions. Such a shared undertaking should be enacted in all fiction since the novel (as Scott believed) is a moral dialogue, "the dual creation by writer and reader" (Scott 1986, 80).[1] This *moral* necessity—to write in such a way as to not only invite but request a dialogue—directly shapes the style and content of his fiction.[2]

Thus when Scott explored the evils of imperialism and the failure of liberal humanism, he did not bully his readers into "a state of vegetable

DOI: 10.7330/9780874219883.c007

acceptance" (Scott 1986, 85) through Manichean judgments or political pronouncements. Rather, he hoped to evoke in readers "a creative and critical response" (114) through a moral dialogue that respects "the *humanity* of those who hold a contrary opinion" (149). In sum, Scott recognizes that undergirding his historical and political views was a moral value that dictated not only his posture toward his subject matter—the British in India—but also his relationship with readers.

This chapter continues our earlier discussions of Michael Ondaatje in terms of what inhospitable encounters between reader and writer involve (chapter 4), for example, a refusal to surrender to the experience and understanding that is being shared. Disconstraints of critics echo those of teachers (chapter 5) when the reader balks at being taught because the writer refuses to conform to expectations or theoretical/political frameworks. The reception of Scott's fiction (as described later in this chapter) validates the fear that our ten student authors expressed (chapter 6), the fear of what might happen when "unfriendly hands" try to possess their texts and reframe their subject in simplified and comfortable terms, and the courage it takes, none the less, for the writer to place his or her text in those very hands.

That is to say, what might be regarded as theoretical arguments in previous chapters now become concrete, with a published author consciously and deliberately attempting to engage his readers hospitably. To demonstrate what this level of engagement (what we have called intellectual hospitality in chapter 3) demands of a writer, we want to examine Scott's motivation and intentions in writing about his subject, his revision process whereby he crafted a style for his narratives that allows for such a dialogue with his readers, and the challenges faced by readers who engage in that dialogue. We shall also see, through evidence from his personal letters, how Scott's hospitality was not merely theoretical, precisely because his readers ceased to be abstract or remote. He knew full well that as important as his "appointment with the muse" might be (Scott 1986, 46), his appointment with his reader-guest mattered just as much. In Levinas's terms, Scott not only awaited an encounter with the Other; he sought it.

SCOTT'S SUBJECT: INDIA AND BRITISH IDENTITY

Paul Scott's openness to dialogue is particularly remarkable given his deep-rooted convictions about the realities of imperialism.[3] His first encounter with India during World War II was as a British officer posted to an Indian supply company, then as a voracious reader of history, and finally as a reflective writer who returned three times to immerse himself in an independent India. No doubt Scott's adjustment from suburban London to India in 1943 was dramatic. By his own admission, he was "extremely ignorant" of the place yet impressed to the point of becoming obsessed with it. He later admitted: "A place grows into your bloodstream . . . I don't think though that I realised how much I'd become attached to India until I went out to Malaya . . . in August 1945 . . . I found myself not homesick for England—which anyway I couldn't expect to see for nearly another year, but for India" (Tulsa, 9:5).[4] Scott could remedy his ignorance, but not the obsession.

Explaining why he devoted his artistic life work to the subject of the British in India, Scott explained: "India, to me, was the scene of a remarkable and far-reaching event. I see it as the place where the British came to the end of themselves as they were" (1986, 48). Most of his thirteen published novels, especially his acclaimed Raj Quartet,[5] provide a stage whereon the cultural, political, and social dynamics of imperialism are enacted. He was conscious at the outset of his writing career that his novels went against the grain of public interest and sentiment. England, believed Scott, was enveloped in "a kind of miasma . . . an infectious or noxious emanation" (93) that emerged in postwar years after Indian independence in 1947. British citizens wanted to forget that imperial experience, to put it and the moral quandary it represented behind them. It is an established pattern, as Scott understood: "When things are going badly, British insularity quickly promotes a passionate belief in the efficacy of everybody looking after his own" (94).

But the subject that the British didn't want to face was for Scott precisely the subject they needed to face if they were to achieve the self-knowledge necessary to break out of insular blindness. He believed that his countrymen had entered into "territorial fragmentation and dangerous racial memory" (1986, 31). According to Scott, the 1950s and 1960s were a period of disenchantment, an age of an "uncharitable" and restive culture "because our old reforming impulses bore fruits that turned out sour." In such a backlash, Scott recognized a fissure that was developing between England's self-image and its reality: "Free and broad of speech, mean of heart. Radical in protestation, reactionary in performance. Active in thought, lazy in habit. Satirical in style, pedagogic in manner. Tolerant on the surface, violently disposed underneath." The English were "alive enough to know that they are not living, but pondering, seeking new definitions of almost every aspect of human exchange" (37).

Written within this context, Scott's novels prove to be antidotes to this miasma. He wanted his fiction to be "a serious statement about reality

. . . a prose work of ideas and images which must be serviceable to man-kind" (Scott 1986, 138). This is one of the signatures of his novels (and a stumbling block to his critics): to offer something "serviceable" to his readers, he focused on people and not politics, choice rather than power. This was an artistic necessity, not a theoretical misstep, for Scott, who believed "a man who is concerned with the realities of power as it may affect men who hold positions in public life, is likely to find himself involved in a less complex relationship of images than is the man who is concerned with the realities of, say, time as part of the human experi-ence" (83).

In a word, politics and power are not fecund enough issues to evoke artistic images that passionately engage writer and reader in a moral dialogue. This isn't to say that Scott dismissed the factor of power out of hand. Power is a cruel fact of history, an appetite of society, a false prom-ise for individuals and nations. And so he set out to explore "just where the corridors of [the Englishman's] power have led him." That journey and the ultimate results for both colonizer and colonized only show that while society believes that power is the means to happiness, what history shows us, through the moral imagination, is that such belief will end only in perplexity (Scott 1986, 28). The dismantlement of empire, marking the end of the road of imperial power, shattered illusions about power, control, and the white man's burden—and so marked the end of the British "as they were" (48).

What exactly does it mean to go against the grain of one's historical moment, to write from the periphery of one's culture? For Scott it meant to write "a literature of *dissent*" (Scott 1986, 140)—we would call it a liter-ature of resistance, of transgression, of disruption. Rather than despair-ing of the future, Scott looked to the present and asked: "What action can be taken that will be, now, for human good?" (144). He was careful not to align himself with prevailing attitudes that promised solutions (or escape) simply because they dominated current perspectives. "When a generality of people know what they are, and what they have, and what they want, they are like an army concentrated in depth on a relatively narrow front. The writer has always been a man with his mind and heart set on penetration of such defences . . . What he opposes must be clear to him. If it is clear to him it will also be clear to the defenders" (28).

As we will see, Scott was accurate in his assessment of his generation. But that did not stop him from writing *his* kind of novel and thereby representing "the collective discontent with established processes that lead to change and social development" (Scott 1986, 28). His charac-ters, especially members of the Raj, feel like spiritual orphans with a superficial or nonexistent sense of value and identity, who lose not only their vision of right and wrong but their sense of purpose as well. Their mission was merely an occupation, "an occupation less and less easy to explain and to follow except by continuing to perform it" (Scott 1998b, 130). Scott dissects a society in a state of moral collapse and watches his characters struggle to find meaning and purpose beyond mere human understanding and design.

Scott's decision to illustrate such a worldview by using the metaphor of the Raj is neither accidental nor arbitrary. The values and beliefs that had informed the work and lives of the British cloaked their action with a noble purpose during their exile, guaranteed the illusion of dignity, and determined both a collective and personal identity that disappeared with the stroke of a pen in 1947. Like Scott's cohorts in the 1950s, members of the Raj in the 1940s were thrown back on themselves, alone in their own hollowness and in their own fragile, personal dignity, inevitably experiencing a sense of "profound spiritual dislocation" (Rubin 1986, 122). The end of the British in India was, for Scott, not a political resolution but a moral challenge that unmasked the personal and global catastrophe of imperialism.

SCOTT'S PASSIONATE POLITICS

Given that in Scott's fiction there are no explicit assertions but rather a series of feasible and varied perspectives, how can a reader construct what Scott's own views are? It is a difficult but not impossible task if one is willing to proceed in dialogue on multiple fronts, working from his published novels, supplementing passages from letters and speeches, and examining textual revisions.

As we will describe in the next section, Scott has been accused of being a pseudo-colonialist, someone nostalgic about the glory days of the Raj. Other scholars, like Peter Childs, have categorized Scott as a liberal humanist[6] because he uses this term unabashedly and deliberately. Both misreadings mark an inability (or refusal) to engage with Scott on his own grounds. Let us address the issue of whether Scott espoused the values and processes of liberal humanism. True, he rejected prejudice and narrow self-interest, affirmed human dignity, and was animated by the conviction that all individual human beings— whether rich or poor, black or white, queer or straight, man or woman, writer or reader, writer or critic—are value-entities. The tag of "liberal humanist" seems justified here, up to a point. Scott himself equated "liberal humanism" with "Fieldingism," based on E. M. Forster's character, involving "a belief in the essentially dynamic nature of man and the structure of society, as one that required of authority within a framework of law guarantees of individual freedom, social justice and equal opportunities" (Scott 1986, 125).

Liberal humanism is amply but critically depicted in the Quartet. Several of Scott's major characters in the Quartet are portrayed as liberal humanists (like Robin White and Nigel Rowan), but perhaps the best example is Edwina Crane, who defines liberal principles in this way: "that fear was evil because it promoted prejudice, that courage was good because it was a sign of selflessness, that ignorance was bad because fear sprang from it, that knowledge was good because the more you knew of the world's complexity the more clearly you saw the insignificance of the part you played" (Scott 1998c, 22–23). Edwina learned these values at her mother's knee, along with "the importance of courageously accepting duties and obligations, not for self-aggrandizement, but in self-denial, in order to promote a wider happiness and well-being, in order to rid the world of . . . poverty, disease, misery, ignorance and injustice" (23).

While Scott would choose these "Fieldingesque" values over the counter-attitude of Forster's Turtons (self-righteousness, snobbery, hypocrisy, and racial bigotry), his own position transcends this simplistic binary. Indeed, Scott relegated his own clear faith in the liberal creed to the days of his youth. "There was the liberal idea alone" (Scott 1986, 125), he admitted, with no other worldview to compete against it. In terms of India, Scott believed that "we ought not to have it but [should] jolly well give it back" (120). But after his return from India in 1946, the shortcomings of his own liberal views, based on little more than ignorance, became increasingly apparent, as his early novels like *Johnnie Sahib*, *The Mark of the Warrior*, and *The Alien Sky* demonstrate (121). As Scott came to realize, there is a great deal of ego beneath the altruism of liberal humanism, an "unfamiliar glow, the effect of something subtler than flattery: the tug of an old sense of responsibility, of the good done to one's soul by doing or trying to do well for other people" (Tulsa II, 9:16). Liberal principles cannot exist apart from what Scott sees as the liberal dilemma: the necessity of using illiberal force to realize the liberal ideal (Scott 1986, 125). Faced with the allegation that his returning to the scene of England's failure was due to nostalgia or guilt, Scott argued: "I return to it because to me the death and internment of liberal humanism is still a living issue" (49).

A sense of Scott's critique of liberal humanism is articulated by William Conway, the main character in *The Birds of Paradise* (Scott

1985a). For Conway, the liberal view of life (that privileges freedom, reason, equality, justice, and benevolence) assumes that human beings who embrace those values are willing to operate habitually and routinely out of their higher natures. But in reality, equality and justice tend to work as abstractions or general principles, and not as a leaven in personal relationships or political realities. This shortcoming creates a fault line between belief and action, a fault line dealt with on a philosophic level in *The Jewel in the Crown*, where the threat of liberalism is shown to be more fundamentally the tension between "policy and its pursuit" (Scott 1998c, 189): the respect and bigotry that exists *within* individuals who espouse the liberal creed. With this tension comes no guarantee that the Raj collectively, nor any individual Englishman, would act out of higher values.

The members of the Raj were not "guardians of a sacred trust" but instead "whoring imperialists" who, when it came to proving true to their promise, found the issue of partition "too hot to handle" (Scott 1985a, 117, 160). Scott is explicit about the link between liberalism and imperialism: "By liberal humanism I mean, broadly, the human consciousness of human dignity that began with the Renaissance & came to an end in the form we knew it in the second world war & its aftermath. *The imperialism was as much an expression of our reforming zeal*" (Austin, 16:1; emphasis added).[7] Instead of being opposites, imperialism and liberalism are next of kin, both emerging from the zeal of superiority.

It is no surprise, then, that Scott (like his character Edwina Crane) could not imagine "something sane and grave, full of dignity, full of thoughtfulness and kindness and peace and wisdom" coming from British rule (Scott 1998c, 63). Scott ruminates:

> We are sure quite properly bent on reforms. But we carry them through, I think, by the power of momentum, dispassionately, more for the sake of a kind of peace of mind. But the mind is detached. It is practical rather than inspired. An act to legalize abortion has nothing to do with a concept of the dignity of unmarried mothers, nor one to legalize unnatural practices between consenting adults with the dignity of queers. Well, how could it, the dignity would be a human dignity & our notions of that have faded. We're no longer certain what a human being is. (Austin, 16:1)

If there is a solution to imperial arrogance, it is not liberal humanism, neither in how it is conceived as an ethic nor in how it is enacted in political and social life. But the issue of liberal humanism allows us to document, without any doubts, Scott's attitudes toward the British dealings with its empire.

SCOTT'S STYLE: HOSPITALITY IN ACTION

We have spent considerable time defining Scott's personal views (as explained in texts apart from his novels) in order to make clear that he was not neutral, sentimental, nostalgic, or cowardly in facing the truth about imperialism. Frustrated with his countrymen's refusal to face the true nature of failure in India—with their desire to bar immigrants from former colonies, with their stubborn indifference and isolationist policies regarding the former empire—Scott resists such cultural currents and offers England a more mature, responsible way to think about India and its own past. While he understood that an honest, self-critical lens was essential to such an approach, he refused to bully his readers into agreeing with him. England had bullied enough.

Thus Scott-as-author offered his novels as foundations of hospitable relationships based on the cornerstone of moral dialogue. As offspring of the "moral imagination," his novels generate a landscape of central images that capture human reality (Scott 1986, 80, 138). The reader, in attempting to decode those images, enters into a "moral dialogue" with the writer (114). Together, writer and reader fructify the images of the novel until the work becomes their "dual creation" (80), with the writer seeking the reader's "own creative response" to those images (85), the reader seeking the writer's own implicit yet passionate attitude about them (57).

To accomplish this, Scott constructed the "building" of his novels with a door "to let people in to use it" (Scott 1986, 86). How did he build such a door for the Other? By incessant revision, a practice that can be traced by comparing holograph and typescript drafts to the published scenes in the Quartet. A simple example involving the character of Mabel Layton, matriarch of the influential Layton family in the hill station of Pankot, will help illustrate both the importance and purpose of his revisions.

As detailed in the published version of *The Towers of Silence* (Scott 1998e), Mabel opens Rose Cottage to a paying guest, retired missionary Barbie Batchelor, during the early years of the war. The officers' wives at the station interpret Mabel's action as a move to co-opt her daughter-in-law's claim to Rose Cottage. The women further agree that such distrust was another indication of a "weakness" about Mabel, which first became apparent years before when she refused to donate to the General Dyer fund after the Amritsar Massacre in 1919. Mabel's self-containment and withdrawal from Raj society invite such criticism, but through the women's responses, Scott carefully displays Mabel Layton's deep love for India, her insistence on treating Indians with respect and deference, and her ability to see through the charade of the English military tradition. As a foil to Mabel's silent resistance, Scott gathers a cluster of dedicated but unreflective, emotionally withered women who place the British military code above all else. Just as Scott allows Mabel's actions (rather than narrative commentary) to alert readers to her political values, he lets the fullness of Mabel's life eclipse the hollowness of the others' lives.

Most of Mabel's rebellion is performed privately, with one exception. On the occasion of Susan Layton's wedding reception, held at the Pankot Mess, Mabel wanders into the "inner sanctuary," where the tables and cabinets of silver enshrine the regiment's history. She reflects: "I thought there might be some changes, but there aren't. It's all exactly as it was when I first saw it more than forty years ago. I can't even be angry. But someone ought to be" (Scott 1998e, 193). Although she shares her thoughts with friend Barbie Batchelor, she does not confront her countrymen but instead maintains her silence.

In the original holograph, however, Mabel is less reticent and more explicitly critical than she is in the published version. In the following excerpt, Mabel comments about Nicki Paynton's mouth: "You can't say its Nicki Paynton's most expressive feature, because they are all . . . conditioned to express the same thing . . . But you look at her mouth you'll notice that it's the only *mobile* feature. Not *very* mobile . . . even when our lips move we often look like ventriloquists dummies" (Austin, 33:2).

This comment, an explicit and caustic condemnation of the vacuous lip service performed by the women, forces the reader to view Nicki and her cohorts only in negative terms early on in the book. It is an example of how Scott would *tell* us what to think of the Raj rather than *showing* us the Raj in action and leaving us to form our own conclusions. It also violates what will become important thematically—Mabel's "gift of silence"—which is as much a symptom of the Raj tradition as the women's "ventriloquistic" show of solidarity.

In the published version, Mildred Layton (Mabel's daughter-in-law) is described rather than Nicki Payton, with the narrator doing the honors: "If the men's eyes were flat the women's—to judge from Mildred's— were slightly hooded as though belonging to the weaker sex they were entitled to this extra protection; and the mouths, again to judge by hers, being less allowably firmed than a man's, were permitted a faint curve down at the corners which could be mistaken for displeasure, in the way that Mildred's languid posture when seated could be mistaken for *ennui*" (Scott 1998e, 33).

The mouth again is important: "the faint upcurve of the downward curving mouth" (Scott 1998e, 44), but the sense of Mildred as both sneering and displeased shows readers the effect and invites us to guess at the cause: the hollowness of her life, her distance, her withdrawal, her hard detachment that allows her to survive. After incessant revisions, Scott shows readers that Mildred is not the object of ridicule, as the original version makes Nicki Paynton to be, but an intelligent, steely woman whose despair is only gradually revealed to the reader through her adultery and her drinking. Ultimately, the reader may well condemn Mildred and the other Raj women, but that criticism might also involve a grudging pity, even respect, at their stubborn resolve to carry on.

HOSPITALITY EXTENDED

It is no surprise that Scott's novels were themselves marginalized by the artistic, cultural, and political mood of the 1950s through 1970s. Before the sequel to the Quartet, *Staying On,* was awarded the Booker Prize in 1977, Scott had received few accolades during his lifetime. In fact, responses in England to the first two novels of the Quartet were mixed, to say the least. Robin Moore (1990) notes that while the public admired *Jewel* and *Scorpion* (each made the best-seller list in England), there were ample negative reviews from critics to cancel out the positive ones. Gerald Hanley, a close friend of Scott's, wrote to him: "I'll be interested in seeing how 'The Jewel' goes in America . . . I would guess they'll read it straight, not bent, as the British are bound to do even now with their blockage about India" (Tulsa, 6:14). During his visit to India in 1969, Scott was asked by an Englishwoman why he felt compelled "to revive all that old bitterness" (Scott 1986, 113). Was he an unrepentant imperialist? A left-wing satirist? Or was he (as some scholars have argued) a student of history yearning for bygone days, nostalgic for, or perhaps guilty about, an age dedicated to duty, encased in moral certainty, draped in glory? Reviewers very often could not decide.[8]

We should remember that fifty years ago, writers were not blessed (or cursed) with instant and widespread digital reactions to new publications. Scott's initial tier of readers, after wife Penny, involved his agents and editors in England and the United States.[9] Once proofs were finalized, advanced copies were distributed to book reviewers in major newspapers and magazines so that with the release of the novel, critical reviews appeared in print as well. Hence the second tier of readers, and the first public response to his fiction, came from paid book reviewers. Those reviews had a powerful effect upon Scott.

Consider one reviewer's comment that Scott's fifth novel, *The Chinese Love Pavilion* (Scott [1960] 1985b), was "parasitical" and "thirty years out of date" (Scott 2011a, 197).[10] Another critic wrote that he enjoyed *Pavilion* but couldn't take it seriously since the style of the novel was "full of ingenious tricks and chances and equivocations that make for *an effect of depth*" (200). Such responses made Scott feel "wretched"—"like some confidence trickster," "dirty and useless, close to that special contemplative suicide writers mock themselves in" (179, 197, 200).[11]

There were positive reviews of every novel, of course. In the case of Richard Lister's review of *The Jewel in the Crown* in the *Evening Standard* (Scott 1998c), Scott felt affirmed by "honest-to-goodness, straightforward praise, with real enthusiasm" (Scott 2011b, 27). Although he obviously valued such positive judgments, Scott more eagerly welcomed responses that appraised his new novel "on the level at which I aim it" (Scott 2011a, 116). For instance, he thanked John Davenport of the *Observer* in 1960 for "judging me by high standards, getting the books *right*, making me feel that I'm not wasting my time" (196). To R. G. G. Price of *Punch*, he wrote that although other reviews had been more positive, "Your reviews of both these novels [*The Mark of the Warrior* and *The Chinese Love Pavilion*] have left me feeling like a human being still, and not like a performing monkey" (202).

Whether the reviews were affirming or discouraging, Scott resolved "to write the sort of novels I write" despite the "wretched slowness" of the drafting and revision process and "the failure of the novels to make much of an impact on the market" (Scott 2011b, 173, 177). It irked him that a writer could put 1,000 words of "crap" together and earn "six million pounds a year" and "hire hacks to put his grammar right" (Scott 2011a, 211). As for himself, he didn't believe that what is said in a novel is more important than the way it is said. "I myself can never properly distinguish between what and how; and I've never yet read a novel that says anything I think important that doesn't emphasise the importance, convey the importance, in the manner of the saying." (Scott 2011b, 75).[12]

In his "dialogue" with critics, thoughtful exchanges could be rare as long as Scott insisted on writing what he needed to write in the style he needed to say it. "It is difficult for a writer to have confidence in his own ability" he wrote to fellow author Arthur Thompson (Francis Clifford), "to put a degree of trust in his instinct—get back then to the pleasure of creating" (Scott 2011b, 13–14).

Some of that confidence was restored when Scott would hear from total strangers, readers who weeks or even months after publication would write to him. Those strangers broke down what often seemed like a "one-way communication" for a novelist, "pretty much like sending a message in a bottle from a desert island in the hope of it arriving somewhere" (Scott 2011b, 153). He especially welcomed letters that revealed how much readers related to his characters and even recognized those characters in their own lives. One reader told him that she in fact knew a real-life Ronald Merrick, which reminded Scott that he wasn't simply writing about a dead issue but "writing for now" (171). He also heard from an Englishwoman who had a Hari of her own in her life; they were in the process of moving from New York to Shillong. Scott told her that "an English teacher told me that she could never believe in the existence of someone like Hari Kumar"; Scott hadn't argued with her though his character was based on someone he met in India during his 1964 visit. To this "Daphne," Scott wished "great happiness" (172). He even shared with a reader what he imagined the future of Hari and Parvati might be. Hari, he thought, "got a post teaching at a Government college, or at one of those Indian public schools run on English public school lines." Parvati, he envisioned, enjoyed a successful career as a classically trained singer. Hari followed her career "with great interest" and attended her first solo recital. "I don't think he intruded on her," Scott reflected (255).

What touched Scott perhaps most intimately were letters from readers who were themselves writers—established or fledgling. For instance, he appreciated the way Violet Wilkinson (a student of his at the Swanwick Writers' Summer School) reacted "to this business of form and shape which, to me, is all important in any art or craft" (Scott 2011a, 228). He counseled her never to consider a book in terms of what would pay off for the publishers. That is not the worry of the writer. "Writing it and believing in it is, of course yours alone, and no one can help you to believe in it unless you show it to them and they say: Yes, this is good" (254).

His support of young writers became a passion for Scott. In his role as a visiting Scholar in Residence at the University of Tulsa (1976–1977), he recommended one of his students to Phyllis Westberg of Harold Ober Associates. "I think it would help him if you are able to like it & say so & one day get more out of him" (Scott 2011b, 339). Hospitalized with cancer yet too weak to undergo surgery in the fall of 1977, Scott spent hours from his hospital bed responding to students in his creative writing seminar, commenting on drafts, assigning readings and exercises, all the while encouraging the potential he saw in those young writers.[13]

THE HOST'S GIFT TO HIS GUESTS

Our own readers might accuse us of appropriating Scott's principle of moral dialogue in the name of hospitality. True, Scott didn't laud hospitality the way he spoke about the novel as a moral dialogue. But certainly he valued the hospitality extended to him during his trips to India. People who entered his life as stranger-hosts (especially Dorothy Ganapathy and Dr. Basanti Dulal Nag Chaudhuri and his wife, Dipali) became lifelong friends. As a traveling writer on a speaking tour in India for the British Council in 1972, he found himself in the sometimes precarious position of ceaseless and needy guest, just as he did on his later tours through New York, Washington, DC, Austin, and Urbana-Champagne. But Scott also played the role of host—not simply by reciprocating the hospitality extended to him in India but in a more formal way, hosting the Swanwick Writers' Summer School in Derbyshire numerous times.

After all, the character who constructs and unifies the story of Bibighar in the Raj Quartet is a traveler—Scott calls him the Stranger—a historian who, after reading the memoirs of General A. V. Reid, goes to India to interview key people in the Bibighar tragedy. On occasions, Scott compared himself (in a limited way) to that Stranger. In July 1966, after the publication of *The Jewel in the Crown*, he wrote to Dorothy Ganapathy: "Wouldn't it be marvelous, though, if some producer decided to make a film of *The Jewel*, and sent me out to India for *ages* to help them work on the script? When I said can you put me up for a week I was only being British. Such hospitality as I had from you, such kindness to the Stranger in the novel, is never forgotten, never presumed upon" (Scott 2011b, 28).

As Scott once observed, "Authors depend a great deal for well-being and peace of mind on the unconscious courtesy of strangers" (Scott 1986, 42). It is a "difficult business," Virginia Woolf knew, for a writer to be intimate with a stranger (Woolf 1988, 34). But it was possible by the very nature of writing, so Scott believed: "To publish a book is to offer it to everyone who cares to read it, and the relationship set up then between reader and writer is a relationship between free thinking and feeling people, each entitled to his or her view, and entitled to express it" (Scott 2011a, 254).

And so Scott set out not to pontificate but to pose questions that cannot be answered with absolute certainty but bear fruit in meaningful dialogue. They are crucial questions, surpassing issues like politics, ideology, and power: Is there a dignity to the human person? Can people love unselfishly? What are the effects of personal choice? How can postwar survivors find meaning in their lives? All he required was a free space to write and a moment of surrender on the part of his readers.

Such surrender is risky for readers, as we have noted. But the potential benefit was, for Scott, worth all of *his* risks. For he offered a remedy for "the defect of our too great nearness to ourselves." That remedy is joy, the joy that "springs from the heightened perception of time and place and people and history—and of oneself revealed mysteriously in an extraordinary and compelling relationship to those things" (Scott 1986, 109).

Scott's refusal to treat his readers as apprentices who should be spoon-fed (or force-fed) his personal ideology and view of history means, in Alasdair MacIntyre's words, that he declined to treat his readers as a means to an end. "To manipulate someone means to use any means available to make another my instrument, to believe what I want him/her to believe by using psychology or sociology, not standards of normative rationality" (1984, 24). In his insistence that his readers become active decoders in the moral and historical situation described in the Quartet, Scott is treating them not as means but as ends in themselves. He aligns himself with MacIntyre's conclusion that "to treat someone else as an end is to offer them what I take to be good reasons for acting in one way rather than another, but to leave it to them to evaluate those reasons" (23).[14] From Scott's perspective, moving the relationship with his readers from "dumb acquiescence" to dialogue might be the only kind of human action he could take "that doesn't directly challenge the *humanity* of those who hold a contrary opinion" (Scott 1986, 138, 149).

What better way to make possible that face-to-face encounter with the Other that Levinas advocates? Scott rejected the totalizing ruse of strident, politicizing fiction for the sake of a fuller, more complex truth that emerges not only in the act of writing but in the act of sharing the text with readers. In Scott's case, his insistence on authoring this kind of fiction ruined his chances (in his lifetime) for a blockbusting best seller, a movie deal, a television script, or a niche in the literary establishment. His philosophy of writing is at once engaged, hard-nosed and, it is to be hoped, still possible in the world of authors, readers, and critics.

Notes

Portions of this chapter are drawn from two previous publications: "Paul Scott's Dialogic Method," *South Carolina Review* 32(5) (2003); and "Images of Rape and Buggery: Paul Scott's View of the Dual Evils of Empire," *Studies in the Novel* 33(2) (2001).

1. From *My Appointment with the Muse* (Scott 1986), edited by Shelley C. Reece, which contains Scott's speeches and formal presentations to British, American, and Indian audiences.

2. There are few words in literary criticism that are more packed than *moral*, as current discourse on the moral dynamics of reading and writing make clear (see Miller 1987; Nussbaum 1998; Newton 1995; Booth 1990; Gibson 1999; Posner 1997; and

Benhabib 1987, 1990, 1992, among others). These theorists are exploring what Scott viewed as "open space," or dialogic exchange in fictional texts that puts readers into a position of shared decisions. At their foundational core, interpretive choice and moral choice cannot be distinguished.

3. Since Scott never made his personal views about history (or about writing) explicit in his novels, we are consulting archival materials (letters, addresses, and essays) to develop this section of the chapter.

4. The Special Collections Department at the McFarlin Library, the University of Tulsa, houses the archives of Paul Scott's letters. Series I includes his correspondence dating primarily from 1940 to 1976 and is cited as Tulsa, with box and folder number. Series II contains his miscellaneous writings and is cited as Tulsa II, then box and folder number.

5. The Quartet consists of *The Jewel in the Crown* (1966), *The Day of the Scorpion* (1968), *The Towers of Silence* (1972), and *A Division of the Spoils* (1975). The Quartet's sequel, *Staying On* (1977) was awarded the Booker Prize (Scott 1998a, 1998b, 1998c, 1998d, 1998e).

6. Peter Childs believes that Scott intended to juxtapose liberalism and paternalism, seeing the demise of liberalism as opening the way to religious intolerance and racism with the policies of Enoch Powell in the 1950s and 1960s (1998, 15). He believes several of the main characters in the Quartet (Sarah and Mabel Layton, Daphne Manners) are "representatives of humanism" (119). Childs also argues that "liberal humanism represented for Scott one set of the laws that Emerson argues pre-exist the facts of history" (81). "Consequently," Childs reasons, Scott "wanted to understand the end of liberal humanism as a counterforce. His chief concerns were therefore with comprehending liberalism's loss of agency and the legacy of that breakdown" (14). It is clear, however, that Scott argues the opposite. India, more than England, was "the scene of the victory of Liberal Humanism over dying paternal imperialism," (Scott 1986, 49) but paradoxically the two are in fact linked, as we will show.

7. We are working here from the holographs and typescripts of the novels in the Quartet housed in the Paul Scott Collection at the Harry Ransom Humanities Research Center, University of Texas–Austin. Materials are cited by "Austin," then box and folder number.

8. More contemporary readers exhibit patterns of misreading that might be divided into two failed engagements. The first involves attacks on Scott's "politics." For instance, Salman Rushdie has accused Scott of being both nostalgic and inept. While Scott pretends to criticize the Raj for hypocrisy and moral failure, he in fact romanticizes the Raj, admiring the ethic he pretends to dislike. Scott is guilty of cashing in on the rise of Raj revisionism during the 1970s and 1980s, argues Rushdie, when conservative members of Parliament like Enoch Powell advocated severe limits on immigration from former colonies (1984, 127–128, 130). In doing so, Scott speaks only in clichés about India, inventing that nation in the tradition of Commonwealth literature: an India that is exotic, barbaric, naturalistic, childlike, erotic to the point of decadent—in short, a country inferior by religion, education, and culture, in sore need of a superior culture to reform it, care for it, guide it.

   Jenny Sharpe also warns against Raj revivalism, which "reanimates the great narrative of the civilizing mission" that weaves a "living tapestry of a forgetting" (1993, 143). Neither Sharpe not Rushdie acknowledge that Scott's interest in India emerged with his first published novel, *Johnny Sahib* (1952), or that there was (in fact) no "cashing in" on India during Scott's lifetime.

   Other, more perceptive readers like Gerwin Strobl have counter-argued that interpreting the Quartet as a defense of colonialism is "fundamentally wrong-headed" (1996, 271; see also J. Haswell 2001, 2002, 2003).

9.   A literary agent by training, Scott knew how and when to sell his ideas for a play, a radio or television script, or a novel. Thus letters to his agents and editors very often are the kind of hard sells that are rarely seen in his letters to other readers. In defending a character or a scene, Scott would often make his design, intent, method, or message explicit. See, for instance, Scott 2011a, 103 (concerning *A Male Child*), 122 (*The Mark of the Warrior*), 150 (*The Chinese Love Pavilion*), 307 (*The Corrida at San Feliu*); and Scott 2011b, 85 (his play *The Situation*), and 109 (*The Towers of Silence*).

10. Scott's published letters are taken from the Special Collections at the McFarlin Library, the University of Tulsa, the Harry Ransom Humanities Research Center, University of Texas–Austin, and the private holdings of Carol and Sally Scott.

11. Scott could mock the critics as well, given enough time and distance. See his letter to Mollie Hamilton (M. M. Kaye) about reviews published in the *Observer* and the *Daily Telegraph* (Scott 2011b, 240–242).

12. There have also been those readers who discredit Scott's novels because of his style. For instance, Benita Parry believes that "only at the end of the quartet is it fully apparent that so enraptured is Scott by the idea of what the British-Indian relationship might have been that he has arranged his material, adjusted his focus and undermined his metaphors and analogues illuminating the association to produce a muted celebration of a concept rather than a critique of a celebration" (1975, 359). Parry also finds Scott's dialogic method a slippery slope, with the political situations and moral choices in the Quartet open to so many possibilities that "the definition of an author's own controlling intelligence is obscured" (359–60). "Where so many possibilities are presented," Parry laments, "the mind of the reader may be replete but the imagination is left undernourished" (360).

   In counterpoint to Parry's view, Eva Brann believes Scott is "unamenable to anything but attentive reading. There *are* discernible narrative devices," Brann insists, "which are not, however, the impositions of an authorial intention but rather the self-shaping of a matter under intense regard . . . There is little critic-fodder here" (1999, 188), In short, Scott is neither ideologue nor propagandist.

13. One final tier of readers was comprised of an increasing number of scholars who were writing master's theses, doctoral dissertations, or scholarly monographs on Scott's novels. He spent hours answering questions from Professor D. M. Burjorjee from Montgomery College in Rockville, Maryland; Professor N. N. Banerji from the British Institute of Technology and Science in Rajastham, India; Professor K. B. Rao at the World University Service in New York; Professor Max Beloff at University College in Buckingham; and doctoral candidate Francine Weinbaum at the University of Illinois at Urbana-Champagne.

14. Alasdair MacIntyre (1984) defines "emotivism" as "the doctrine that . . . all moral judgments are *nothing but* expressions of preference, expression of attitude or feelings" (12). Because moral judgments are neither true nor false, their implementation depends upon an advocate's persuasive (or coercive) powers. As a consequence, social relations are manipulative by nature, and "others are always means, never ends" (23, 24).

8

OUTSIDE HOSPITALITY
The Desire to Not Write

Richard Haswell

Thought, in its essence, is pure potentiality; in other words,
it is also the potentiality to not think.

—Giorgio Agamben

The very stone one kicks with one's boot
will outlast Shakespeare.

—Virginia Woolf

Some places do not fit print very well. Nor do they fit hospitality very well. It's a truth that people commissioned to write official tourist guides may not convey. The *Documental* for the Peruvian department of Ayacucho actually says about its chief urban center, "Ayacucho, once the ancient Incan town of Huamanga, is one of the most pleasant and beautiful cities in Peru." Maybe the authors of this *Documental* had never visited Ayacucho, or maybe they had lived there all of their lives. Maybe they knew of a hospitality that I did not find.

When I visited Ayacucho in the spring of 1970, it seemed anything but pleasant, friendly, or even accommodating. Ayacucho squats at 9,000 feet elevation on an arid shelf of the eastern Andean slopes. In March, with the rainy season just tailing off, the late afternoon storms drop blackly down from even higher country and leave ridges of silt across the street intersections. By noon the next day the winds sweeping up from the rocky washes of the Montaro valley 2,000 feet below swirl the dust up and down the cobbled alleys. Especially around midafternoon when the grit is the worst, Ayacucho, with its population of 27,000, has the air of an abandoned place on the first step toward dilapidation. It seems determined to catch up to the pre-Incaic ruins of Huari, acres of stone heaps that lie on a neighboring shelf of the Montaro only twenty miles away. In 1970 from Ayacucho to Huari was a wretched two-hour drive over axle-breaking roads.

DOI: 10.7330/9780874219883.c008

The whole region, in fact, was wretchedly depressed. Another Peruvian documentary, the *Anuario éstadístico*, forced to use numbers in place of adjectives, cannot hide the fact (*Anuario éstadistico del Perú, 1966*, 1969). In 1966 only 4 percent of Peruvians lived in the Department of Ayacucho but they suffered 9 percent of the cases of typhoid and amoebic dysentery, 23 percent of diphtheria, and 31 percent of human rabies. About the same time, in the early 1960s, a spasm of land seizures set whole Indian communities marching to the haciendas of their landlords holding up their seventeenth-century Spanish titles like banners. By 1965 large-property owners were simply abandoning buildings, land, and crops to their rebellious serfs. Five years later we found the Ayacucho market a huddle of Indian ladies, hunkering by a cloth with a small mound of barley grain or a few stacks of cactus fruit or a dish of blackening avocados. It lacked the grand fruit and vegetable stalls familiar in markets everywhere else in Peru.

These are facts that I suppose tourist guides, even those called *documentales*, do not feel bound to register. According to the Statistical Yearbook, fifty-six people served the entire department (population 410,772 in 1966) with electricity, gas, water, and "sanitary services." There was no telephone service beyond the town, even to Lima, and, as we were told rather proudly by the bilinguist in residence, in town there were only seven flush toilets. The bilinguist, who had one of them, did not ask us why we were staying in Ayacucho. Maybe he assumed we were waiting for Easter week when the place overflows with tourists from Lima who come up to watch the religious processions famous all over Peru for their size and frenzy.

But the assumption would have been wrong. I was not ambitious to see Easter week anywhere in South America, much less in Ayacucho. So what was a novice professor of English literature doing in the town? I would not have been able to say. My wife and I had spent four days driving our VW van from Cuzco over one of the worst roads in Peru. That road too was lying in a state of ruin, since the new route from Lima to Cuzco via Puquio had bypassed Ayacucho and the appalling mountain gorges that slash northeastward down into the Amazon basin. Along the passes at 13,000 and 14,000 feet, miles of this old Inca road from Cuzco to Ayacucho were eroded away to its foundation of basalt boulders. We had coasted down into Ayacucho, our van's gas tank nearly empty and I with a bad case of diarrhea. So Ayacucho first seemed a welcome oasis, a chance to recuperate, maybe to finish *Remembrance of Things Past*, which I had transported from the States as part of my sabbatical reading. By the time I had recovered my digestion and we had discovered the lean of the town, it had taken on the cast of a challenge. We would stay here a month—despite Ayacucho.

Beyond this there really was no reason why I was not properly settled in the book-lined study of a scholar instead of in what the World Health Organization called the center of the most poverty-stricken region in the hemisphere. Certainly the last thing I intended was for Ayacucho to thrust upon me my scholarly ambitions. But that is exactly what happened. Within a few days the Department of Ayacucho held out to me my yearned-for article in *Comparative Literature* and with it assurance of fame in my own department—well, at least tenure. As it turned out Ayacucho itself kept me from accepting Ayacucho's gift.

MARIO VARGAS LLOSA AND JAMES JOYCE IN AYACUCHO

Of course I was not looking for anything to excite or even mollify a scholar in the bookstores of the town. Despite the presence of the University of San Cristóbal of Huamanga, the so-called *librerías* cater almost exclusively to schoolchildren, supplying them with colored pencils and wide-lined tablets and cheap tin compasses. We would call them stationery stores. Beyond the racks of comic books and *foto-novelas*, the only adult literature is a scattering of nonfiction—dream interpretation, juvenile sex manuals, counsel on writing love and business letters, collections of snappy street remarks for girl watchers, advice on how to hypnotize oneself and others. The only fiction I saw were translations of Maupassant and biographies of Kropotkin and Trotsky. What else would one expect in a region where only a fourth of the population could write or read and only a third could speak Spanish? Consequently, one day when buying some airmail envelopes, I was astonished to see, propped up between a book on electrical chemistry and *El libro de esplendores* by Eliphas Levi, the handsome two-volume Barral edition of Mario Vargas Llosa's new novel, *Conversación en la catedral*. By coincidence I had met Vargas Llosa a year earlier when he was still writing the novel in the States. How it got to Ayacucho so quickly from the publisher in Spain is still a mystery to me, but it may have been a bit of publicity to prepare for subsequent and cheaper editions. One of the characters in the novel drives an ice-cream truck from Lima to Ayacucho.

The presence of *Conversación en la catedral*, which I bought and started reading at once before my wife could lay claim to it, was only half, and not the most miraculous half, of the scholarly inspiration that Ayacucho had prepared for me. The other half lay in the closet of one of the sons of Señora Adolfa Zavala Gutiérrez. We had arrived at the señora's—a labyrinth of peeling walls smelling of bleach and dog excrement—after three days of searching for a place to stay. Evidently the few rooms that Ayacucho rashly expected to rent were already committed to relatives arriving at the end of the month for Holy Week. Señora Zavala showed us a tiny bedroom jammed with a huge desk, a trunk, an armoire, a stack of old mattresses, and a scratchy, sagging double bed. The room belonged to a son now studying in Lima, and in the top of the closet I found some books—his school texts, a translation of three Chekhov stories about peasants, St. Pierre's novel (*Pablo y Virginia*), and a stack of *Carreta* magazines. Except for the Chekhov, it was a discouraging lot, but then the boy was expected to be a doctor like his father, like Chekhov, come to think of it. Having reluctantly arrived at the end of *Conversación* and bogged down in the middle of the second 1,000 pages of Proust, I took to leafing through the copies of *Carreta*. In imitation of the European slicks, the magazine had some celebrity gossip and lively photographs on the first and last pages.

So it was that Ayacucho, whose ladies prefer to cover their ankles with the dirt-stiffened hems of three or four skirts, led me to a decidedly non-Indian thigh and thence to my article for *Comparative Literature*. For next to the thigh was a column by Mario Vargas Llosa, and the column was an account of his visit to Ireland, and there, approximately at the knee, was his remark that the Irish Sea was not, as Joyce had famously written, "snot-colored" (*color de moco*). And I remembered, like a gift from heaven, Vargas Llosa's description in the first pages of *Conversación* of an adobe wall in Lima: "*color de caca*," shit-colored.

I sat on the trunk resting against the pile of mattresses with the copy of *Carreta* in my hands, listening to the slap of wet clothes being knocked against a concrete trough by one of the señora's Indian girls, and I knew I was famous. Joyce's epithet "snot-colored," as everybody knows, deliberately evokes Homer's image of the "wine-colored" sea at the beginning of the *Odyssey*. It is one of a thousand parallels in Joyce's *Ulysses* with Homer's epic. Vargas Llosa's epithet in *Conversación en la catedral* must evoke in turn Joyce's, and signal the fact that his novel parallels *Ulysses*. From the direction of the market came the hollow, doubled cry of a harassed donkey.

There was no doubt of it. Vargas Llosa's novel, written, as was *Ulysses*, in exile from the country it describes, experiments with similar tricks of narration. Despite a multitude of flashbacks, the action takes place around the capital (Lima) during one entire day. Also as in *Ulysses*, the names and places around the city are scrupulously exact. There are two main characters whose conversation forms the novel, a reporter obviously reminiscent of the author (compare Stephen Dedalus), and a down-and-out ex-chauffeur living by his wits (compare Leopold Bloom). The novel even ends with a long internal monologue of the chauffeur's wife (compare Molly Bloom). As I sat on the trunk, the donkey's persistent lament beginning to get on my nerves, the comparisons started coming so thick I knew it was an assured thing. It was only a question of paging systematically through *Conversación* and recording all the parallels I could find before my memory of the book grew stale. My memory of *Ulysses* was stale enough, but that could wait until I got back to the States. The English translation of *Conversación* would take two or three years and not many English-speaking scholars would have dipped into *Carreta.*

The señora's teenage son began singing on his guitar and his mother herself came out of the kitchen to tell the girl to hang up the clothes as she finished with each piece instead of leaving them wadded up on the ground. It was clear that I needed some place to tabulate my inspiration in peace.

Señora Zavala's room, unfortunately, would not do. It was not so much that to sit at the desk one could hardly pull out the chair without knocking against our breakfast table (the trunk). But Señora Zavala had troubles and in Peru troubles mean a racket. Three of her four sons were gone and her husband's practice was in Lima. This left her alone with her youngest—a moody brat who spent a lot of his time learning to play the guitar. To say "learning" is generous, for he seemed satisfied with combining march rhythms, atonal chord clusters, and the wail of radio love ballads. The rest of his time he spent shouting politics with his mother. He wanted her to let him attend the Marxist-leaning San Cristóbal University in Ayacucho instead of conservative San Marcos in Lima. (Neither he nor she nor I, of course, would have known that a mile away at San Cristóbal one of the teachers was Manuel Rubén Abimael Guzmán, future leader of the bloody "Shining Path.") It was during these arguments that I first noticed how "¡Bueno!" could be projected like a bullet. When the boy wasn't home, the señora was usually out berating her girls in the high-pitched, weepy voice of the sierra matron. Like all the ladies of her class, she was taxed with the thankless job of keeping a set of nine- and ten-year-old Indian girls, hired for a few centimos a day, at their tasks of watering the garden with pails, beating the washing at the trough, scrubbing the patio, throwing the dog manure over the walls. My wife suggested I try the public library in the morning.

THE SILTS OF AYACUCHO

A walk through the streets of Ayacucho, one would think, should be an exercise in pity. But even in the moist, clean air of the morning, there is something about Ayacucho that thwarts the more self-flattering of the affections. Pity descends to a certain level, as Simone Weil (1947) wrote, and not below. Something about the townward cant of the surrounding hills, the stubborn tilt of the rough and cobbled alleys, and the relentless scabrous walls seems to block speculative thrusts of any sort. As I crossed the bridge over the dry ravine that splits the town, my glance was returned by the curious stares of people squatting in the sand and garbage.

I've called Ayacucho inhospitable. This was not entirely true. There were the two old sisters: Dominga stocky and corseted, Ximena skinny with no upper teeth and slightly deaf, both widowed and lively. We had heard they had a room to rent. They hadn't, but they invited us in and over lemonade and biscuits considered the local possibilities. Without them we would never have found Señora Zavala. But Dominga and Ximena were the exceptions. We understood that Señora Zavala was offering us her room free, but within a day she was whining about how much our stay was costing her. Ayacucho was an impoverished place. Hospitality was calculated in *soles*. And those without *soles* were humiliated and angry. We couldn't drive a block off of the main square without boys in tatters pressing against the big VW windows shouting, "¡Gringos!" and "¡Puta!"

It was even harder to look at the Indians, trudging to and from the town market. Need had stripped away the color and the old craft and wrapped them in layers of gray rags. They tended to stare back like the country dogs that stood, lopsided and diseased and mad-eyed, by every maguey patch along the country roads. I even stopped looking through Ayacucho's doorways in hopes of catching a glimpse of geraniums and blue tile and the greenery of a well-washed courtyard, a common sight throughout Peru. I did not see many sanctuaries of this sort in Ayacucho. Instead I was rewarded with dirt yards and sagging lines of wash, porches collapsed under the weight of cracked roof tiles, the trash and accoutrement of three or four families.

The museum housing the library did not open until nine. I stepped down into a restaurant with four tables and grimy sawdust on the floor. The room was not much larger than a pre–World War II American bedroom, the walls bare except for the flies and the usual calendar with a photograph of the Colorado Rockies and a single shelf behind the counter with a row of Fanta bottles. Inside the glass counter I could make out a pile of round breads, a plate of white cheese patties, and another plate of soupy butter. The glass of the counter looked like a chicken had been roasted in it. On top was nothing but an olive-pitter and a gallon jar of green olives. Although the restaurant was on the corner of an intersection with a fine view of the Montaro valley, there were no windows and only one door out and I began to feel as if I were ordering coffee as a last request.

Two soldiers came in, and we all three drank our coffee in silence and watched a couple of small boys begin slicing bread and cheese, pitting olives, slapping on butter, throwing the sandwiches into the counter. As usual there was no money in the shop, and we had to wait twenty minutes while change was sought. The soldiers grew impatient but their cries of *"Eh, mozo!"* brought no one out of the kitchen.

Finally out of the restaurant and at the museum door, I stared at the two bright volumes of *Conversación* in my hand and for a second wondered why I had them with me. But the sight of the museum courtyard revived my enthusiasm. No one was about, and two replicas of stone pumas from the ruins of Huari across the valley stared through the potted plants at the visitors' ledger. The room containing the library was also empty. Even better, a huge bare table waited in the middle. Here was a friendly sanctuary from Ayacucho where I could get some work done. Not that the room had much of an air of a library about it. I had expected walls of books, but only three cases waist high ran along one side for perhaps eight feet. I went over and squatted down. It was a depressing lot—pamphlets on local history, antiquarian journals from the nineteenth century, an 1873 encyclopedia, a scattering of religious tracts. *Account of the Merits and Services of Don Miguel de Otermin, Director General of the Tobacco Tax in the Kingdom of Peru. Genealogical Tree for the Dardano Family from Noah to Carlos II, and for the Corebanto Family Continued to Narnes Cortés, King of Lombardy.* Here were *Novenas* and *Pastoral Letters* and *Orations* and *Meditations* and *Royal Catechisms* and more *Accounts of Merits and Services.*

Did anyone read these books anymore? For some reason the case containing the encyclopedia was locked. How depressing the volumes seemed, with their flimsy paper covers or tight black bindings, their tiny print, their indigestible blocks of facts. No, they were more pitiful than depressing. They'd never had many readers. They had not really been written to be read. *Letters to My Fellow Seminarists.* The title was just another cover, and the text had been written in some book-lined cubbyhole and sent to be fitted, uncut, into the wall of other book-lined cubbyholes. Or eventually to find its way into those back corridors of the great university libraries, those dark unvisited cul-de-sacs where the stacks are lined with commentaries on the Psalms and long rows of the *Nineteenth Century* and the *Library World* and *Mercure de France.*

I went back to *Conversación* and my sheets of airmail stationery. But I had momentarily lost the heart for it. The black books in the case had too much brought back the graduate-student feel of those early black, squat volumes of *PMLA* with the inner margins lost in the binding, always slewing around when carried in a stack to the checkout desk. What would next year's bound volumes of *Comparative Literature* feel like in seventy years?

On one wall was a row of framed antique photographs. Nineteenth-century hacienda owners sat on horses, looking like Mexican bandits from a low-budget Italian western. Behind them were lined up their serfs, 80 or a 100, standing meek or sullen or stupefied or open-mouthed like a class of schoolchildren. Some photographs were of haciendas in the La Mar province, on the Rio Pampas, thirty-five miles east of Ayacucho. In fact, here was the famed swinging bridge over the Pampas, a photo taken in 1899, not Thornton Wilder's bridge of San Luis Rey but the one that replaced it. I remembered stopping three weeks earlier on the modern concrete structure and looking, stupid with twenty-four hours of diarrhea, up the bare walls of the canyon for the abutments that must remain from the old bridge. The region is viciously inhospitable—hot, narrow, eroded hills swarming with forests of cactus.

Would Wilder have written his book had he ever been there? Even in his day the *hacendados* of the Pampas were renowned for their harsh rule. In 1960, of 40,000 people in La Mar province, only 8,000 could speak Spanish, and ten years later the rebel activity and military pursuit and land seizures had reduced the monolithic haciendas to great hulks of adobe. La Mar province. I thought of Homer's phrase the "wine-colored sea" and remembered looking down the canyon of the Pampas, down the dirt-yellow rapids sluggishly moving past some cane huts and a corral. The Pampas flows north into the Apurímac and then into the Ucayali, which flows past Iquitos and into the Amazon at 600 feet above sea level, still in Peru. Then into Joyce's "snot-colored" Atlantic.

At the door of the museum I looked up the street, where I could see a corner of Ayacucho's main plaza. A man was sweeping a border of grass with a besom made of twigs. Already the wind was swirling the dust up and across the intersections. Down the street three small boys played baseball with a rubber bolus, using their arms for a bat. The cobbled street descended crazily for three or four blocks and then disappeared against the hill of Kikipata, scored with paddle cactus, maguey, goat paths, and adobe huts, and spiked at the top with a cross of concrete wired for electrical display. The pale blue beyond seemed less like a sky than an optical illusion of solid metal.

I suppose specialists should never leave home with their specialties. If they have a hankering to fare about the menacing ways of the world, they should lock their occupations up safe inside the sanctums where they prosper. Otherwise, their preoccupation will be brutalized or scandalized by a life that offers them little hospitality. The stamp collector will discover countries that simply burn mounds of mail backed up during seasonal rushes. The man who designs machines to bleach flour will find himself in a town where the side lanes are treacherous with puddles of diarrhea full of cactus-fruit seeds. The woman who sets the hair of her neighbor in a room she has equipped for a few thousand dollars will be told that the comb she found in a market, with the wonderfully fine teeth, is used to strip out fleas—and not from the hair of poodles.

And the scholar of literature—can anyone's specialty be more vulnerable? How many people in Ayacucho had heard of Vargas Llosa, their country's best-known writer? How many would ever read *Conversación en la catedral?* Would it make any difference to anybody in Ayacucho that Vargas Llosa read Joyce? Would the knowledge of epic parallels between two books do one person in Ayacucho one iota of good? I watched an Indian woman, wrapped in a patched black shawl, creep brokenly up the street on bare feet that looked like cracked clods of dirt, carrying a slice of yellow squash in hands that did not look like hands at all, more like two rolls of chicken skin. Simone Weil (1947, 221) must have seen peasants like this. "Un malheur trop grand met un être humain au-dessous de la pitié: dégoût, horreur, et mépris," she wrote. "Too much of a misfortune puts a human being below pity: repugnance, abhorrence, contempt." Too much of life lies outside hospitality.

Back at Señora Zavala's, I found that more plans than my own had been thwarted. The señora's hospitality had come to an end. One of her sons and her husband were coming from Lima with four friends to see Holy Week, and we would have to leave in two days. We decided to drive out to Huari and camp for a week.

That night we began filtering water to fill our five-gallon container. But the señora's filter was so old and clogged with dirt that it looked like the process would take until Easter. We finally filled the can directly from the tap, trusting that most of the dirt would sift to the bottom. Since the rains had stopped, Ayacucho's water had cleared to a certain degree. The bilinguist had told us we could purify it with 1 part iodine to 2,000 parts water. Calculating a best as I could remember from teaspoon to cup to quart to gallon, I concluded that we should put thirty-two tea-spoons of the 3 percent solution of iodine we had bought in a drugstore into our five gallons. This seemed improbable, so we decided to go by the bilinguist's alternate standard, to put in iodine until it just began to taste. But we put in too much and the water tasted horrible. We poured some out, replaced it with tap water, and so on until we had no idea how much iodine was in the water. It occurred to me that the alcohol in our solution of iodine might conduct the taste better than the pure iodine used by the bilinguist. We gave in to our five gallons of Ayacucho water and went to bed.

THE RUINS OF HUARI

I was thinking that the isolation of the Huari ruins would offer a refuge where I could tackle my article for *Comparative Literature*, a place more open to us than Ayacucho with its noise and dirt. On the road out of town we could see across the Chacocc River to the great Huari pampa, an appealing green shelf stretched out against the dusty grays and yellows of the surrounding mountains. Two hours later, at the trail end of a hacienda road, we found a spot to camp. It was a knoll perched at the top of the pampa, a haven of grass, molle trees, and Druidic basalt boulders. The ruins descended gradually in three directions, six square miles of stone walls, bouldery outcrops, and plots of peas and oats and peppers. The forests of paddle-cactus trees made it a jungle that only the Indian paths allowed one to penetrate. Huari was greener than the neighboring pampas because the ancient terracing had resisted erosion for centuries.

Isolated Huari was, at least from the raw presence of Ayacucho. But I found it as impossible to work there. Huari lay so buried in the centuries that to scribble away at Joyce and Vargas Llosa seemed as foolish as putting on a tie to scramble about the rock walls. From our clump of boulders I could just make out, ten miles to the northeast, the thick white obelisk marking the plains of Quinua, where Sucre won an improbable victory for independence in 1824. To the south lay Ayacucho, that ruined city, a smear of ocher against the gray hills. To the west, across the gorge of Pacaicasa and the valley of the Montaro, I thought I could see the cave, a mouth in a hillside, where MacNeish and other archeologists were finding the oldest human remains in the Americas mingled with giant sloth bones.

I lazed under a molle tree on a boulder, the top of which had once been pecked rather flat, and breathed the pure sierra air. Around our red van dirty white sheep were nibbling the grass, the greenest grass in the world. The Indian boy herding them sat on a stone wall that had been put up 3,000 years ago and put up repeatedly for 3,000 years since. Comparative literature, indeed. An Indian came trudging up from the pampa, on his back a crate of cactus fruit covered from the sun with cactus paddles. It seemed nonsensical to open up *Conversación.* Spanish had never been the language of this American place. It spoke Quechua or Aymará, if it spoke in words at all.

Huari is one of those ruins that archeologists love but tourists do not visit. Tello and Lumbréres and Bennet and Menzel had found it a treasure of history, one of the oldest continuously occupied sites in Peru, but it lacks the remains of temples or pyramids or decorated priest dwellings or intricate stonework. There are several burial chambers of stone slabs, dressed but uncarved, so lost in the maze of walls and cactus that we never ran across them except by chance. The last time they held a litter of pigs. There is also a natural cave called Infiernillo that Bennet says still is used for burials, and indeed the stink of it kept us out. But beyond these eccentricities, Huari offers nothing but the debris of a great urban sprawl, five millennia of anonymous living and dying that left nothing but a labyrinth of loose stone walls and a soil choked with potsherds. Thousands of like ruins lie around the world—mute, impenetrable, autistic.

Sitting on my boulder like an ascetic sloth and gazing at Huari, I thought that before such a momento mori the literary scholar must fall silent. If the millions who lived here over the centuries had any literature, it had dissipated into the air. And before these ruins, the idea of literary criticism is an inanity. Huari neither lived for it nor died for lack of it.

But does any living city offer a better prospect for the scholar? Living or dying or dead, what is the difference? Toward the end of his life, living in Amalfi, Kenneth Grahame was showing a visiting American girl around, impressing her with his encyclopedic knowledge of the place. Decades later she remembered him saying that "the strongest human instinct is the desire to impart knowledge, and the second strongest is the desire to resist such knowledge." Grahame forget to mention the third instinct, although he had rendered it indelibly in a famous chapter of *The Wind in the Willows*, the desire not to impart knowledge. Now I understood why the scholars I knew preferred to have their book-lined studies at home in basements without windows or in nooks at the rear of the house with a view no further than the back fence. No scholar ever wrote at a window with a vista. So it was that at Huari I finished Proust— that great city of a book built in a room lined with cork—and spent hours with my wife picking our way through the cactus and collecting potsherds from the plots that had been recently plowed.

Ironically, it was the shards that revived my belief in my article for *Comparative Literature*. The way it happened was odd. The pottery from Huari rewards the eye with stylized motifs painted in reds and browns and black. White was also used, but it had deteriorated badly. We figured out a few motifs: a jaguar, a bird of prey, a foot with claws—and eyes. The Huari artists loved eyes. We offered the Indian children a sol for every eye, and ended up with a sackful. But one motif, though common, continued to puzzle me. There was an oval area of cross-hatching beneath two dots, but since the design had been painted in white, I could make out little else from the few flakes that were left. Our fragments included not much of the rest of the design, but from their strong curvature they must have come from a glass or a cup or perhaps a small bowl.

The enigma was solved the day before we left Huari. A woman on her way back from a day's work in the pampa told us she had some potsherds at her house if we wanted to come look at them. She led us up the road past the empty Huacaurara hacienda, where the original stone jaguars of the copies in the Ayacucho museum still sat in a row on the veranda. We took a rough path that zigzagged up a ravine to the woman's house, a humped stack of rocks too small for more than two people to sleep in, guarded by a mongrel growling and snapping, yellow-eyed, from the entrance. The lady brought out a shawl full of ceramic fragments, and as I squatted down to look I saw a large piece that instantly explained the puzzling motif. Above the cross-hatched oval were two indentations that could only be eye sockets. It was a death's head. All over Huari lay pieces of ceramic skulls. As in civilizations before and since, the people of Huari drank their beer or milk or water from bowls that celebrated the most ugly and adamant fact they knew.

The bilinguist had told us a pleasing story. When he first got to know the Ayacuchan Indians, they tried to point out for him the figures they saw in the constellations. But he never could see them. Then one night he suddenly realized that the Quechua constructed their mythic shapes—the deer, the bow—out of the dark spaces between the stars. As I looked at the potsherds on the blood-red cloth, something similarly flip-flopped for me. The Huari potters had not hoped to alter the fact of death. They had not intended to help themselves or others escape death or enjoy it or even accept it. The fact of death had simply affected them and they had responded, no differently than when a struck person cries out. Artists do not create to effect the world; they create because the world has affected them. Though art may change things a little, it does not do so often, for artists, being human, are largely moved by things that cannot be changed or that they would not want to change—death, land and economy and their fixed ties, the fatalities of character and culture, the inevitability of joy.

And so it is, I thought, with literary scholars as well. Whatever the excuse they make, whatever the light they see themselves in, as historian or philosopher or scientist or belletrist, their subject always will remain something they cannot change. In a sense, everything written is written in despair. The critic as well as the artist must always write about a past, a world that is inalienably *perdu*. In the exuberant climax to his work, Proust wrote that the work of art is our only way save the present, that is, to recapture the past. But surely the capture succeeds only if it seizes a past that is true, that has not changed. So writers write in despair, though not necessarily out of despair. It just as well may be out of joy.

I nudged the potsherds about and thought that the trouble had been that I had forgotten to ask, before wondering how Vargas Llosa had been influenced by Joyce, why he had remembered Joyce at all. Surely it was not to enlarge the meaning of his novel, *Conversación*, or to provide a mythic structure for it, or to graft it onto a stock of literary fame. It was simply to celebrate the memory of a book he had once read and could not get out of his mind. For the same reason I might celebrate two books that had affected me, albeit in my dry-as-dust scholarly way. No matter that my article would add not one drop of good to the world. Let it lie like a shard in some potter's field of a library. Auden said that poetry is a "mouth," like MacNeish's cave. Literary criticism need be no more, or even less, a few teeth painted on a fragment of clay, so long as it expresses a singular vitality that once was.

As I abruptly stood up by the cloth, the dog broke with a snarl and laid hold of my leg.

THE SILENCE OF AYACUCHO

I never wrote the article. I think I came to believe, perhaps mistakenly, that if I did I would never write again. So maybe it was to protect myself. It certainly wasn't to protect Ayacucho. In fact, when our month was up and it was time to return to Lima, we went out of our way and drove the two bone-jolting hours back to Ayacucho to see Holy Week, and that was certainly a mistake.

That night as we stood jammed in the crowd around the main square, I noticed that the wealthy middle-class girls from Lima had found it stylish to wear *fajas*, woven Indian belts. I thought how unpredictably and quirkily people react to the wonders and tragedies of the world. Señora Zavala, who believed that the Incas had built their tight-fit basalt walls out of a dough that then hardened into stone. The Quechuan students of the bilinguist, who wrote and produced plays that always had the same plot of the "dumb" Indian tricking and making a fool of the white without the white knowing it. The artists of Huari, who painted eyes on their bowls as if they had made a mirror. Vargas Llosa, who had seen a squalid adobe wall and had thought of a book.

And now this procession. The image at last was nearing, life-size, a plaster Christ lifting the cross. It was preceded by a group of upper-class ladies dressed in black suits and white lace mantels, laughing and gossiping and glaring back with disgust and hatred at a mob of Indians fighting their way between the crowd and the procession in an effort to keep up with the Christ. The image swayed and bounced on the litter, oblivious, encased in columns frosted like a wedding cake.

Before leaving Ayacucho that evening, we stopped to say good-bye to Dominga and Ximena. We found them exhausted and sick from entertaining a houseful of haughty relatives from Lima, members of a younger generation full of themselves. Afterward, walking back to our car along a peaceful side street, we met a terrible sight. Just inside the entrance to a shop stocked with a tub of beer, illuminated by the light from the street, sat two men. Behind them in the dark were three or four small children, eyes agog. And facing them on the other side of the entrance sat an old lady, talking and weeping and holding a large glass of beer. Her left leg, stretched across the doorway with her skirts drawn up to the thigh, was swollen twice its normal size, yellowish-black and streaked with red. We did not stop but walked on to the car and drove out of town to camp for the night in a field.

"Hay golpes en vida tan fuerte que, ya no sé." The line is from César Vallejo, who grew up not too far from Ayacucho. "Some of life's blows are so heavy that—I just don't know." When I see again that tableau, with that leg slanting across the light like the monstrous limb in Picasso's *Guernica*, all I can do is tell myself that among the ways that humans react to life perhaps not the least human is to remain silent. If it happens to be the least hospitable, so be it. As I say, much of life, and some of the worst, lies outside hospitality. No doubt there are some of life's misfortunes beneath pity about which only artists rage out. But as a scholar, without the means to express sensitivity and courage, maybe without the necessary sensitivity and courage, I give in. Someone else with a different potential can write my article on Joyce and Vargas Llosa. Ayacucho probably has received stranger returns for its hospitality than my silence.

9

BEYOND HOSPITALITY
The Desire to Reread

Janis Haswell

It is but the smaller number of books that become more instructive by a second perusal: the great majority are as perfectly plain as perfect triteness can make them. Yet, if time is precious, no book that will not improve by repeated readings deserves to be read at all. And were there an artist of a right spirit . . . what task could there be more profitable than to read him as we have described, to study him even to his minutest meanings? For, were not this to think as he had thought, to see with his gifted eyes, to make the very mood and feeling of his great and rich mind the mood also of our poor and little one?

—Thomas Carlyle

In chapter 2 we examined Levinas's understanding of hospitality, which emphasized that the self desires rather than needs the Other. A relationship with the Other doesn't satisfy the self, as does a nutritious meal, for instance. Indeed, the self doesn't use the Other for his or her own purposes but instead must "let be" what is infinite and radically exterior. Thus the act of welcome is "peaceable from the first" because it marks the self's "unquenchable Desire for Infinity" (Levinas 1969, 150). Paradoxically, in desiring yet letting be, "I attend to myself" (178).

Levinas captures the weighty potential of what happens at the threshold of a classroom when teacher and student meet for the first time. We have argued that such a moment has moral dimensions, that our encounter with students (and they with us) can be life changing. Our challenge is to ensure that students retain their own rich uniqueness while being open to our offerings, and that we as teachers seek ways to learn with and from them.

In most cases, this is a onetime opportunity. As an instructor of first-year composition in particular, I will never again teach most of these students because they will pursue majors that don't require another

DOI: 10.7330/9780874219883.c009

English course. Which is to say, the most meaningful and affirming relationship I might ever have with many of our students is a hospitable one—the interaction of host and guest that is temporary since we move along different paths once a course is completed.

When teaching courses in the major, though, the chances for reencounter are far better. I could, for instance, meet a young English major in the beginning course, later in an upper-division course, eventually in a capstone course, then even in a graduate course. In this case, the hospitable dynamic we have discussed throughout this study gradually will be superseded once teacher and student, over the course of several years, no longer relate to each other as strangers but interact as equals, as fellow scholars, as coauthors, as friends. Such a longer-term relationship gradually divests itself of the risk taking of hospitality. Continual encounters—mutually desired and planned—replace chance meetings. Moving beyond hospitality, of course, does not necessarily lose the beneficial effects of hospitality. Trusted exchanges and intimate conversations may even deepen the possibility of fulfillment and revelation through the Other.

The same patterns can be found in the writer-reader relationship. There are encounters that are the first and only, as when I read a book for the first time and then never return to it. But there are also instances when I enter the same book again and again, attend to the same author over and over, and thereby develop a long-term relationship.

In this essay for the English profession, we have explored the hospitable relationship between teacher and student, writer and reader. The question I raise toward the close is this: what does the hospitable encounter make possible? What kind of foundation does it lay? Where might it lead? In this chapter I will look at what might emerge when reader and writer move beyond their initial meeting. Using Michael Ondaatje and J. R. R. Tolkien as examples, I will argue that many authors write not to be *read*, but to be *reread*.[1] By rereading I don't mean what is sometimes required of students by teachers, which assumes that students are too dumb to get it the first time. Nor do I mean that students need to grapple with a text for the first time on their own, listen to the teacher's explication, then read it a second time to apply the teacher's superior interpretation.

The kind of rereading that Ondaatje and Tolkien lend themselves to goes beyond the response from a guest who will remain (fundamentally) a stranger. The relationship they *desire* is more like familiarity, if not friendship—kinship based on a shared desire for meaning. These authors design a writing space within which their own uniqueness (and their readers') has free play. In such cases, both writer and reader need time to make discoveries, time for truths to be revealed, time and space to be changed through the experience of writing and of reading. Both are open to psychological effects such as recovery and consolation, to slowly evolving relationships such as partnership, to philosophical and spiritual ends such as contemplation, to social ends such as action, to personal ends such as getting in touch with oneself.

All of this goes beyond hospitality. But such experiences are also made possible by the initial hospitable encounter that becomes a pathway to subsequent practices and patterns. Thus an examination of rereading is one way of envisioning the full potential of hospitality in our encounter with the Other, both as writer and reader, teacher and student.

READING, WRITING, AND DESIRE

Arundhati Roy (1997) observes in *The God of Small Things* that "Great Stories" are the ones we have heard and want to hear again, "the ones you can enter anywhere and inhabit comfortably" (218). Even chronic rereaders like myself will admit that not every story, not every novel, entices the reader back. I return to certain novels because I feel comfortable there. I feel welcome. They comprise a world where I want to be. They capture a truth about life, about the human heart, that resonates with me. That truth is complex enough to require repeated study and extensive exposure beyond an initial reading. But such labor is rewarded; here is meaning that I not only assent to but embrace in how I live.

Critic Peter Brooks (1984) has argued that the act of reading is a form of *desire*, a passion both *for* meaning and *of* meaning (19, 37). Certainly there are echoes of Levinas here: the self's desire for the Other, for something or someone outside myself who opens a door, who releases me from my personal limitations, experiences, and perspectives. But I would go a step further. Both reading and authoring rest upon *the same desire for meaning*. That is, in the act of writing, the author discovers something about life and the human condition. That discovery is then offered to the reader, who (it is hoped) shares the same hunger.

With the lens of hospitality, we have seen that the initial writer-reader encounter involves a gift. But what exactly is given when author and reader meet? Is the gift the text itself? It might seem so. But how then could readers ever reciprocate? We can welcome the message and insights of the author, and in that sense host the text. But this is certainly an asymmetrical encounter that cannot change. More important, if the text is the gift, then the text—by itself—is the end point of the host-guest relationship and not, instead, the potential interchange of author and reader that the text makes possible. This may satisfy some writers who know before page 1 what it is they mean to say and don't allow the message to change in the process of telling the story.[2] Nor do they allow the promise of a reader to become a formative influence in what and how they write. By contrast, in a hospitable encounter the author makes a place for the reader, has the reader in mind during the process of creating the text, so that the presence of the reader—the prospect of the stranger—directly impacts the substance of the novel.

What if we think of the text not as a gift but as a path created by the author? Free entry onto the path is the hospitable act, the gesture whereby author (as host) invites the reader (as guest) to engage, reflect, enjoy, grieve, affirm. For the author, following the path has to be more personal, hidden, and utterly human: the need to create a story in the first place, the desire for meaning that prompts discovery—in the act of writing—of something fundamentally true about human experience, often at great cost, but a cost the author is willing to pay. The authoring, then, is indisputably singular. The accompanying reading is similarly singular. The intersection of these singular acts—authoring and reading—promises the potential of a unique interaction, of two companions traveling together, that cannot be duplicated, predicted, or formulated.

That intersection is not something that can always happen in a first encounter. It may require many renewed meetings extended over a long time. By way of illustration, I turn to two authors: Michael Ondaatje and J. R. R. Tolkien. It is first necessary to examine what these writers say about their process of authoring, and later discuss the kind of relationship they seek with readers. In the cases of both Ondaatje and Tolkien, the act of authoring is intense, personal, protracted, and (it may seem) exclusionary. But as we will discover, the reader in fact plays an important role in their writing processes.

Ondaatje says that he became a writer because he loves to read. "'There's nothing I like so much as to disappear into a book, or with a book,'" he told John Stone (quoted in Stone 1996, 258). Ondaatje's enjoyment of "disappearing into a book"—whether reading one or writing one—stems, in part, from an appetite for travel through "discovery." Don't readers open a book to follow a story line, or meet new characters, or consider a unique perspective? We *expect* to sniff out something placed there, something made possible by another's imagination. In the same way, Ondaatje sets out to discover plot, character, and theme in the act of writing.

In *The English Patient*, for example, the reader is involved in a quest to discover the truths about Hana and her patient. Ondaatje (1992) offers two whole and intuitively graspable images. One is of a man on fire, falling out of the sky, the other an image of a woman catching rainwater in her cupped hands. They may be immediately accessible, but what is the story behind these images or, better put, what is the story within which the images cohere? How did the man come to fall out of the sky? Who is this woman who loves water, and how is it that she enjoys this moment of pleasure and tranquility? What is the connection of one image to the other? What is her connection with the man? It might seem that readers can answer such questions simply enough: through an initial, one-time-only knowledge of the plot. But knowledge and understanding are quite different things.

For Ondaatje, the initial images—the man on fire, the woman who loves water—cannot be explained by a simple plot outline. It isn't what happens that defines the characters. Rather, this mysterious man and woman determine what happens. "When I write a book," Ondaatje told actor Willem Dafoe, "I'm sitting down to discover what the story is, as opposed to telling the story. I don't have that story yet" (quoted in Dafoe 1997, 19). Ondaatje doesn't know Hana or the patient but discovers his characters "in the actual act of writing, in the actual scene of writing" (quoted in Stone 1996, 248). The desire for meaning, in this case, leads first to discovery and only later to expression and communication.

Once Ondaatje learns more and more about his characters, the original path his story might have followed changes direction. *The English Patient* at first included only Hana and the patient. Ondaatje (1992) had no idea "it was going to be Kip's story or Caravaggio's story or Katharine's story. It was the patient and Hana; I thought that was the book" (254). In fact, the characters took on a life of their own, developing personalities apart from the author.[3] But what happens *to* the characters pales in comparison to what happens *between* characters and author. "The book is more a debate, a meditation between characters and with the author," Ondaatje explained to Maya Jaggi about *The English Patient* (quoted in Jaggi 2000, 11). That is, Ondaatje creates texts to engage in an argument *through* his characters, *with* himself. "That's why you're writing the book. It's why you create characters; so you can argue with yourself." Argue about what? "It's not an abstract discussion," Ondaatje told David Welch. "The issue is what these characters or anyone, will do *with the truth*" (quoted in Welch 2006; emphasis added).

I will have more to say about the truth in Ondaatje's novel in a moment. Here the important point is that Ondaatje writes to discover something about himself that may have been there all along but needed these particular characters to reveal. Or perhaps these characters evoked something new in the author, changed him, because of their experience and perspective. Ondaatje himself looks, as does Hana, "upon books as the only door out of [his] cell" (Ondaatje 1992, 7).

We might say, then, that for Ondaatje the process of authoring is a self-directed act. It draws him into a new place, face-to-face with characters he has not met but will become intimate with in order to speak convincingly as those characters. Entering into those Others enlarges him. "Once you get the voice, you're saying what you know, and after that you start saying what you don't know" (quoted in M. Moore 1994).[4] The act of authoring, in essence, places Ondaatje on the threshold—at home, knowing who he is, confident of what he knows—then beckons him to cross into the foreign, the new, the strange, and be changed through that experience.

J. R. R. Tolkien confessed that he was compelled to write, "driven to it by the scarcity of literature of the sort that I wanted to read" (1981, 211). But his creative urge went far deeper, as he wrote to fellow Inkling C. S. Lewis: "I have something I deeply desire to *make*" (126). Human beings, as images of God, yearn to create in their own right and in their own image. As "subcreator," an artist's personality is always evident in the subcreation (Tolkien 1966, 68, 87). In its final form, *The Lord of the Rings* had become, in Tolkien's words, "a monster . . . immensely long, complex, rather bitter, and very terrifying, quite unfit for children" (1981, 136).

Tolkien's preferred genre—fairy stories or fantasy—works like a dream "that some other mind is weaving" (Tolkien 1966, 72). The "bones" of that dream in his "Cauldron of Story" are independent invention; "inheritance," or borrowing in time; and "diffusion," or borrowing in space (47). A substantial aspect of his borrowing occurred as Tolkien developed the various languages of Middle Earth (Quenyan, Sindarin, and so on) from his study of Finnish, Welsh, Icelandic, Gothic, West Midlands, Anglo-Saxon, and Middle English as well as Greek, Latin, and French. Language, Tolkien wrote, "affects me emotionally like colour or music" (1981, 212). What kind of species would speak Quenyan, he wondered. How would Sindarin shape perspectives and behavior? What does the Black Speech reveal about the character of its utterer? The characters and story line emerged gradually as Tolkien created worlds of the Perilous Realm "in which my expressions of linguistic taste could have a function" (214; see also 219).

As in Ondaatje's experience, Tolkien's writing process is one of discovery. His characters lead him in unforeseen directions. As the hobbits reach Bree, Tolkien "met a lot of things on the way that astonished me . . . Strider sitting in the corner at the inn was a shock, and I had no more idea who he was than had Frodo . . . Fanghorn Forest was an unforeseen adventure" (1981, 216). Most disquieting of all, Tolkien observes, was the treachery of Saruman. "I was as mystified as Frodo at Gandalf's failure to appear on September 22" (217). In fact the characters—their choices and their actions—create a momentum of their own, so much so that the events on Mount Doom were "unforeseen" to Tolkien, who had sketched earlier trial versions but never used them (325). Like Ondaatje, then, Tolkien discovered characters, events, and consequences of actions *with* and *through* his characters.[5]

It might seem from this discussion of process that these authors work solo. But this is not the case. Although it is self-directed, authoring is not self-contained. The author's path to discovery during the early stage of the writing process is like the reader's first entry into a novel. We want to find out who these characters are (where they came from, what their names are), then what happens to them. But a deeper understanding requires much labor from the writer as the novel proceeds. Clearly, Ondaatje and Tolkien have to spend a long time getting to know their characters before those characters can speak for themselves. If we think about the primary encounter not between writer and reader but between writer and character, the acquaintance of Ondaatje and Tolkien with their books goes beyond hospitality to friendship and deep understanding. In fact, after long years of production, Tolkien came to appreciate "the pain that may enter into authorship" (1981, 126).

The result? Ondaatje and Tolkien have written books that ask for more than hospitality on the part of the reader, something akin to long-term engagement, even companionship. That takes rereading.

THE ANTICIPATED READER

Once Ondaatje's own discoveries are realized, another presence makes demands on him. "I think about the reader a lot, but later on . . . when I'm editing . . . I turn myself into the reader" (quoted in Stone 1996, 249). And what does a reader experience? Ondaatje thinks of reading as a journey, and he depicts that journey through his character Hana Lewis in *The English Patient*. Hana falls "upon books as the only door out of her cell. They became half her world. She sat at the night table, hunched over, reading of the young boy in India," the boy seeking the solution to a "tremendous puzzle" (Ondaatje 1992, 7, 111). Hana doesn't read the pages of *Kim,* or of *The Charterhouse of Parma, Anna Karenina, The*

Last of the Mohicans, and *Lorna Doone,* but rather enters them. Books act as hospitable doorways, beyond which "Parma and Paris and India spread their carpets" (93). Once she enters those geographic spaces in her imagination, she feels immersed in the lives of others. In the same way, readers of *The English Patient* are invited into the novel. We walk through Ondaatje's doorway into the desert of North Africa, the Italian landscape, the asylum at San Girolamo where each refugee is welcomed with hospitable graciousness.

In their own journey, readers encounter the main characters as they are caught up in the public sphere: the carnage of war and the politics of nation-states. But there is the private drama as well—Hana's grief for her father, the patient's lost love, Caravaggio's maimed hands, Kip's disillusionment with the West after the bombing of Hiroshima. Readers committed to entering the text and receiving the gift of the author over the long-term place themselves in the characters' situations. What will *we* do with the truth?

Such a truth certainly bears the imprint of the author. The encounter of readers and writers is a real one for Ondaatje. "I believe books are communal acts," he told Maya Jaggi. "That's how you can escape into something that is not you when you are writing. It is when you become more than yourself; speak from a different perspective" (quoted in Jaggi 2000, 9). Self and Other meet. It is as if writer and reader meet at Caravaggio's moon dial, a place of magic, of safety, of suspended time. But that moon dial is communal at its core (Ondaatje 1992, 261).

In the "narrative folds" of *The Lord of the Rings,* Tolkien realized, are caught up "visions of most of the things that I have most loved or hated" (1981, 257). Something of his own reflections and values "inevitably get worked in" to a novel (233). Yet he also admitted: "No one can really write or make anything purely privately" (211), for "solitary art is no art" (122). The truth must be offered to someone else. During the composition of *The Lord of the Rings,* Tolkien did not envision his "reader" in the abstract, some future stranger-guest still unknown to him. He wrote to close family and friends, with his son Christopher "most in mind" (103). But there were also his fellow Inklings—C. S. Lewis in particular—who listened to early drafts and provided for Tolkien immediate (and positive) feedback. Such "recognition," some level of understanding, was for him an "essential part of authorship" (128). Real readers. Real rereaders.

After working "alone in a corner," with only the input "of a few like-minded friends," Tolkien sought a wider audience of fresh minds that could validate "any wider value" of his legendarium (Tolkien 1981, 135).

In his foreword to *The Fellowship of the Ring*, Tolkien remarks: "The prime motive was the desire of a tale-teller to try his hand at a really long story that would hold the attention of readers, amuse them, delight them, and at times maybe excite them or deeply move them" (ix). What would he offer those readers? That which pleases him—his mind, heart, and conscience: "only my own feelings" (ix).

Those feelings comprised a secondary world that readers can enter (Tolkien 1966, 60). Both "designer and spectator" can be equally enchanted (73). In fact the term *spell* means both "a formula of power over living men" and "a story told" (55). Tolkien believed that fairy stories are concerned not primarily with possibility but rather with desirability. If they awaken desire, "satisfying it while often whetting it unbearably," they succeed (63). Desire for what? Desire for other creatures, "Other-worlds" (64), and perhaps for places that we make our own over time.

As a writer of fairy stories, Tolkien consciously offered his readers four things: fantasy or the magical in nature, escape, recovery, and consolation (Tolkien 1966, 67). Fantasy allows us to enter into a secondary world that produces "an alteration in the Primary World" (73). "Uncorrupted," Tolkien explains, fantasy "does not seek delusion or bewitchment and domination; it seeks shared enrichment, partners in making and delight" (74). We need to escape from the weariness of triteness and familiarity, from the factual as given and never resisted or renewed, from the appetite of possessiveness and appropriation, from a sense that the given is inevitable (77, 80). Once we escape, we can recover a "clear view" of things as not of our making, our possession, our extension. Things are "apart from ourselves" (77)—are Other, as Levinas would say.

It might be possible for an attentive reader to appreciate the possibilities of escape through the magical in an initial reading, that is, in a hospitable encounter. But Tolkien offers more gifts. After escape comes recovery. We can recover the world of other beings that we have set ourselves outside of, have made war upon (Tolkien 1966, 84). Then we are open to consolation, to the "eucatastrophe" of the Happy Ending—that joyous turn in fantasy that is "beyond the walls of the world" because it brings us to a vision of "underlying reality or truth" (86). Recovery and consolation, I would argue, are the fruits of deep and prolonged engagement.

While Tolkien drew comparisons between Europe's "dark age" of the 1930s and 1940s, "in which the technique of torture and disruption of personality [rivaled] that of Mordor" (Tolkien 1981, 234), he insisted that his legendarium should not be understood as an allegory. "I have no didactic purpose, no allegorical intent" (298). Why not, given his decidedly moral focus? One reason is that allegory reduces characters to types, and Tolkien wanted his characters to exhibit the "incalculable element in any individual real or imagined" (233).

The second reason that Tolkien disliked allegory is the kind of relationship the author necessarily forces upon the reader. While many aspects of his subcreation might prove applicable to events of the 1930s and 1940s, applicability cannot be confused with allegory. The first "resides in the freedom of the reader, and the other in the purposed domination of the author" (Tolkien 1970, xi). He wanted his readers to be "partners" rather than "slaves" to how things in the world appear to be (53, 55). Readers, too, have a place in Middle Earth—a free place Tolkien called partnership—a role that involves more than just passing through.

To judge from Ondaatje and Tolkien, authoring is not for the faint of heart. It begins with an act of hospitality, which is risky enough, but it bears that risk far beyond, sometimes for years. That is true for both author and reader. Authoring requires a desire to leave the comfort and familiarity of reality and embark on a journey into a new place, with new companions—characters and readers—who are inscribed by the place yet also shape it. As Ondaatje observes: "Writers themselves are immigrants; every time you write a new novel you're coming to another place" (quoted in Jaggi 2000, 10). The full *potential* of authoring cannot be realized apart from the reader, who creates and delights with a writer such as Tolkien and who wonders with a writer such as Ondaatje about what he or she will do with the truth.

A REREADER'S RESPONSE

At some point in the creative process, these authors consciously prepared for their readers—strangers who would soon be guests, guests welcomed, respected, anticipated, needed, challenged—guests who would, the authors hope, accept with goodwill the proffered gift. But what if the guest returns again and again, or camps out, refusing to leave?

I may be one of the few readers who in the act of reading broke their neck. One summer I spent pouring over Yeatsian criticism for my dissertation. My head was bent over a book so many hours of the day that I ruptured a disk in my neck. Three surgeries later, I often tell my students that reading is a hazardous undertaking. Perilous, to use Tolkien's term. But the physical risks pale in comparison to the psychological, moral, and emotional consequences. If reading entails entering another's world, another's subcreation, then there is always a chance that readers can find themselves in a place that is uncomfortable, unwelcoming, disruptive, antithetical in terms of values. I choose not to reenter such texts, and hope that their vestiges will not linger.

I've come to think of academic life as contemplative, not in the sense of withdrawn or isolated, but in the sense of wanting to enter, to allow into my life the kinds of worlds I want to be influenced by, the kinds of ideas and views that nourish who I am and who I want to become. Once I feel that I belong in a novel, I can never leave it behind but choose to return to it again and again. Rich responds quite differently, rarely rereading even a novel he thoroughly admires. "There is so much more to read," he says. Tolkien admitted that he seldom read a work twice: "Nothing, not even a (possible) deeper appreciation, for me replaces the bloom on a book, the freshness of the unread" (Tolkien 1981, 249).

True. But I don't feel that I am losing out on potential hospitable encounters with other authors. Instead, I feel privileged to cultivate a long-term relationship with an author or a novel that (paradoxically) ensures I am never "fully in balance" (Ondaatje 1992, 93). That is, the truth that they offer is substantive enough, deep enough, *human* enough, that every reading provides something both new and familiar. In such a relationship, the writer and reader no longer are strangers and thus fall out of the host-guest paradigm. What the writer thought of as potential or future readers gives way to readers who can prove, as Tolkien realized, "a constant source of consolation and pleasure" (Tolkien 1981, 221).

As a writer-reader relationship develops over time, the gift still remains: the singular message via the text, a "truth" and the challenge to do something with it (harking back to Ondaatje's reflection). Perhaps it will help to think of the gift as what Wolfgang Iser calls the fictive, or the bridge between the imaginary and the real. The imaginary is "a featureless and inactive potential" (1993, xvii). The real is the given world and seems immoveable, unnegotiable—the reality of facts, of politics, of bombs, of rings of power and desire to dominate. The fictive for Iser is "an operational mode of consciousness that makes inroads into existing versions of the world. In this way, the fictive becomes an act of boundary-crossing [that] simultaneously disrupts and doubts the referential world" (xiv–xv). Rooted in the imaginary but far more potent, the fictive is the first step to assessing and amending the world.

Disrupting the totality of the referential world, infinitely crossing boundaries between what is and what might be, the fictive brings authors in touch with themselves, readers in touch with authors and, finally, readers in touch with themselves. The fictive, in Iser's terms, allows us to "lead an ecstatic life by stepping out of what we are caught up in, in order to open up for ourselves what we are otherwise barred from" (1993, 303).

Let's return now to Ondaatje's claim: "The issue is what these characters or anyone, will do *with the truth*." Anyone—author, character, reader. In the case of *The English Patient*, Ondaatje examines what motivates one person to care for another, how love can transform but also oppress, how nations can erase the presence and importance of individuals. He also tells of the transitory nature of happiness, the hazards of detachment, and the kind of love that stays in the heart forever. Tolkien writes about the power of will and the desire to dominate the Other (the essence of evil). But his primary themes are death and mortality: "the mystery of the love of the world in the hearts of a race 'doomed' to leave and seemingly lose it; the anguish in the hearts of a race 'doomed' not to leave it, until its whole evil-aroused story is complete" (Tolkien 1981, 246).

Both Tolkien and Ondaatje have carved out unique landscapes for their readers, raising fundamental questions, delving into the human heart and challenging behavior and assumptions that pervade their time. Once they have offered their gift, *they* move on. Is the debate that drives *The English Patient* different from *In the Skin of the Lion* or *Anil's Ghost?* Probably not, Ondaatje believes. His art is one long, interwoven, interior dialogue. "Each book is a rewriting of what you didn't quite get to in the previous book" (quoted in Dafoe 1997, 16). But there is always another, always *must* be another. In Tolkien's case, once he completed *The Lord of the Rings*, he felt he had finally "'exorcized'" his fantasy world through decades of labor (Tolkien 1981, 137). But of course his last years involved revising his true love, *The Silmarillion*—the story of the First and Second Ages—for publication.

Even though Tolkien moved on, he left something of himself behind. In commentary to one of the later drafts of *The Silmarillion*, Tolkien (1977) described "the mystery of 'authorship'": "by which the author, while remaining 'outside' and independent of his work, also 'indwells' in it, on its derivative plan, below that of his own being, as the source and guarantee of its being" (Devaux 2007, 105). Thus those readers whose hearts are hungry for "eucatastrophe" will find that hunger appeased in *The Lord of the Rings*. Other readers, "wholly devoted to machines," will not find Tolkien's subcreation to their taste (Tolkien 1981, 122).

Such an indwelling is one of the most mysterious and alluring aspects of a novel ripe for rereading. I have talked about rereading as a choice on the part of the reader, an invitation on the part of the writer. On occasion, we can even encounter a kind of challenge from the writer, a situation wherein a conclusion cannot be understood without rereading. An example would be the closing pages of Arundhati Roy's *The God of Small Things*. Why does Roy end her novel with Velutha and Ammu together on their first of fourteen nights of love making? Readers have known for many pages about this illicit alliance between the Untouchable Velutha and Ammu, the twins' mother. It is anticlimactic in terms of Sophie Mol's drowning, Baby Kochamma's conniving, or the events of the Terror. It is an episode that belongs neither to the twins' memories (for it is a scene they never witnessed) nor to the present telling moment. It isn't even the bridge that joins past and present. Still, Roy shows us the first of a handful of nights when this "luminous woman" opens herself to a "luminous man" (Roy 1997, 318). They can leave each other only with the promise of "tomorrow." But too quickly a tomorrow will bring "smashed smiles." That is their future—the Terror. Readers know this full well. The twins, once an "I" and "we," will be violently divided, with Estha returned to his father and Rahel separated from her mother. Ammu will be thrown out on the streets, Velutha beaten to death, and Estha forced to falsely accuse him. The final scene is itself a kind of rereading, a going back and in the preceding action finding one particular moment that lasts.

The key to the last scene comes earlier in the novel when the three children (Estha, Rahel and cousin Sophie Mol) visit Velutha's home. They have dressed up as "real ladies" in saris with kohl around their eyes, introducing themselves as Mrs. Pillai, Mrs. Eapen, and Mrs. Rajagopalan. Velutha graciously addresses them as Kochamma, gives them a tour of the hut, and chats with them about the weather. As an adult, Rahel realizes the "sweetness" of Velutha's gesture: "A grown man entertaining three raccoons . . . instinctively colluding in the conspiracy of their fiction." It is so easy to shatter a story, the narrator reflects, so easy to ruin a dream. "To let it be, to travel with it, as Velutha did, is much the harder thing to do" (Roy 1997, 181).

In the same way, Roy as author has elected not to shatter the dream. It is her *gift* to the reader, allowing us to remain at the end of the novel in the one tranquil, joyous moment of love freely given and reciprocated—love unmeasured, uncalculated, unforbidden, unrestrained—the only love of its kind in this novel otherwise depicting a world that determines who will be loved and how much. We might call it Roy's "conspiracy of fiction," her choice to prolong this fragile moment so that we can run our hands across these last pages, go back and forth over the scene, sit beside these still waters.

BEYOND HOSPITALITY IN THE CLASSROOM

Understanding the nature of the gift and the potential for a deeper-than-hospitable relationship can radically alter our approach to working with students. Among the authorial virtues of hospitality are risk taking, openness, curiosity, compassion, and turn to the Other. Among the authorial virtues beyond hospitality are challenge, exploration, perseverance, renewal, consolation, and friendship with the Other. If in teaching authoring we tend to neglect the first set, the second set seems to lie totally outside our pedagogical imagination. We tend to teach students how to write and read; we don't teach them how to author or to reread. To travel with a reader or an author is a choice one makes, and makes often, if one is an avid writer or habitual rereader. But teachers of English are unwilling to travel with their students and extend the "unconscious courtesy of strangers." Evidence of this sad truth has recurred again and again in previous pages. As we said in *Authoring* (Haswell and Haswell 2010), teachers and student do not normally look beyond the last day of the course.

How would our expectations change if we responded to our students as authors, not just as readers or writers, if we involved them in the act of authoring, not just in the "reading or writing process"? Reading, of course, involves authoring, as literacy studies have shown for decades. Consider just writing as authoring. First, we would expect that our students would begin with an image or idea (or situation, action, person, problem), then develop (through exploration) and discover (through joining experience, memory, and imagination) the potential that such an image or idea promises. Second, we would expect that the meaning that emerges from the image or idea is singular to the author, rooted in his or her knowledge, experience, needs, and ongoing, interior dialogue about the truths of our human condition. We would also expect that such meaning carries the imprint of the characters or persons, situations, notions, time and place unique to *this* particular text. Third, and perhaps most important, we would understand that the student has not written a text as if filling the private pages of a diary. Instead, the student has authored a text with the promise of a reader in mind, a coauthor and codesirer who will seek and make meaning of the text, reread months or even years later with pleasure, and may remain influenced by that text for years into the future.

It is chancy, this act of authoring, for it does not exist in a solipsistic world. Authors are drawn out of themselves because they are not the only meaning maker of their text. At the same time, they assume tremendous responsibility—to welcome each reader who comes to their threshold and to maintain that welcome as long as their writing is read and reread. In return, they have the singular pleasure of being gift givers to their readers.

What author would not desire that?

Notes

1. My choice of authors is somewhat arbitrary. I could also use material from Paul Scott, W. B. Yeats, John Gardner, Graham Swift, and many others who are subject to my constant rereading. Ondaatje and Tolkien are typical in this case rather than distinctive.

2. John Gardner calls this form of fiction "propaganda." Serious writers who insist on operating this way can turn out "first-class propaganda." Cited from the papers of John Gardner housed at the University of Rochester, box 49b, folder 31.

3. Ondaatje also discovers the structure of his novels in the process of writing. He insists that he has no plan in mind. "These things are discovered in the actual writing . . . If I had it planned beforehand, why would I bother executing it?" But once the characters come to life, their perspectives not only shape the story line but dictate the structure. "The perceptions and ironies double and triple and quadruple. You're getting everyone's point of view at the same time, which for me, is the perfect state for a novel, a cubist state, the cubist novel" (quoted in Welch 2006).

4. Specifically, Ondaatje is speaking of the English patient's ideas about nationhood. "There was stuff said about nations that I had never imagined before. It's absolutely thrilling. Like putting two and two together and getting six" (quoted in M. Moore 1994).

5. "I have long ceased to invent," Tolkien wrote to an admiring reader in 1956. "I wait till I seem to know what really happened. Or till it writes itself. Thus, though I knew for years that Frodo would run into a tree-adventure somewhere far down the Great River, I have no recollection of inventing Ents. I came at last to the point, and wrote the 'Treebeard' chapter without any recollection of any previous thought: just as it now is. And then I saw that, of course, it had not happened to Frodo at all" (Tolkien 1981, 231).

10

TROPES OF LEARNING CHANGE

It's not about empty minds waiting to be filled, nor about flatulent
teachers discharging hot air. It's about the opposition of teacher and stu-
dent. It's about what gets rubbed off between the persistence of the one
and the resistance of the other. A long, hard struggle against a natural
resistance. Needs a lot of phlegm. I don't believe in quick results, in
wand-waving and wonder-working . . . But I do believe in education.
                                                              —Graham Swift

In his 2006 Nobel lecture, novelist Orhan Pamuk (2006) offers a mixture of reasons why he writes. At first reading, one of his motives is a
touch startling: "I write because I like to be read." Well, who doesn't? Yet
imagine the range of ways this motive can be appeased: showing your
draft to a friend, sending copies of your poem around a writers' group,
e-mailing your article to a colleague, checking how many libraries have
bought your book, looking for marks that your teacher has put on your
paper. Writing this paragraph?

In these final two chapters we reaffirm hospitality as one way that
writers who like to be read can be made happy and readers who like to
appreciate writers can do so. As the previous two chapters testify, hospitality as a social praxis supporting the act of writing and reading may fail
or may not last long. But the failure of hospitality may open the way to
success, and its natural transience may transform into something more
permanent. After all, Rich did eventually write his essay on Vargos Llosa,
in the form of chapter 8, and Jan has changed from a guest to a permanent resident in many a book over the years. Furthermore, as we will see
in this chapter and the next, hospitality can assume more lasting forms,
ones that will easily hold for an academic course and beyond.

The persistence of hospitality as a trope for learning we will take up
in this chapter. Chapter 11 will explore its lasting presence in physical space. Students resist and teachers persist, says Graham Swift, and
between the two learning sometimes happens. Hospitality affords a location for the persistence of teachers that also accommodates, amiably and
easily, the resistance of students.

DOI: 10.7330/9780874219883.c010

LEARNING CHANGE AND ITS TROPES

For outsiders to the professional field of biology, Leah Ceccarelli (2004) offers a Homeric catalogue of metaphors used by science writers to describe the human genome system: "a legacy one carries of disease, heirlooms, the mother lode, gems, low-hanging fruit, hieroglyphs, words, text, books in a library, an instruction book, a recipe, a blueprint, order forms, coded instructions for manufacture and operation, software code, building blocks, a toolbox, pieces of a kit, defective parts, workers dispatching order forms, slaves, immigrants, alien parasites, triggers, territory to be mapped, malfunctioning machines, and life itself" (93). The list on its own offers insights into the dynamics of biological study. For instance, it betrays contradictions in the implied attitude of genetics writers toward their topic. Is the sought-for genome treasure or trickery?

Over the last half century, professionals in composition studies have set forth a similar feast of root metaphors to describe the dynamics underlying the teaching of writing:

Table 10.1

banking money	getting over the hump
battling the Goths	governing the masses
being a handmaid	handling a crisis
being married	instrumenting voice
bridging a chasm	investing capital
bringing into the fold	keeping a family functional
building a barn together	keeping physically fit
claiming ownership	liberating the enslaved
climbing a ladder	maintaining a conversation
coaching athletes	mapping a terrain
conducting a symphony	negotiating a contract
constructing a net	offering physical therapy
consuming goods	offering psychotherapy
controlling the violence	parenting
corralling the kids	rehabilitating the maimed
crossing a border	saving the pagans
curing maladies	taking physical risks

continued on next page

Table 10.1—*continued*

dancing socially	tending a garden
directing actors	tending a plant
discovering riches	training the troops
exploring space	traveling together
extracting the ore	unclogging the pipeline

We could cull a comparable list from discussions of teaching literature over the same decades, with many of the same metaphors.

We are not proposing any parallel between biological gene structure and English classroom structure. Nor are we questioning the length of the composition-instruction list, since each trope casts its distinctive light. Note that in Table 10.1, where these metaphors of English instruction include two or more people, one of the persons is pictured as in control. The alpha member is always the teacher, seen as leading the troops, shepherding the flock, conducting the musicians, counseling the disturbed, healing the sick, directing the barn building, tending the garden plants, liberating the oppressed, and so forth. In only three tropes is the English classroom imaged through two people of equal status: marriage partners, traveling companions and, debatably, social dancers.

To that small cluster we have proposed a fourth pair: host and guest. We are proposing hospitality—traditional hospitality, where host and guest are equals—as an alternative metaphor of teacher-student dynamics in literature and writing courses. Of course, as we note in chapter 3, hospitality in the English classroom serves as social praxis as well as metaphor, a point to which we will return in the next chapter.

In this chapter we will focus on disciplinary metaphors of change. We modestly argue that as an image for educational change, hospitality serves better than a number of established English-discipline images. The argument may not seem trivial, however, when the consequences are considered. For example, one of the results of instituting hospitality in the English classroom is an increase in enjoyment. The connection of change, teaching, and joy isn't so surprising when we remember a larger relationship, that of change to learning itself. True learning, no different from true hospitality, entails change. True learning—that is, learning that stays learned—is accompanied by the most basic motivation of humans, what in the 1800 Preface to *Lyrical Ballads* Wordsworth (1800, 255) called "the grand elementary principle of pleasure." "Only in enjoyment," agrees Levinas (1969), "does the I crystallize" (144). You can always tell when people are learning. They are happy. This applies as much to teachers as to students. Hence there is an educational maxim that has stayed learned with us. Are you unhappy? Learn something. Or teach somebody.

IMAGES OF CHANGE

The five traditional images of educational change we want to critique are *clearing the hurdles, crossing the border, climbing the ladder, marking the door frame,* and *learning the ropes.* Doubtless, these images of change cross over into the discourse of assessment and accreditation, a discourse that saturates institutions of higher education. We will not address the tropes of student learning outcomes here or of other measurable acts that attract some educational assessors because they are so reductive and simplistic. The images we address are common metaphoric ways of depicting learning and, as familiar and unselfconscious as they may seem, promise insights into how courses, programs, and curricula in general might operate.

All of these images are somewhat dysfunctional, though in different ways. For each one, we offer a counter-story, a real-world tale of educational change that doesn't fit the common image and thus puts it into question, paving the way, we hope, for a better image: teacher and student, host and guest, *welcoming the stranger.*

Let's begin with *clearing the hurdles.* Meet the challenges one at a time, do the assignments on schedule, work your way through the required courses—here is a common educational narrative. It stresses linearity. It tells students that you learn by passing an assignment or course or test so you can go on to study for the next assignment, next course, next test. It underpins the academic system of prerequisites and the lockstep curriculum of many majors.

But do people best learn in a straight line? Carolina sits in Jan's office, crying. She is a senior and dropping out of college. Her parents had wanted her to become a registered nurse, had paid her college tuition on the condition that she do well in the prenursing program. And she had done well, passing each course with an A or a B. But by her sophomore year she had known that the program was not for her. She just couldn't find good reasons to drop out of it. Each academic success seemed to lead only in one direction, the next courses in the curriculum. And the more credits earned, the more motive to carry on. Now she had passed the breaking point, was abandoning college, getting married. She could see the waste and what could she tell her parents?

An archetypal story of clearing the hurdles. Passing tests is, of course, the most widespread and institutionalized register of change in education. If to the many institution-mandated barrier examinations across the nation we add the thousands of course tests given every day in our classrooms, we are not surprised when we hear students talk about "getting done with courses" or "getting through" requirements rather than learning from them.

The fact is that getting over hurdles just does not fit any natural act or process of learning. Hurdle requirements work against learning because they dismiss things already learned. Once cleared, the hurdle is forgotten in the need to focus on the next hurdle. The process is not about learning—true learning—but about coping. Students know this. For several years Rich and colleague Glenn Blalock gathered opinions from first-year students at Texas A&M University–Corpus Christi about the Texas state-mandated TAAS testing.[1] The students had passed this barrier exam in their sophomore or junior year of high school. Three years later, over 80 percent of them express negative feelings about that particular set of hurdles. The most common comment is that it was "a waste of time," that the students had already learned what was tested so that preparation for the test *kept* them from learning new material. "My results were good," one student related. "I was distinguished and above average, and I guess I was finally smart enough to proceed to another grade, but I wonder—they couldn't have determined that a long time ago?"

Hurdle requirements also work against natural learning because they prematurely set in place the hurdles ahead. But no one knows, neither the teacher nor the learner, what the next best step in a learning process will be. As Alfred North Whitehead (1967) long ago said about education, in human learning antecedents are set but subsequences are free. "We know what we are, but we know not what we may be," says not-so-mad Ophelia. As we will see, Ophelia's line refers directly to the act of traditional hospitality, where host and guest willingly make sure they do not know what they may learn from their encounter.

This positive experience of passing over or passing through is also an element of our second image of educational change, *crossing the border*. We all know the trope. It's in our educator bones. Students travel through the curriculum as through a series of bordering countries, with rites of passage at the borders. We tell them, "You have to *get through* freshman composition before you will be *allowed into* technical and professional writing." The central point of change, of course, is situated at the border, where your papers are checked: "Yes," the registrar says, "you are qualified to *enter* journalism."

So what is counter-educational about this image of change? The main problem is that usually in English departments it doesn't live up to its billing. Promised is a qualitative transformation from one state, old and familiar, to a new state, new and exciting. Actually experienced is a time-consuming ritual that documents a student passing from one educational status to another not much different. The literature courses the student takes after officially being accepted as an English major are not much different than the ones taken before. The GRE exam is costly and stressful but it transfers the student into graduate courses not instructionally different from undergraduate English courses, and sometimes with undergraduates enrolled in them. Victor Turner (1969), scholar of social rituals, would call these humdrum border crossings "status reversing." There may be a threshold moment when novices feel elevated to a new level, but that is quickly reversed and the novices find themselves returned to their previous state. On Halloween night kids can pretend to be adults, but the next day they are kids again. Compare what Turner calls "status-elevating" rituals, such as confirmations or weddings, where mentors prepare applicants for a novel public test that, passed successfully, places them in a permanent higher social or spiritual world.

In Texas students studied every year for the TAAS, beginning in the sixth grade. Did the test live up to this five- or six-year preparation? Looking back, the high-school test takers said they found TAAS "eighth-grade stuff." "I went in thinking that I was going to be doomed, that I would completely fail, and when I was handed the test I thought it was a joke." "Anyone with an arm that held a pencil could pass it." Did the students feel any sense of status elevation through the test? The majority expressed little change, pride, or even surprise in the results. "I remember my mom telling me that my scores had come in and I told her, 'OK, what is your point?' And when she told me that I passed and that I did very well, I said, 'Tell me something new.'" TAAS testing is typical of English-department border crossings in later years. In English the only traditional assessment rites that might warrant the term "status elevating" are three, each seemingly in the slow historical process of dying out—the senior project, the MA thesis, and the dissertation.

Now *climbing the ladder*, our third image of change, rejects the notion of border crossing but embraces the notion of status elevation. In college-catalogue lingo that goes back to the nineteenth century, climbing the ladder is "curricular course of study." Courses border each other not like one country abuts another but like one step of a ladder stands above or below another. Supposedly, courses follow a learning sequence—what is learned in the course below prepares the student for the course above. The ladder-climbing trope underlies expressions such as "That course may be too far *above* you," "You are *rising* quickly in the major," "I think you are ready for *upper*-division courses."

Unfortunately, rarely will ladderlike ordering of courses be found in English-department offerings. The departments try. They say first-year composition should precede "advanced" composition—but then many students are successful in the "higher" course without having taken the first one. Departments see British and American surveys as prerequisites to period courses—but how often is that sequence broken? They number courses to create the illusion of movement from first to fourth year—yet how many times has an advisor explained to an overpunctilious student that 300-level courses are not restricted to juniors? On paper such curricular ladders provide a misleading and even dangerous image of change because such laddering doesn't fit the content of the courses. Moreover, it is never going to fit many students. And when it doesn't fit a student, the educational outcome may be worse than if the ladder had never been there.

Mark—tall, blond, with a touch of the saturnine—sat in the back row next to the door of Jan's 200-level Introduction to World Literature classroom. He was an "older student." He had been in the navy, but in order to marry he and his fiancée had been forced to resign since he was an enlistee and she a commissioned officer. One day in the middle of class discussion, Mark gathered his books and walked out of the room. Later he told Jan he couldn't stand hearing eighteen-year-old students assuming that William Blake was a born-again Christian. (Jan replied that if he had been patient he would have heard her say exactly that later in class.) Mark never felt at home in college and dropped out during his second year to take a job that paid him well for his exceptional computer skills.

Mark's tale might seem to confirm ladderlike sequencing in the English curriculum but it does the opposite. He is not the exception that tests the rule but the rule itself. For how many students in a 200-level world literature class, even those nineteen years old, is the course the right one at the right time? Probably not many, given their individual differences in social background, educational preparation, personal history, and learning style. The nineteen-year-old sitting next to Mark might very well have got more pleasure and learned more from a 400-level course in Dostoevsky. Why assume that survey courses are "introductory" and should be taken before period courses? Might English majors learn more about literary history by taking Survey of American Literature as a capstone course for seniors after having taken various period courses such as Colonial Literature and American Modernism?

Sequencing in composition courses is even more arbitrary, since the natural act of composing—circular, recursive, holistic—offers few universal sequences of its own. And were there such sequences, who is to say that the natural act of learning to write should follow them?

English studies just do not have the kind of vertical content that positions algebra before calculus or calculus before astrophysics. The best candidate for establishing verticality in the English curriculum might be cognitive complexity or cognitive maturity, although we know of no college department offerings so organized. Besides, cognitive development itself hardly climbs a tidy ladder. Thoroughly documented is vertical dis-laddering (*décalage*), in the form of backsliding, and horizontal dis-laddering, where new concepts are acquired in connection with one part of a person's life but not with other parts. Teachers all know that the right course at the right time will do wonders for learning that no particular teacher of the course can match. But what is the right time? No doubt the commercial-educational testing complex has erected elaborate ladders for putting students into the "next" or "right" course. The mechanism has machines doing quite a bit of it, in fact. But in whatever course—and it is teachers who are the best ones to judge—how many of the students really belong there, belong there in the sense that they are ready, eager, and pleased to learn what it teaches?

Marking the door frame. A quarter of a century ago, in a piece called "Two Ways of Thinking about Growth," Joseph Williams (1989) described "a model of growth that is map-able onto the door-jam that we use to measure our children's increasing height." Remember the birthday ritual? How many houses still have door frames with annual pencil marks showing a heartwarming regularity of growth? The model is familiar and consoling, a picture of physical change mentally graphed as a "smooth curve," as Williams says (254). The trouble is that as a model for learning change it is false.

Actually, it is false even as a picture of physical growth. Here's an appealing story from science. In 1992, three years after Williams published his essay, Michelle Lampl, a behavioral anthropologist at the University of Pennsylvania, was studying her friend's five-month-old baby. Lampl had attended a physical anthropology conference on bone growth and, on a whim, decided to start measuring the length of the baby. She took two measurements two days apart and was amazed to discover that the baby had grown half an inch. Despite her first assumption that she was just inept at measuring the length of a squirming baby, she persisted, and the results were so astonishing that she set up a formal study with two other scientists. Understand that then the received

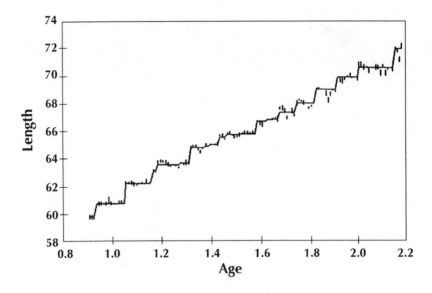

Figure 10.1. Daily measurements of length, from 90 to 218 days of age. For one day, the largest jump is almost three-fourths of an inch (Lampl, Veldhuis, and Johnson 1992, 802). Used by permission.

opinion of doctors and growth experts was that human growth proceeds along Williams's "smooth curve." *Natura non facit saltus*: nature doesn't proceed by jumps. Lampl and her coresearchers measured several babies for a year, some every day, and discovered that nature pays no attention to Latin and in fact does proceed by jumps. At least babies do. Babies would remain the same size for irregular intervals, from two days to two months, and then grow anywhere from a fifth of an inch to a full inch in less than twenty-four hours. Graphed here in figure 10.1 are the daily body length changes in one baby for a period of four months.

The same jerky pattern has now been found elsewhere in biological growth, and is called episodic, discontinuous, punctuated, pulsatile, or saltatory. (The discovery of a new phenomenon seems to generate a competition among scientists to find the most learned or, as Shakespeare would say, inkhorn term.) But here's an additional finding, less well known. For ten years after her discovery, Lampl tried to find a statistical procedure that will locate some regularities in saltatory growth. She used the most sophisticated measurement formulas, such as finite mixed distribution analysis and nonlinear dynamic approximate entropy, and her conclusion, so far, is that "growth patterns are statistically unique and cannot be reconstructed or identified from group data" (Lampl,

Johnson, and Frongillo 2001, 403). Change in body length—and it's as true of eleven-year-olds as of babies—is as singular as fingerprints.

What is true about bone growth probably fits every other aspect of human development. Marked at long intervals, growth may appear to progress in even increments, but in the intervals by which we teach, day to day, week to week, month to month, semester to semester, nothing develops that way. There are idea spurts, understanding spurts, imagination spurts, motivation spurts. Saltation is recorded in detail in the acquisition of every complex skill ever mapped over time. Yet think of the way teachers map out their courses: a row of chapter readings as even as fence posts, a new essay expected every fourth week like the cable bill, a revision due on this Monday, an examination due on that Friday. So far the field of English has largely resisted developmental theory—physical, cognitive, social, emotional—as being too time bound and lockstep. Yet you couldn't have predicted this resistance from the working documents of the trade: for instance, syllabuses posted on the Internet or lists of first-year writing criteria.

What the profession *has* bought into is the second of Joseph Williams's (1989, 254) two ways of thinking about growth, what we call *learning the ropes* and what he, and many after him, calls "socialization into a community of discourse." We are not going to spend much time on this familiar image of change. It's empowering to think of writing teachers showing students the way into the discourse practices of engineering, business, science, and other prestigious academic fields and on into the workplace, where the money is. We will raise just one hand of caution about this image. It concerns the phrase, which falls so easily onto the page, "showing students the way." Is that what we really do? Or is it more like we showing them the water and then someone else throwing them in? "Socialization" is an appealing notion, but how does a teacher help an individual student become socialized into a community of which the teacher is not a member?

Learning the ropes is a metaphor from the days of sailing ships. And the tricky maneuvers by which a skilled sailor ties knots and climbs rigging are learned not through socialization within a group of first-year sailors but through individual mentoring by veteran sailors. In the writing arena, the image of socialization has misled many teachers, including ourselves, into what is called "group work," where we assume apprentices will lead each other into a community of discourse none of them yet belongs to.

That may be harsh. It certainly oversimplifies. But consider the story of Ji, a Korean student in Rich's first-year composition course. She had been in the country for two years. At the beginning of the semester, Ji asked Rich to mark every one of her mistakes in grammar and idiom. He agreed on one condition: that in turn she come to his office every other week and tell him the ways she was using her first language, Korean, to learn English. She agreed. With the third draft of her last paper came an amazing jump in quality. Her topic was cosmetic surgery, and the piece was full of disturbing facts about Asians undergoing face surgery in order to appear more Western; the essay was also full of complex, unresolved thoughts about those facts. Here was the kind of change in writing we want to see in our writing students but rarely do. Rich was curious about how it happened with Ji and, if he had played any part in the process, how he might allow it to happen with other students.

Images of educational change should come to our aid here, but in truth the ones we have so far considered don't deliver much insight. What had happened? Ji laughed and then got embarrassed. "I don't learn much from the peer evaluation," she said, "so I travel to Houston." Houston? Well, that's where her cousin lives, *five* years in the country, a senior at the University of Houston, and they just sat around and talked, in Korean, about the ideas in Ji's second draft. Rich had not played any part. Could this be the true image of change that we call "socialization into a discourse community"—not the way of classroom instruction and group critique but another way, age-old, one-on-one, master and apprentice?

Ji's story of change fits better our last and counterimage of change in learning, *welcoming the stranger*. As we outlined in chapter 1, traditional hospitality is an act of sharing or exchange. The essential principals are just two people, usually strangers, usually unequals in social rank, always equals in personal worth, one on the move and asking for help, the other in residence and offering assistance. In welcoming the stranger, learning is not the primary object, but learning is a customary outcome. Hospitable learning is individualistic, erratic, serendipitous, unpredictable, gratuitous. It is sui generis, outside the pale, or at least outside the syllabus.

That doesn't mean English courses can't be designed to better the chances that hospitable learning will happen in them. Safe space can be found for more open-ended, one-on-one encounters. Teachers can increase office hours and encourage students to drop in, and not only when they have a paper due or a paper to be diagnosed. Assigned readings can be relaxed, allowing room for individual choices. Above all, more work in the course can be not targeted directly at course exams but generously broadcast toward the unknown, seeds tossed toward life beyond the course. Hospitable learning is proleptic, future directed. Since it fits the idiosyncratic, current, and ongoing developmental motives of students and teachers, it is less likely to be forgotten.

Such learning attracts, in part, because it valorizes a condition of being human that our other five images neglect. In a word, that condition is *potentiality*. Potentiality is simply what each of us uniquely *could* become. It is the degree to which subsequences are not entirely dependent upon antecedents. To set subsequences in education is to deny the student traits or capabilities that make a person truly human—creative, free, and singular (see Haswell and Haswell 2010, chapter 2). As Levinas would say, educational subsequence setting puts the individual outside of infinity and inside totality. Potentiality sounds anti-institutional, and it is. For that reason it sounds inconsequential, which it is not. What we have been and what we now are, the actual or nonpotential, can be described, recorded, compared, and acted upon by all those institutions that want to control us, from the IRS to the ACT to the bursar's office. What we might become is precisely what can't be described, recorded, compared, and acted upon, because it is unknowable. Like saltatory growth, it cannot be extracted from group data. As we say, it is outside the syllabus.

It is also outside current trends in education. This has been evident long before Duke's MOOC in first-year writing. For decades our class-rooms have been increasingly shaped for teachers by others to match every image of change except that intrinsic to hospitality. The forces that back testing, ceremony, curriculum, and socialization are going to insist that we keep adding tests, keep hewing to the mandated or legalized syllabus, keep adding more students to our classes, keep carving our grading system in stone, keep surveying our students with outside assessors—keep doing the things that erect barriers against the individual student and the individual teacher together acting as guest and host. Currently, these forces have designed, intentionally or not, the educational apparatus in such a way that the great majority of what we teach, at great labor and with good intentions, is forgotten by students, is never really learned.

Yet hospitable learning, despite this opposition, or maybe because of it, does happen in the classroom. It happens despite the efforts of hard-working teachers to keep it from happening. This is a great contradiction, little noticed. Moments of learning, real learning, learning that lasts, do occur, but those moments sometimes happen beyond the intentions of the teacher, outside the syllabus, beyond the parameters of the tests or the assignments in reading and writing. A first-year composition student dislikes topic A taken from an anthology of readings and deliberately writes on topic B, which means he has to study an essay not assigned. A junior sees a book that her parents have mentioned on the shelves of her teacher's office, borrows it, reads it. A graduate student mishears an assignment on Theodor Reik's theories of the unconscious as underlying literary works and instead reads, enthusiastically, a good deal about Wilhelm Reich's theories of the orgone. These are actual instances. At Harvard University Richard Light and his coresearchers found that students remembered best one kind of teaching moment in their undergraduate careers—when a teacher invited them to join in the teacher's individual project. Notice how these cases also lie outside the boundaries of our first five images of learning. The scoring machines are programmed to give a zero to any essay that records as off topic. The borrowed book does not help the student pass from one course to another. Learning about Reich's orgone box on one's own doesn't much look like socialization into a community of discourse.

Something else unintended happens when teachers start welcoming students as strangers. In this case, it happens to teachers. The more they shape their courses in the image of hospitality, the happier they are. Some of this comes from shedding old frustrations, frustrations due to false expectations. Paper after paper, students don't change in their writing. What else should we expect? If babies spend 90 percent of their time in growth stasis, why should we expect anything else with the writing growth of composition students? Week after week, most of our students appear unenthused about the reading, the topic for discussion, or the next assignment, and only a few catch fire. What else should we expect, if everyone's potential, the power source for future change, is unique, singular, and by definition unknown? And there is a relief and a joy in walking into every class or starting every student conference asking not, "Do I have the knowledge to teach the students?" but rather, "What do these students know that I want to learn?"

IMAGES OF LEARNING CHANGE AND COURSE STRUCTURE

How students learn and how teachers teach should be coordinated. They rarely are, of course. What teachers do coordinate, often, is their image of learning change and the way they structure their courses. The two are so tightly integrated, in fact, that it is impossible to know if the image built the structure or the structure created the image. Let's say one tends to authorize the other. One also shares the same strengths and weaknesses as the other.[2]

We might combine the strengths of these five images into an ideal model of learning change for the English profession (see Table 10.2). Such change will be self-evident to the student, publicly marked with status-elevating events, fitted to the individual student's readiness, sociable, saltatory, and serendipitous. This model would not match many familiar

Table 10.2

Image	Major strength	Major problem	Course structuring
Clearing the hurdles	Provides an opportunity to show one's advance in learning to self and others	Encourages learning that is bound to passing contexts and therefore easily forgotten	Through tests, each marking the end of one section of the course
Crossing the border	Ritualization of change in learning helps authorize future change	Pictures learning as a threshold ritual, whose import is trivial and difficult to grasp or remember	Through ceremonies such as post-test celebrations or end-of-course parties
Climbing the ladder	Provides educational scaffolding for students who are ready for it	Will not fit all or even many students in the time allowed for coursework	Through content sequences such as sentence/paragraph/essay, or early/late Victorian
Marking the door frame	Lodges learning in developmental changes that are normative for people through their life span	Pictures these changes as regular, which they never are on a day-to-day basis	Through dubious cognitive sequences such as concrete to abstract or biographical to interpretive
Learning the ropes	Pictures learning as group promoted and future oriented	Usually lacks the context or the experts of that future	Through socialization practices such as peer critique or team reports
Welcoming the stranger	Sees learning as taking place through a serendipitous exchange between two strangers	May be difficult to implement within the current educational trend toward large classes	Through hospitable events such as one-on-one tutoring or faculty office visits

tropes of educational change, in any profession. No trope comes closer to the model than hospitality. And, as we will next argue, no trope better conjures up a fit location for writers who like to be read and readers who like to be written to.

Notes

Parts of this chapter are based on a keynote address Richard Haswell gave at the Missouri Colloquium on Writing Assessment, St. Joseph, MO (October 2001).

1. TAAS stands for Texas Assessment of Academic Skills tests. It was predecessor to the TAKS (Texas Assessment of Knowledge and Skills), which has been replaced by the State of Texas Assessments of Academic Readiness (STAAR). TAAS was the forerunner of the national No Child Left Behind legislation. The entire corpus of student opinion can be found at Blalock and Haswell (2002–2003).

2. As shown by the catalogue of imagery that begins this chapter, English faculty operate with other pedagogical tropes than just these six. See chapter 13 of our *Authoring* (Haswell and Haswell 2010) for a number of concepts of writing growth that the literature side of the English department might offer the composition side.

11

THE MULTIPLE COMMON SPACE CLASSROOM

*The paradox of hospitality is that it wants to create emptiness, not a
fearful emptiness, but a friendly emptiness where strangers can enter
and discover themselves as created free.*

—Henri Nouwen

Events, even learning events, don't just take place in thin air. They take
place. They happen in a physical surround, rife with its own meaning and
poised with its own influence.

Any trope of learning change worth its salt, then, will inscribe location as well as temporality, and the location will be appropriate for the
aspect of learning that is stressed. So *clearing the hurdles* suggests a track
meet, befitting an emphasis on testing; *crossing the border* a transit no-
man's-land between countries, where ceremony reigns; *climbing the ladder*
a building under repair, where scaffolding and other sequential struc-
turings function; *marking the door frame* a family residence, traditionally a
place where norms and regularities are first instilled; *learning the ropes* a
sailing ship, traditionally a locale illustrating group socialization; *welcoming the stranger* a living quarters, transitory or permanent, traditionally
the locale for open hospitality.

Spatially the last of these metaphors, however, contrasts with the
other five in one major way when it is applied to English-department
teaching and learning. *Welcoming the stranger* is not only an informative
metaphor for a distinctive place in English instruction. It is also a living social praxis that can be put into place there. The English classroom, for instance, cannot *be* a track meet, a transit area, a building in
construction, a family home, or a sailing ship. But it can *be* a location
for hospitality.

A working idea of hospitable instructional space in English overlaps
and competes with at least three other concepts. One is linguist Mary
Louise Pratt's (1993) notion of "contact zone," a distinct social territory
where cultures, societies, languages, and discourses clash and construct

DOI: 10.7330/9780874219883.c011

ways of dealing with each other. According to Pratt, contact zones are
not necessarily friendly, equitable, or instructional. They include situations of heavily imbalanced power relations, such as slavery or colonialism.[1] Composition scholars have appropriated Pratt's term, perhaps
sometimes bowdlerizing it. They argue that the contemporary writing classroom is a contact zone where cultures clash—cultures such
as school and college, Western and non-Western, Hispanic and non-
Hispanic, lower class and middle class, native speaker and nonnative
speaker—and where the clash can be tamed, embraced, explored, and
in other ways turned to pedagogical use (see Gaughan 2001 or a number
of the essays collected in Wolff 2002). Hospitable instructional space,
however, is not first and foremost a contact zone. If guest and host are
from different cultures, hospitality tries neither to hide nor to expropri-
ate that cultural difference. What guest and host may learn from their
encounter may or may not connect with that difference. The essence of
the hospitable act, it will be remembered, disregards any group affilia-
tion. The contact that hospitable space allows occurs between two singular people. As Derrida says, it happens "before any determination,
before any anticipation, before any identification" (2000, 76).

Nor does hospitable instructional space necessarily reproduce the
pedagogy of what is called "sheltered English." Designed for limited
English proficient (LEP) students, the sheltered classroom combines
instruction in content and language. The instruction is an alternative to
"immersion," a well-named pedagogy where such students are placed in
mainstream courses and expected to sink or swim. In a sheltered content course, teachers apply a number of strategies that recognize where
students are in their language proficiency, strategies such as correcting
content rather than language, using visual aids, making connections
with cultural background, and pairing LEP students with English-fluent
students. All of this assumes a vaguely hospitable stance toward LEP students, who often are recently arrived in the United States. But sheltered
teaching does not emerge from the center of the hospitable act, where
the stranger and the host engage as equals. Strangers may be seeking
shelter, but it is a shelter that protects them from the elements, not from
other people (for example, students with a language advantage). In the
veritable hospitable encounter, host and guest experience not so much
shelter as exposure.

In English departments, closer to the hospitable classroom is a mode
of instruction called "safe house" (or safe place, safety net, halfway
house, haven, harbor). For students, the safe classroom is so in any
number of ways. Safe from grading standards applied to first-language

students. Safe from unrealistic expectations of mechanically perfect papers held by content teachers. Safe from counter-educational values imposed by institutional culture. Safe from ideologies forced on minorities by mainstream students. Not surprisingly, safe-house pedagogy is most often encouraged in second-language classrooms, basic-writing group tutorials, and writing centers (see Canagarajah 1997; Baker 2006; and Owens 2008). Writing centers in particular take pride in their "culture of welcome," call their tutorial space "the hospitality room," or advertise the ways that they further their college's LaSallian or Benedictine mission of hospitality. Probably, if we could put numbers on it, over the years more acts of genuine hospitality have been initiated by writing-center tutors than by any other postsecondary faculty (for writing-center work as traditional hospitality, see Davis 2001). Still, safe-house instruction differs from that based on traditional hospitality. Safe-house space tries to minimize risk; hospitable space makes risk an essential condition. In a safe-house classroom that optimizes learning change, instructors remove inhibitions and other barriers for their students. In a hospitable classroom that optimizes learning change, instructors and students remove those barriers for themselves.

MULTIPLE COMMON SPACE

In the English curriculum, however, can we honestly speak of a hospitable classroom in the same way that we can speak of the contact-zone classroom, the sheltered classroom, or the safe-house classroom? As chapters 1 and 3 make clear, true hospitality operates in the margins of society, and it is in the margins of the instructional course that hospitality most naturally takes place. It is not hard to imagine hospitable welcome, stranger to stranger, shown by the teacher in the teacher's office to a late-enrolling student, or by the members of a study group in a dorm room to an international student who feels alienated in class, or by a tutor in a writing-center cubicle to a student sent there by the teacher. But is it possible for true hospitality to be enacted by a literature class of 40 or even a composition class of 25? (We won't speak of Duke's MOOC of 67,530.) And if such classwide hospitality were possible, what would we call it?

Let's entertain the possibility, and let's call it a "multiple common space" classroom. We base our speculation and our name on the sixth chapter of Giorgio Agamben's (1990) *La communità che viene* (17–19). In this astonishing essay-chapter of little over 600 words, Agamben describes a community that is united by each member's respect for every member's unique potential, that is, respect for the actualization or taking-place of each singular being (*l'aver-luogo di ogni essere singolare*). How is this unified community achieved? Agamben relies on the great Islamic scholar Louis Massignon and his notion of "sacred substitution." Sacred substitution is a vow to stand in place of another—not in order to correct, better, convert, or save that person but to offer a space to that person as he or she is (*in lui tale qual è*), that is, in order to help that person achieve his or her singular future (*l'avvenire a se stessa di ogni singolarità*). What this vow of substitution sacrifices, then, is one's own space in order to create an empty space in which someone else can achieve his or her potential. Massignon, who happened to have been Catholic, saw the empty space as an opportunity to offer Christ's own hospitality, but Agamben's reading is not religious. What is opened up is space for a unique and irrevocable hospitality (*all'unica, irrevocabile ospitalità*), a space that is already always common (*è già sempre comune*). Agamben points out that this unconditioned substitutability has no representation nor possible means of representation (*senza rappresentanza né rappresentazione possibile*), and therefore creates a community that cannot be pinned down with identifications or subjectivities.

Henri Nouwen (1966) says much the same thing. "The paradox of hospitality is that it wants to create emptiness, not a fearful emptiness, but a friendly emptiness where strangers can enter and discover themselves as created free; free to sing their own songs, speak their own languages, dance their own dances, free also to leave and follow their own vocations. Hospitality is not a subtle invitation to adopt the life style of the host, but the gift of a chance for the guest to find his own" (51).

Try substituting "instruction" for "hospitality," "teacher" for "host," and "student" for "guest." How many U.S. classrooms this very moment would fit Nouwen's rewritten passage? Dale Jacobs, who quotes the passages from Nouwen, adds, "As hosts, we should not seek to re-make guests (students, colleagues, and so on) in our own image, but should instead create an atmosphere where change can occur" (2008, 571).

Agamben calls such a community a multiple common space (*multiple luogo comune*). The English translator of *La communità che viene*, Michael Hardt, quite reasonably renders this phrase as "multiple common place" (Agamben 1993, 24). We have chosen "multiple common space" in order to avoid confusion with the rhetorical term "commonplace." The commonplaces (topoi) are the traditional argumentative appeals of classical rhetoric held in common by speaker and audience, and for us offer too much of a contradiction with the transgressive space of traditional hospitality. But we would not like our name to erase Virginia Woolf's (1988) remarkable anticipation of Agamben when she writes of the hospitable meeting of reader and writer, "It is of the highest importance that this common meeting-place should be reached easily" (34).

Indeed, Agamben's name for the quality that defines this common space, this sacrificing of room for the potentiality of others, is agio: ease, opportunity, coziness. It's an inspired choice, a word whose etymology is almost as rich as that of *hospitality* itself. *Agio* is cognate with the French *aise*, Provencal *aizin*, and English *ease*. Ultimately all derive from the Latin *adjacens*, which means adjacency, proximity, or neighborhood (*ad + jacens*, lying next to), and they all retain some sense of opportunity and room to maneuver, as most obvious in the English legal term *easement* (or French *aisance*) and the military command "at ease" (that is, one foot fixed, the other free to move). In English *ease* largely has become internalized into a psychological state. With Agamben we would like to recapture some of the earlier meaning, maybe something akin to the Old French *aise*, which means a comfortable place with elbow room.[2] Ease is the state of a group of place-bound people when each gives everyone else private space to change.

So a multiple common space is a most opportune place for learning change. Can an English classroom be turned into a hospitable multiple common space, in this deep sense? In this deep sense, how do English teachers in their classrooms achieve a community of hospitable ease?

First by offering themselves as substitution for each student. This simply means sacrificing some of the teacher's space to open up space, learning space, in the students. It might mean giving up coverage of certain authors in favor of authors students want to read. It might mean making writing assignments elastic enough to allow students their own interests and enthusiasms. It might mean relaxing the teacher's professed interpretation of a poem or essay to leave room for the differing interpretation of students. But it will also mean teaching students genuine hospitality. Because a multiple common space cannot be formed unless it is truly multiple. Students will have to learn to imitate Massignon and offer themselves as substitution for other students. In class discussion, peer-evaluation groups, collaboration groups, coauthoring groups, and study groups, even in the daily classroom give-and-take that comes from brushing against each other, students will have to learn to give easement to other students, give them elbow room to follow their singular learning potentials. Is it too far-fetched to imagine students occasionally giving easement to the teacher, rather than just accepting the teacher's authority to do what he or she wants?

In a sense, for all these strangers who find themselves close neighbors (*adjacens*) in a room three times a week, a multiple common space classroom would be no more than everyone applying the ordinary tactics of traditional hospitality—friendly welcome, generous offering of assistance, openness to others, free exchange of information and other gifts, allowance of privacy, sacrifice of elbow room for others, setting aside of social rank, acceptance of difference, mutual respect, unforced talk, willingness to learn from strangers, acceptance of the unpredictable. If this seems of little consequence and maybe of little relevance to instruction, think what an English class looks like without hospitable ease. Assignments are given without any concern for the way they will be received, teacher talk is purely for student absorption, teacher status is irrevocably elevated over everyone else's, student needs are defined by the syllabus, student privacy is of no account since student lives do not enter into the course, class discussion, when allowed, is no more than separate students trying to show that they have understood more of the teacher's knowledge than have other students, social cohesion is little more than everyone protecting her or his own private space, and learning in the course is strictly confined to what the teacher dispenses or expects. The picture looks outmoded, but how much of it still fits the large majority of English classrooms today? The picture is altered with contact-zone, sheltered, and safe-house classrooms, and the multiple common space classroom joins with them in trying to give back to students their singular potential for learning, real learning, learning that stays learned.

As with the temporal metaphors for learning change, these spatial metaphors lure as concrete models to pursue concretely. The hospitable or multiple common space classroom, however, can flout one piece of evidence arguing that its lure is less an ignis fatuus and more an attainable goal. That is the long-documented fact that students tend to shift over the undergraduate years in the direction of what human developmentalists call allocentricism, personal autonomy, and political and religious tolerance (for example, Chickering 1969; Kimmel 1980), that is, in the direction of Agamben's agio. Compared to a classroom of first-year students, a classroom of third-year and fourth-year students is more a room of distinct people. The older students are more their own person. Somehow in two years these students are more comfortable with themselves as different from one other, and with others as different from them. The hospitable classroom, it seems, is a natural bent, though surely it can be pushed. At least teachers know that they will be paddling with the current.

GOD'ILD YOU

The year Rich was five, while his father and older sister and brother were in town at work or at school, he spent his day at home with his mother. Home was a farmhouse on a narrow gravel road, eleven miles from town and six miles from the nearest highway. One day in the middle of the afternoon, a stranger knocked on the door asking if there was any work he could do in exchange for food. The year was 1945. Without knowing it, Rich was witnessing a sight common enough ten years earlier during the Great Depression but thereafter rapidly vanishing in the United States, the homeless itinerant asking for hospitality.

Here is what Rich remembers, or imagines he remembers. The man had a walking stick taller than his head and a bedroll secured at the small of his back. He didn't ask to come in the house and quite likely wasn't invited in—he courteously sat on the concrete step of the front porch while Rich's mother prepared a plate of food. It was late summer in southern Missouri and still hot and humid. The man ate his hand-out and talked with Rich's mother for a long time, or what seemed a long time to a five-year-old. And then he was gone. What did he want? Rich remembers asking his mother. "Just a bit of food and a bit of rest, and then the road again." At least that is the phrase lodged or grown in Rich's memory.

Isn't this the essence—metaphoric and real—of hospitality in the classroom? Doesn't this suggest the most sociable and most pedagogical way to deal with the actual condition of students? They want a little learning, they want it freed from distracting and constraining contingencies so they can have the space to develop it according to their peculiar wonts, and then they want to be released, out of there, on their singular ways. What does it mean to deny them this?

There is a moment in *Hamlet* when this educational hospitality is poignantly shown. Ophelia is befuddling Claudius and Gertrude with her faux-mad ramblings. Remember, as daughter of the dead chief counselor, she is now a guest in a castle where formerly she had been a host. "Well, God'ild you! They say the owl was a baker's daughter. Lord, we know what we are, but know not what we may be. God be at your table!" (IV.v.).

"God shield you" is what one says to the roofless wanderer. As for the owl and the baker's daughter, in the Celtic legend Christ asks for some bread at a baker's shop. The hospitable baker's wife puts an oat-cake in the oven for him, but the inhospitable baker's daughter thinks it too much and cuts it in half. Christ's half suddenly grows in size. In surprise the daughter exclaims, "Heugh, heugh!" and turns into an owl. Comments Ophelia, "We know what we are, but know not what we may be."

Apt enough to describe her plight, Ophelia's line is also a concise definition of human singularity. No one can be documented or otherwise penned in by ideological, group, institutional, or curricular definitions since no one's future is ever known. Therefore Ophelia's words also define potentiality, because we don't know whether the stranger at our door, perhaps an angel unawares, may be our future. "May God be at *your* table," concludes Ophelia, speaking to Claudius. May you be hospitable, she means, you who are now host but who has been the most ungrateful of guests at your brother's table.

Notes

1. Similar is the sociological notion of shatterzone or shatterbelt, an area historically so mixed in ethnicity, class, or economic status that no single group dominates, with largely unexplored ramifications for educational institutions located there (see Haswell and Haswell 2010, 167–172).

2. Agamben (1990) mentions the refrain that appears in a number of Provençal poems, *Mout mi semblatz de bel aizin*: "Much to me you seem of good *aizin*." Apparently it could be a phrase of welcome to a stranger, the first cracking open of the door of hospitality. But what exactly *aizin* meant is in considerable dispute. *Bel aizin* is variously translated as "friendly ease," "respectable status," "fine character," "near neighborhood," and "garden of love." Take your pick.

REFERENCES

Agamben, Giorgio. 1990. *La communità che viene.* Turin: Einaudi.

Agamben, Giorgio. 1993. *The Coming Community.* Trans. Michael Hardt. Minneapolis: University of Minnesota Press.

Allen, Marin Pearson. 1985. "The Guest-Host Archetype as a Rhetorical Constraint on the Modern American Presidency." PhD diss., University of Maryland. *Dissertation Abstracts International* 46.08A, 2128.

Alterman, Eric. 2004. *When Presidents Lie: A History of Official Deception and Its Consequences.* New York: Viking.

Anuario éstadistico del Perú, 1966. 1969. Lima: Impresa del Ministerio de Hacienda y Comercio.

Aristarkhova, Irina. 2012. "Hospitality and the Maternal." *Hypatia* 27(1): 163–181. http://dx.doi.org/10.1111/j.1527-2001.2010.01147.x.

Baker, Brooke. 2006. "Safe Houses and Contact Zones: Reconsidering the Basic Writing Tutorial." *Young Scholars in Writing* 4:64–72.

Beck, Lois. 1982. "Nomads and Urbanites, Involuntary Hosts and Uninvited Guests." *Middle Eastern Studies* 18(4): 426–444. http://dx.doi.org/10.1080/00263208208700524.

Benhabib, Seyla. 1987. "The Generalized and the Concrete Other: The Kohlberg-Gilligan Controversy and Feminist Theory." In *Feminism as Critique,* edited by Seyla Benhabib and Drucilla Cornell, 77–95. Minneapolis: University of Minnesota Press.

Benhabib, Seyla. 1990. "Afterward: Communicative Ethics and Current Controversies in Practical Philosophy." In *The Communicative Ethics Controversy,* edited by Seyla Benhabib and Fred Dallmayr, 330–369. Cambridge, MA: MIT Press.

Benhabib, Seyla. 1992. *Situating the Self: Gender, Community and Postmodernism in Contemporary Ethics.* New York: Routledge.

Bennett, John B. 2000a. "The Academy and Hospitality." *Cross Currents* 50(1/2):23–46.

Bennett, John B. 2000b. "Hospitality and Collegial Community: An Essay." *Innovative Higher Education* 25(2): 85–96. http://dx.doi.org/10.1023/A:1007520705448.

Benveniste, Emile. 1973. *Indo-European Language and Society.* Translated by Elizabeth Palmer. Coral Gables: University of Miami Press.

Birkerts, Sven. 1995. *The Guttenberg Elegies: The Fate of Reading in an Electronic Age.* Winchester, MA: Faber and Faber.

Bishop, Wendy, and Kevin Davis. 1986. *The Reading/Writing Relationship: A Selected Bibliography.* ERIC Document Reproduction Service, ED 272 848.

Blake, William. 1973. *The Marriage of Heaven and Hell.* Miami: University of Miami Press.

Blake, William. 2008. "Proverbs of Hell." In *The Complete Poetry and Prose of William Blake,* edited by David V. Erdman, 35–38. Berkeley: University of California Press.

Blalock, Glenn, and Richard Haswell. 2002–2003. *Student Views of TAAS Testing.* http://comppile.org/TAAS/index.html.

Boisvert, Raymond D. 2004. "Ethics Is Hospitality." *Proceedings of the Catholic Philosophic Association* 78:289–300. http://dx.doi.org/10.5840/acpaproc2004789.

DOI: 10.7330/9780874219883.c012

Bok, Christian. 1992. "Destructive Creation: The Politicization of Violence in the Works of Michael Ondaatje." *Canadian Literature* 132:109–125.

Booth, Wayne. 1990. *The Company We Keep: An Ethics of Fiction.* Berkeley: University of California Press.

Borradori, Giavanna. 2003. *Philosophy in a Time of Terror: Dialogues with Jürgen Habermas and Jacques Derrida.* Chicago: University of Chicago Press.

Bourdieu, Pierre. 1984. *Distinction: A Social Critique of the Judgment of Taste.* Translated by Richard Nise. Cambridge, MA: Harvard University Press.

Brann, Eva. 1999. "Tapestry with Images: Paul Scott's Raj Novels." *Philosophy and Literature* 23(1): 181–196. http://dx.doi.org/10.1353/phl.1999.0009.

Brooks, Peter. 1984. *Reading for the Plot: Design and Intention in Narrative.* Cambridge, MA: Harvard University Press.

Burke, Kenneth. 1966. *Language as Symbolic Action: Essays on Life, Literature, and Method.* Berkeley: University of California Press.

Cable News Network. 2003. "US Troops Topple Saddam Statue." *CNN.Com/WORLD,* April 9. http://www.cnn.com/2003/WORLD/meast/04/09/sprj.irq.int.war.main1400/.

Canagarajah, A. Suresh. 1997. "Safe Houses in the Contact Zone: Coping Strategies of African American Students in the Academy." *College Composition and Communication* 48(2): 173–196. http://dx.doi.org/10.2307/358665.

Carey, Cynthia. 2001. "Re-inventing (Auto)-biography: The (Im)Possible Quest of Michael Ondaatje in *Running in the Family.*" *Commonwealth* 24(1): 41–51.

Carini, Patricia F. 1994. "Dear Sister Bess: An Essay on Standards, Judgment and Writing." *Assessing Writing* 1(1): 29–66. http://dx.doi.org/10.1016/1075-2935(94)90004-3.

Ceccarelli, Leah. 2004. "Neither Confusing Cacophany nor Culinary Complements: A Case Study of Mixed Metaphors for Genomic Science." *Written Communication* 21(1): 92–105. http://dx.doi.org/10.1177/0741088303261651.

Chickering, Arthur W. 1969. *Education and Identity.* San Francisco: Jossey-Bass.

Childs, Peter. 1998. *Paul Scott's Raj Quartet: History and Division.* English Literary Studies Monograph 77. Victoria, BC: University of Victoria.

Chomsky, Noam. 1966. "Some Thoughts on Intellectuals and the Schools." *Harvard Educational Review* 36(4): 484–491.

Chomsky, Noam. 1967. "The Responsibility of Intellectuals." *New York Review of Books,* February 23. http://www.chomsky.info/articles/19670223.htm.

Chomsky, Noam. 1973. *For Reasons of State.* New York: Pantheon Books.

Chomsky, Noam. 2005. *Imperial Ambitions: Conversations on the Post–9/11 World.* New York: Metropolitan Books.

Chouliaraki, Lilie. 2007. "Spectacular Ethics: On the Television Footage of the Iraq War." In *The Soft Power of War,* edited by Lilie Chouliaraki, 129–144. Philadelphia: John Benjamins. http://dx.doi.org/10.1075/bct.3.08cho.

Coleman, Daniel. 1993. "Masculinity's Severed Self: Gender and Orientalism in *Out of Egypt* and *Running in the Family.*" *Studies in Canadian Literature* 78(2): 62–80.

Coleridge, Samuel Taylor. 1983. *Biographia Literaria.* Edited by James Engell and W. Jackson Bate. Princeton, NJ: Princeton University Press.

Coll, Steve. 2014. "The Unblinking Stare: The Drone War in Pakistan." *The New Yorker* (Nov. 24): 98–109.

Crawford, Lawrence. 1984. "Viktor Shklovskij: Différance in Defamiliarization." *Comparative Literature* 36(3): 209–219. http://dx.doi.org/10.2307/1770260.

Dafoe, Willem. 1997. "Michael Ondaatje." *Bomb* 58 (Winter): 14–19.

Davis, Jeffry C. 2001. "Pitching a Tent, Welcoming a Traveler, and Moving On: Toward a Nomadic View of the Writing Center." *Writing Lab Newsletter* 25(10): 12–15.

Debord, Guy. 1983. *Society of the Spectacle.* Detroit: Black and Red.

Derrida, Jacques. 1993. *Aporias.* Translated by Thomas Dutoit. Stanford, CA: Stanford University Press.

Derrida, Jacques. 1999. *Adieu to Emmanuel Levinas.* Translated by Pascale-Anne Brault and Michael Naas. Stanford, CA: Stanford University Press.

Derrida, Jacques. 2000. *Of Hospitality.* Translated by Rachel Bawlby. Stanford, CA: Stanford University Press.

Devaux, Michael. 2007. "The Origins of the Ainulindalë: The Present State of Research." In *The Silmarillion Thirty Years On,* edited by Allan Turner, 81–110. Zollikofen, Switzerland: Walking Tree.

Diprose, Rosalyn. 2009. "Women's Bodies between National Hospitality and Domestic Biopolitics." *Paragraph* 32(1): 69–86. http://dx.doi.org/10.3366/E0264833409000418.

Dower, John H. 2010. *Cultures of War: Pearl Harbor, Hiroshima, 9-11, Iraq.* New York: Norton.

Elbow, Peter. 2008. "The Believing Game—Methodological Believing." Paper presented at the Conference on College Composition and Communication, New Orleans, April 4.

Emig, Janet. 1983. *The Web of Meaning: Essays on Writing, Teaching, Learning, and Thinking.* Montclair, NJ: Boynton/Cook.

Engelhardt, Tom. 2006. "In the Rubble." *Truthout.org,* April 16. http://www.tomdispatch.com/post/77789/.

Foucault, Michel. 1967. "Of Other Spaces: Heterotopias." http://foucault.info/documents/herteroTopia/foucault.herteroTopia.en.html.

Foucault, Michel. (Original work published 1970) 1972. "Discourse on Language." Translated by A. M. Sheridan Smith. In *The Archaeology of Knowledge and the Discourse on Language,* 215–237. New York: Pantheon Books.

Fussell, Paul. 1989. *Wartime: Understanding and Behavior in the Second World War.* New York: Oxford University Press.

Ganapathy-Dore, Geetha. 1997. "Total Fiction: Biography in Ondaatje and Le Clézio." In *Biographical Creation,* edited by Marta Dvorak, 119–126. Rennes: University Press of Rennes.

Gaughan, John. 2001. *Reinventing English: Teaching in the Contact Zone.* Portsmouth, NH: Heinemann Boynton/Cook.

Gibson, Andrew. 1999. *Postmodernity, Ethics, and the Novel: From Leavis to Levinas.* New York: Routledge.

Giltrow, Janet, and David Stouck. 1992. "'Mute Dialogues': Michael Ondaatje's *Running in the Family.*" In *Postmodern Fiction in Canada,* edited by Theo D'haen and Hans Bertens, 161–179. Amsterdam: Rodopi.

Green, M. Christian. 2010. "From Saint Martha to Hurricane Katrina: A Feminist Theopolitical Ethic of Hospitality." In *Feminism and Hospitality: Gender in the Host/Guest Relationship,* edited by Maurice Hamington, 91–106. New York: Lexington Books.

Gregorious, Zelia. 2001. "Does Speaking of Others Involve Receiving the 'Other'? A Postcolonial Reading of Receptivity in Derrida's Deconstruction of *Timaeus.*" In *Derrida and Education,* edited by Gert J. J. Biestra and Denise Egéa-Kuehn, 134–149. New York: Routledge.

Grice, H. 1975. "Paul." In *Logic and Conversation,* edited by Peter Cole and Jerry L. Morgan, 3:41–58. Syntax and Semantics. New York: Academic.

Groome, Thomas H. 1988. "The Spirituality of the Religious Educator." *Religious Education* (Chicago) 83(1): 9–20. http://dx.doi.org/10.1080/0034408880830102.

Guardian UK. 2003. "Bush Disavows 'Mission Accomplished' Link." *The Guardian UK,* October 29. www.guardian.co.uk/world/feedarticle/3321684.

Haas, Christina. 1993. "Beyond 'Just the Facts': Reading as Rhetorical Action." In *Hearing Ourselves Think: Cognitive Research in the College Writing Classroom,* edited by Ann M. Penrose and Barbara M. Sitko, 19–32. New York: Oxford University Press.

Haggerty, Daniel. 2010. "Shame in Feminine Hospitality." In *Feminism and Hospitality: Gender in the Host/Guest Relationship,* edited by Maurice Hamington, 5–69. New York: Lexington Books.

Haswell, Janis E., and Richard H. Haswell. 2010. *Authoring: An Essay for the English Profession on Potentiality and Singularity.* Logan: Utah State University Press.

Haswell, Janis E., Richard H. Haswell, and Glenn Blalock. 2009. "Hospitality in College Composition Courses." *College Composition and Communication* 60(4): 707–727.

Haswell, Janis Tedesco. 2001. "Images of Rape and Buggery: Paul Scott's View of the Dual Evils of Empire." *Studies in the Novel* (Summer): 202–223.

Haswell, Janis Tedesco. 2002. *Paul Scott's Philosophy of Place(s): The Fiction of Relationality.* New York: Peter Lang.

Haswell, Janis Tedesco. 2003. "Paul Scott's Dialogic Method." *South Carolina Review* 35(2): 72–87.

Haswell, Richard H. 1991. *Gaining Ground in College Writing: Tales of Development and Interpretation.* Dallas: Southern Methodist University Press.

Hayslip, Le Ly. 1989. *When Heaven and Earth Changed Places: A Vietnamese Woman's Journey from War to Peace.* New York: Penguin.

Heard, Matthew. 2010. "Hospitality and Generosity: A Response to Dale Jacobs." *JAC: Journal of Advanced Composition* 30(1/2): 315–335.

Heble, Ajay. 1994. "'Rumours of Topography': The Cultural Politics of Michael Ondaatje's *Running in the Family.*" *Essays on Canadian Writing* 53:186–203.

Hedges, Chris, and Laila al-Arian. 2007. "The Other War: Iraq Vets Bear Witness." *The Nation,* July 9. http://www.thenation.com/article/other-war-iraq-vets-bear-witness-0#.

Huggan, Graham. 1996. "Exoticism and Ethnicity in Michael Ondaatje's *Running in the Family.*" *Essays on Canadian Writing* 57:116–127.

Irigaray, Luce. 1999. *Between East and West: From Singularity to Community.* Translated by Stephen Pluhácek. New York: Columbia University Press.

Iser, Wolfgang. 1993. *The Fictive and the Imaginary: Charting Literary Anthropology.* Baltimore, MD: Johns Hopkins University Press.

Jabès, Edmond. 1991. *Le livre de l'hospitalité.* Paris: Gallimard.

Jacobs, Dale. 2008. "The Audacity of Hospitality." *JAC: Journal of Advanced Composition* 38(3/4): 563–580.

Jaggi, Maya. 2000. "Michael Ondaatje in Conversation with Maya Jaggi." *Wasafiri* 32:5–11. http://dx.doi.org/10.1080/02690050008589693.

Johnson, Susanne. 1993. "Reshaping Religious and Theological Education." *Religious Education* (Chicago) 88(3): 335–349. http://dx.doi.org/10.1080/0034408930880302.

Jolly, Andrew. 1976. *A Time of Soldiers.* New York: W. P. Dutton.

Kanaganynkani, Chelva. 1992. "A Trick with Glass: Michael Ondaatje's South Asian Connection." *Canadian Literature* 132:33–42.

Kawash, Samira. 1997. *Dislocating the Color Line: Identity, Hybridity, and Singularity in African-American Narrative.* Stanford, CA: Stanford University Press.

Kearney, Richard. 1999. "Aliens and Others: Between Girard and Derrida." *Cultural Values* 3(3): 251–262. http://dx.doi.org/10.1080/14797589909367166.

Kegan, Robert. 1994. *In over Our Heads: The Mental Demands of Modern Life.* Cambridge, MA: Harvard University Press.

Kimmel, Douglas C. 1980. *Adulthood and Aging: An Interdisciplinary Developmental View.* New York: Wiley.

Kristeva, Julia. 1991. *Strangers to Ourselves.* New York: Columbia University Press.

Krog, Antjie. 1988. *Country of My Skull.* New York: Three Rivers.

Lakoff, George. 2001. "Metaphors of Terror." In *The Days After.* Chicago: University of Chicago Press, January 23. http://www.press.uchicago.edu/sites/daysafter/911lakoff.html.

Lampl, Michelle, Michael L. Johnson, and Edward A. Frongillo Jr. 2001. "Mixed Distribution Analysis Identifies Saltation and Stasis Growth." *Annals of Human Biology* 28(4): 403–411. http://dx.doi.org/10.1080/03014460010016662.

Lampl, Michelle, Johannes D. Veldhuis, and Michael L. Johnson. 1992. "Saltation and Stasis: A Model of Human Growth." *Science* 258(5083): 801–803. http://dx.doi.org/10.1126/science.1439787.

Langer, Judith A., and Sheila Flihan. 2000. "Writing and Reading Relationships: Constructive Tasks." In *Perspectives on Writing: Research, Theory, and Practice*, edited by Roselmina Indrisano and James R. Squire, 111–139. Newark, DE: International Reading Association.

Lapham, Lewis H. 2005. "Notebook." *Harper's Magazine* (August): 7–9.

Leahy, David. 1992. *"Running in the Family, Volkswagen Blues* and *Heroine:* Three Post/ Colonial Post-modernist Quests?" *Kunapipi* 14(3): 67–82.

Levinas, Emmanuel. (Original work published 1961) 1969. *Totality and Infinity: An Essay on Exteriority.* Translated by Alphonso Lingis. Pittsburgh: Duquesne University Press.

Mabey, Richard. 1990. *Home Country*. London: Random Century House.

MacIntyre, Alasdair. 1984. *After Virtue.* Notre Dame, IL: University of Notre Dame Press.

Manzi, Joachim. 1999. "Accueillir, aimer, nommer la femme étrangère." In *Mythes et représentations de l'hospitalité*, edited by Alain Montandon, 325–339. Clermont-Ferrand, France: Presses Universitaires Blaise Pascal.

Marine Corps News. 2007. "Famed 'Lion of Fallujiah'—Major Douglas A. Zembiec USMC Dies in Combat." *Military.com,* May 31. http://forums.military.com/eve/forums/a/tpc/f/97 51945704/m/8520022031001.

Matthews, S. Leigh. 2000. "'The Bright Bone of a Dream': Drama, Performativity, Ritual and Community in Michael Ondaatje's *Running in the Family*." *Biography* 23(2): 352–371. http://dx.doi.org/10.1353/bio.2000.0015.

McAvoy, Jane. 1998. "Hospitality: A Feminist Theology of Education." *Teaching Theology & Religion* 1(1): 20–26. http://dx.doi.org/10.1111/1467-9647.00004.

McNulty, Tracy. 1999. "Israel as Host(ess): Hospitality in the Bible and Beyond." *Jouvert: A Journal of Postcolonial Studies* 3(1/2). http://english.chass.ncsu.edu/jouvert/v3i12 /mcnult.htm.

Miller, J. Hillis. 1987. *The Ethics of Reading.* New York: Columbia University Press.

Miller, Susan. 2007. *Trust in Texts: A Different History of Rhetoric.* Carbondale: Southern Illinois University Press.

Montandon, Alain, ed. 1999. *Mythes et représentations de l'hospitalité.* Clermont-Ferrand, France: Presses Universitaires Blaise Pascal.

Moore, Miriam. 1994. Interview with Michael Ondaatje. http://list.gatech.edu/archives /LCC2401D/old/0062.html.

Moore, Robin. 1990. *Paul Scott's Raj.* London: Heinemann.

Moyers, Bill. 2007. "On Impeachment." *Bill Moyers Journal,* July 13. http://www.pbs.org /moyers/journal/07132007/transcript2.html

Mukherjee, Arun P. 1985. "The Poetry of Michael Ondaatje and Cyril Dabydeen: Two Responses to Otherness." *Journal of Commonwealth Literature* 20(1): 49–67. http://dx.doi.org/10 .1177/002198948502000106.

Nelson, Nancy, and Robert C. Calfee, eds. 1998. *The Reading-Writing Connection.* Chicago: National Society for the Study of Education.

Newton, Adam Zachary. 1995. *Narrative Ethics.* Cambridge, MA: Harvard University Press.

Noddings, Nel. 1984. *Caring: A Feminine Approach to Ethics and Moral Education.* Berkeley: University of California Press.

Norris, Kathleen. 1993. *Dakota: A Spiritual Geography.* New York: Houghton Mifflin.

Nouwen, Henri J. M. 1966. *Reaching Out: The Three Movements of the Spiritual Life.* New York: Doubleday.

Nouwen, Henri J. M. 1972. "Education to the Ministry." *Theological Education* 9(1): 48–59.

Nussbaum, Martha C. 1998. "Exactly and Responsibly: A Defense of Ethical Criticism." *Philosophy and Literature* 22(2): 343–365. http://dx.doi.org/10.1353/phl.1998.0047.

Nystrand, Martin. 1989. "A Social-Interactive Model of Writing." *Written Communication* 6(1): 66–85. http://dx.doi.org/10.1177/0741088389006001005.

Ogletree, Thomas W. 1991. *Hospitality to the Stranger: Dimensions of Moral Understanding.* Philadelphia: Fortress.

Ondaatje, Michael. 1982. *Running in the Family.* New York: Random House.

Ondaatje, Michael. 1987. *In the Skin of a Lion*. New York: Random House.

Ondaatje, Michael. 1992. *The English Patient*. New York: Random House.

Ondaatje, Michael. 2000. *Anil's Ghost*. New York: Random House.

O'Reilley, Mary Rose. 1984. "The Peaceable Classroom." *College English* 46(2): 103–112. http://dx.doi.org/10.2307/376856.

O'Reilley, Mary Rose. 1993. *The Peaceable Classroom*. Portsmouth, NH: Boynton/Cook.

Owens, Derek. 2008. "Hideaways and Hangouts, Pubic Squares and Performance Sites: New Metaphors for Writing Center Design." In *Creative Approaches to Writing Center Work*, edited by Kevin Dvorak and Shanti Bruce, 71–84. Cresskill, NJ: Hampton.

Oxford English Dictionary. 1971. Compact ed. Oxford: Oxford University Press.

Palmer, Daryl W. 1992. *Hospitable Performances: Dramatic Genre and Cultural Practices in Early Modern England*. West Lafayette, IN: Purdue University Press.

Palmer, Parker. 1998. *The Courage to Teach: Exploring the Inner Landscape of a Teacher's Life*. San Francisco: Jossey-Bass.

Pamuk, Orhan. 2006. Nobel lecture. *The Official Web Site of the Nobel Prize*. http://www.nobelprize.org/nobel_prizes/literature/laureates/2006/pamuk-lecture_en.html.

Parry, Benita. 1975. "Paul Scott's Raj." *South Asian Review* 8(4): 359–369.

Pease, Donald E. 1990. "Author." In *Critical Terms for Literary Study*, edited by Frank Lentricchia and Thomas McLaughlin, 105–117. Chicago: University of Chicago Press.

Pesch, Josef. 1998. "Cultural Clashes? East Meets West in Michael Ondaatje's Novels." In *Across the Lines: Intertextuality and Transcultural Communication in the New Literatures in English*, edited by Wolfgang Klooss, 65–76. Amsterdam: Rodopi.

Pilardi, Jo-Ann. 2010. "Domestic Hospitality: Self, Other, and Community." In *Feminism and Hospitality: Gender in the Host/Guest Relationship*, edited by Maurice Hamington, 71–89. New York: Lexington Books.

Pitt, William Rivers. 2003. "Without Honor." *Truthout.org*, November 10. http://www.truth-out.org.

Plato. 1997. "The Republic." In *Plato: Complete works*, edited by John M. Cooper, 971–1223. Cambridge, MA: Hackett.

Pohl, Christine D. 1995. "Hospitality from the Edge: The Significance of Marginality in the Practice of Welcome." *Annual of the Society of Christian Ethics* 15:121–136.

Polanyi, Michael. 1958. *Personal Knowledge: Towards a Post-critical Philosophy*. Chicago: University of Chicago Press.

Ponsonby, Arthur. 1940. *Falsehood in War-time*. London: George Allen and Unwin.

Posner, Richard A. 1997. "Against Ethical Criticism." *Philosophy and Literature* 21(1): 1–27. http://dx.doi.org/10.1353/phl.1997.0010.

Pratt, Lonni Collin, and Daniel Homan. 2002. *Radical Hospitality*. Brewster, MA: Paraclete.

Pratt, Mary Louise. 1993. "Arts of the Contact Zone." *Profession* 91:33–40.

"President Bush Announces Combat Operations in Iraq Have Ended: Remarks by the President from the USS *Abraham Lincoln* at Sea off the Coast of San Diego, California, May 1, 2003." 2003. http://www.gwu.edu/~action/2004/bush/bush050103sp.html.

Puleston, Dennis. 1976. "Ospreys and the DDT Ban." *Environmental Defense Fund Newsletter* 7(2): 1.

Ray, Sangeeta. 1993. "Memory, Identity, Patriarchy: Projecting a Past in the Memoirs of Sara Suleri and Michael Ondaatje." *Modern Fiction Studies* 39(1): 37–58. http://dx.doi.org/10.1353/mfs.0.1093.

Reece, Steve. 1993. *The Stranger's Welcome: Oral Theory and the Aesthetics of the Homeric Hospitality Scene*. Ann Arbor: University of Michigan Press.

Renan, Yael. 1984. "Disautomatization and Comic Deviations from Models of Organizing Experience." *Style* (DeKalb, IL) 18(2): 160–176.

Rilke, Rainer Maria. 1962. *Letters to a Young Poet*. Translated by M. D. Herder Norton. New York: Norton.

Rosello, Mireille. 2001. *Postcolonial Hospitality: The Immigrant as Guest*. Stanford, CA: Stanford University Press.

Roy, Arundhati. 1997. *The God of Small Things*. New York: Random House.

Rubin, David. 1986. *After the Raj: British Novels of India since 1947*. Hanover, NH: University Press of New England.

Rundin, John. 1996. "A Politics of Eating: Feasting in Early Greek Society." *American Journal of Philology* 117(2): 179–215. http://dx.doi.org/10.1353/ajp.1996.0029.

Rushdie, Salman. 1984. "Outside the Whale." *Granta* 11:124–138.

Russell, John. 1991. "Travel Memoir as Nonfiction Novel: Michael Ondaatje's *Running in the Family*." *Ariel* 22(2): 23–42.

Russell, Letty M. 2009. *Just Hospitality: God's Welcome in a World of Difference*. Louisville, KY: Westminster John Knox.

Salvatori, Mariolina. 1996. "Conversations with Texts: Reading in the Teaching of Composition." *College English* 58(4): 440–454. http://dx.doi.org/10.2307/378854.

Sanders, Mark. 2002. *Complicities: The Intellectual and Apartheid*. Durham, NC: Duke University Press. http://dx.doi.org/10.1215/9780822384229.

Sander-Staudt, Maureen. 2010. "Su casa es mi casa? Hospitality, Feminist Care Ethics, and Reciprocity." In *Feminism and Hospitality: Gender in the Host/Guest Relationship*, edited by Maurice Hamington, 19–38. New York: Lexington Books.

Scarry, Elaine. 1985. *The Body in Pain: The Making and Unmaking of the World*. New York: Oxford University Press.

Schérer, René. 1993. *Zeus hospitalier: Eloge de hospitalité; Essai philosophique*. Paris: A. Colin.

Scott, Paul. (Original work published 1962) 1985a. *The Birds of Paradise*. London: Granada.

Scott, Paul. (Original work published 1960) 1985b. *The Chinese Love Pavilion*. London: Granada.

Scott, Paul. 1986. *My Appointment with the Muse*. London: Heinemann.

Scott, Paul. (Original work published 1968) 1998a. *The Day of the Scorpion*. Chicago: University of Chicago Press.

Scott, Paul. (Original work published 1975) 1998b. *A Division of the Spoils*. Chicago: University of Chicago Press.

Scott, Paul. (Original work published 1966) 1998c. *The Jewel in the Crown*. Chicago: University of Chicago Press.

Scott, Paul. (Original work published 1977) 1998d. *Staying On*. Chicago: University of Chicago Press.

Scott, Paul. (Original work published 1972) 1998e. *The Towers of Silence*. Chicago: University of Chicago Press.

Scott, Paul. 2011a. *Behind Paul Scott's Raj Quartet: A Life in Letters*. Vol. 1, *The Early Years (1940–1965)*, edited by Janis Haswell. Amherst, NY: Cambria.

Scott, Paul. 2011b. *Behind Paul Scott's Raj Quartet: A Life in Letters*. Vol 2, *The Quartet and Beyond (1966–1978)*, edited by Janis Haswell. Amherst, NY: Cambria.

Sennett, Richard. 1990. "The Rhetoric of Ethnic Identity." In *The Ends of Rhetoric: History, Theory, Practice*, edited by John Bender and David E. Wellbery, 191–231. Stanford, CA: Stanford University Press.

Shanahan, Timothy. 1998. "Readers' Awareness of Authors." In *The Reading-Writing Connection*, edited by Nancy Nelson and Robert C. Calfee, 88–111. Chicago: National Society for the Study of Education.

Shapiro, Kam. 2003. *Sovereign Nations, Carnal States*. Ithaca, NY: Cornell University Press.

Sharon-Zisser, Shirley. 1999. "From 'Guest' to Occupier? Unstable Hospitality and the Historicity of Tropology in the Discourse of Rhetoric." *Philosophy & Rhetoric* 32(4): 309–333.

Sharpe, Jenny. 1993. *Allegories of Empire: The Figure of Woman in the Colonial Text*. Minneapolis: University of Minnesota Press.

Silva, Neluka. 2002. "The Anxieties of Hybridity: Michael Ondaatje's *Running in the Family*." *Journal of Commonwealth Literature* 37(2): 71–84.

Sirc, Geoffrey. 2011. "The Salon of 2010." In *Beyond Postprocess*, edited by Jeff A. Rice and Michael Vastola, 195–218. Logan: Utah State University Press.

Smith, Frank. 1984. "Reading Like a Writer." In *Composing and Comprehending*, edited by Julie M. Jensen, 47–56. ERIC Clearinghouse on Reading and Communication Skills, ED 243 139.

Snelling, Sonia. 1997. "'A Human Pyramid': An (Un)Balancing Act of Ancestry and History in Joy Kogawa's *Obasan* and Michael Ondaatje's *Running in the Family*." *Journal of Commonwealth Literature* 32(1): 21–33. http://dx.doi.org/10.1177/0021989497 03200103.

Solecki, Sam. 1985. "An Interview with Michael Ondaatje (1984)." In *Spider Blues: Essays on Michael Ondaatje*, edited by Sam Solecki, 313–327. Montréal: Véhicule.

Stone, John. 1996. "Being as Intimate as You Can: A Conversation with Michael Ondaatje." *Revista española de estudios canadienses* 3(1): 247–264.

Strobl, Gerwin. 1996. "*Quartet* and *Four Quartets*: The Influence of T. S. Eliot on Paul Scott." In *Trends in English and American Studies: Literature and the Imagination*, edited by Sabine Coelsch-Foisner, Wolfgang Görtschacher, and Holger M. Klein, 269–284. Lampeter, UK: Edwin Mellen.

Sugunasiri, Suwanda H. J. 1992. "'Sri Lankan' Canadian Poets: The Bourgeoisie that Fled the Revolution." *Canadian Literature* 132:60–80.

Suleri, Sara. 1991. *Meatless Days*. Chicago: University of Chicago Press.

Tannock, Stuart. 2007. "To Keep America Number 1: Confronting the Deep Nationalism of US Higher Education." *Globalisation, Societies and Education* 5(2): 257–272. http:// dx.doi.org/10.1080/14767720701427186.

Taylor, W. C. 1831. *Of the Civil Wars of Ireland*. Vol. 2. Edinburgh: Constable.

Telfer, Elizabeth. 1995. "Hospitableness." *Philosophical Papers* 24(3): 183–196. http:// dx.doi.org/10.1080/05568649509506530.

Tillich, Paul. 1954. *Love, Power, and Justice: Ontological Analyses and Ethical Applications*. Oxford: Oxford University Press.

Toelken, Barre. 2014. *Oral Patterns of Performance: Story and Song*. Boulder: University Press of Colorado. http://dx.doi.org/10.7330/9780874219531.c001.

Tolkien, J. R. R. 1966. "On Fairy-Stories." In *The Tolkien Reader*, 33–84. New York: Ballantine Books.

Tolkien, J. R. R. 1970. *The Fellowship of the Ring*. New York: Ballantine Books.

Tolkien, J. R. R. 1977. *The Silmarillion*. Boston: Houghton Mifflin.

Tolkien, J. R. R. 1981. *The Letters of J. R. R. Tolkien*. Edited by Humphrey Carpenter. Boston: Houghton Mifflin.

Turner, Victor. 1969. *The Ritual Process: Structure and Anti-structure*. Amsterdam: Walter De Gruyter.

Tutu, Desmond. 1999. *No Future without Forgiveness*. New York: Doubleday.

Wallace, David L., and Helen Rothschild Ewald. 2000. *Mutuality in the Rhetoric and Composition Classroom*. Carbondale: Southern Illinois University Press.

Ward, Irene. 1994. *Literacy, Ideology, and Dialogue: Towards a Dialogic Pedagogy*. Albany: State University of New York Press.

Weil, Simone. 1947. *La pesanteur et la grâce*. Paris: Librairie Plon.

Welch, David. 2006. "Michael Ondaatje's Cubist Civil War." *Powells.com* Interviews, October 10. http://www.powells.com/blog/interviews/michael-ondaatjes-cubist-civil-war -by-dave/.

White, Brian. 2003. "Caring and the Teaching of English." *Research in the Teaching of English* 37(3): 295–328.

White, Edward M. 1970. *The Writer's Control of Tone*. New York: Norton.

White, Edward M. 1985. *Teaching and Assessing Writing*. San Francisco: Jossey-Bass.

Whitehead, Alfred North. (Original work published 1929) 1967. *The Aims of Education and Other Essays*. New York: Free Press.

Williams, Joseph M. 1989. "Two Ways of Thinking about Growth: The Problem of Finding the Right Metaphor." In *Thinking, Reasoning, and Writing*, edited by Elaine P. Maimon, Barbara F. Nodine, and Finbarr W. O'Connor, 245–255. New York: Longman.

Winslow, Rosemary. 1996. "Hospitality, Community, and Literary Reading and Writing." In *Civil Society and Social Reconstruction*, edited by George McLean, 176–193. Washington, DC: Council for Research in Philosophy and Values.

Winslow, Rosemary. 1999. "Poetry, Community and the Vision of Hospitality: Writing for Life in a Women's Shelter." In *The Literacy Connection*, edited by Ronald A. Sudol and Alice S. Horning, 181–204. Cresskill, NJ: Hampton.

Winslow, Rosemary. 2004. "Between Two Circles: 'Host' as Metaphor of Identity in the Language of Inclusion and Exclusion." In *Civil Society: Who belongs?* edited by William A. Barbieri, Robert Magliola, and Rosemary Winslow, 195–216. Washington, DC: Council for Research in Values and Philosophy.

Winterson, Jeanette. 1998. "Orion." In *The World and Other Places: Stories*, 57–61. London: Jonathan Cape.

Wolff, Janice M., ed. 2002. *Professing in the Contact Zone: Bringing Theory and Practice Together*. Urbana, IL: National Council of Teachers of English.

Woodward, Bob. 2006. *State of Denial*. New York: Simon and Schuster.

Woolf, Virginia. (Original work published 1925) 1981. *Mrs. Dalloway*. Orlando, FL: Harcourt Brace.

Woolf, Virginia. 1988. "Mrs. Bennett and Mr. Brown." In *Essentials of the Theory of Fiction*, edited by Michael Hoffman and Patrick Murphy, 24–39. Durham, NC: Duke University Press.

Wordsworth, William. 1800. Preface to *Lyrical Ballads, with Other Poems*. London: T. N. Longman and O. Rees.

Zinn, Howard. 2010. *The Bomb*. San Francisco: City Lights Books.

ABOUT THE AUTHORS

RICHARD HASWELL, Haas Professor Emeritus at Texas A&M University–Corpus Christi, thinks of himself as a teacher first and a researcher second. At Corpus Christi and at Washington State University, he taught courses in composition, rhetoric, British romanticism, postmodern literature, contemporary poetry, young-adult literature, and language in society. He has been writing program administrator and director of cross-campus writing assessment. He is author or coauthor of *The HBJ Reader* (1987), *Gaining Ground in College Writing* (1991), *Comp Tales* (2000), *Beyond Outcomes: Assessment and Instruction within a University Writing Program* (2001), *Machine Scoring of Student Essays* (2006) and, with Janis Haswell, *Authoring: An Essay for the English Profession on Potentiality and Singularity* (2011). Currently he coedits the *WPA-CompPile Research Bibliographies* and *CompPile*, an online bibliography of scholarship in composition and rhetoric.

JANIS HASWELL is Professor Emerita at Texas A&M University–Corpus Christi. She taught undergraduate and graduate courses in modern and contemporary British literature for the English department and composition in the university's First-Year Program and Honors Program. She is the author of *Introduction to the Raj Quartet* (1985), *Pressed against Divinity: W. B. Yeats and the Feminine Mask* (1997), *Paul Scott's Philosophy of Place(s): The Fiction of Relationality* (2002), and *Behind Paul Scott's Raj Quartet: A Life in Letters* (2011) in two volumes. She has also published some thirty-three articles and book chapters in both literature and composition. She received numerous college and university teaching awards and was recognized by the A&M System for teaching excellence. She was also a faculty fellow at the United States Holocaust Memorial Museum.

INDEX